Volunteers in Research and Testing

Volunteers in Research and Testing

EDITED BY

BRYONY CLOSE

ROBERT COMBES

ANTHONY HUBBARD

AND

JOHN ILLINGWORTH

Taylor & Francis
Publishers since 1798

UK Taylor & Francis Ltd, 1 Gunpowder Square, London, EC4A 3DE
USA Taylor & Francis Inc., 1900 Frost Road, Suite 101, Bristol, PA 19007

British Library Cataloguing in Publication Data

A catalogue record for this book is available from the British Library.

ISBN 07484-0397-3

Library of Congress Cataloguing in Publication data are available

Cover design by Jim Wilkie

Typeset in Times 10/12pt by Keyset Composition, Colchester, Essex

Printed in Great Britain by T. J. International Ltd, Padstow, Cornwall

Contents

Foreword

This book is based on a conference that took place over two days in April 1995 and was arranged because of an anonymous private donation by someone who considered that the full potential of using volunteers in medical research and product evaluation had not been realised. Volunteers fall into two classes: healthy volunteers and patients. All should be helped to make an informed, unpressured choice about taking part in research testing and evaluation and many of the contributions to this symposium have concentrated on the safeguards that need to be put in place to protect their interests and ensure that any consent given is genuine. Some people are legally incapable of consent and cannot be recruited as volunteers. In the case of children and notwithstanding the existence of a form of proxy (parental) consent, rigorous professional safeguards operate. No one has legal authority to consent on behalf of legally incompetent adults. Directive 91/507/EEC incorporated into UK domestic law by virtue of the Medicines (Applications for Grant of Product Licences – Products for Human Use) Regulation 1993 (S.I. 1993/2538), although only applying to research done with a view to making an application for a product licence, appears to have the effect that non-therapeutic research may only be conducted on those legally competent to consent. The Law Commission has considered the issue of research on the mentally incapacitated, concluding that research of no therapeutic benefit would currently be unlawful. It does, however, propose a new legislative scheme to safeguard and permit it. Clearly, research on mentally incapacitating conditions is desirable, subject to appropriate ethical control. Research involving patients in the National Health Service is overseen by Local Research Ethics Committees (LRECs) as described here. Straightforward, 'user-friendly' written explanations to prospective volunteers are plainly necessary but often require detailed scrutiny before being achieved. Payment to volunteers has attracted much discussion. The altruism of volunteers must be nourished and encouraged, and monetary and other inducements should be avoided in the interests of risk containment and in the furtherance of genuine consensual arrangements. The risks of volunteer studies are described here, and it is to be remembered that the impetus for the *Red Book* relating to LRECs arose, in large part, from the deaths of two volunteers in 1984, in Ireland and Wales, a matter discussed in Parliament and leading to guidance from the Medicines Commission and professional organisations. Studies on healthy volunteers do not attract statutory control under the UK Medicines Act (1968). Indemnity for injury received by volunteers has also attracted much debate, although the principle is widely accepted.

Quite apart from more general work on therapeutic agents in healthy and patient volunteers, especially in early pharmacokinetic and pharmacodynamic assessment, volunteer studies play an important role in psychiatric and psychological research, and in the study of the performance of military personnel over a range of climatic and environmental conditions. Ethical and other difficulties inherent in such programmes are discussed. Non-invasive, and relatively non-invasive, techniques of study in physiology are also described.

The Conference was supported generously both by industry and by voluntary organisations.

ROSALINDE HURLEY DBE

Acknowledgements

The editors would like to thank David Guinness who first suggested holding the conference in April 1995, the papers upon which this book is based. We would also like to thank Pamela Brown who kindly gave her time to read and check the entire manuscript prior to submission to the publishers. The work of the members of the organising and scientific advisory committees is gratefully appreciated as without them the conference could not have taken place: Riad Ayesh, Pamela Brown, Jayne Buffey, Bryony Close, Robert Combes, Anthony Dayan, Julia Fentem, David Guinness, David Healy, Anthony Hubbard, John Illingworth, Maggy Jennings, Gill Langley, Walter Nimmo, Michacl Ormc, Denis Parke, L. Prescott, Patrick Vallance, Glyn Volans and David Webb. Special thanks must go to Anthony Frew, chairman of the scientific advisory committee who gave up much of his time to provide assistance and advice during the preparation of the conference.

We would also like to thank the following sponsors who provided funding for the conference which allowed publication of this book: Boots Contract Manufacturing, Boots Pharmaceuticals, Dr Hadwen Trust for Humane Research, European Centre for the Validation of Alternative Methods (ECVAM), Fund for Replacement of Animals in Medical Experiments (FRAME), Glaxo Research and Development Ltd, Inveresk Clinical Research Ltd, Lederle Laboratories, Procter and Gamble (Health and Beauty Care) Europe, Royal Society for the Prevention of Cruelty to Animals (RSPCA), St Andrew Animal Fund, Status of Animals Conference Funds, and The Body Shop International plc.

List of Contributors

David Basketter, Unilever Environmental Safety Laboratory, Sharnbrook, Bedfordshire
Christine Bendall, McKenna & Co., London
Stanley Blenkinsop, Vice-Chairman, East Cheshire NHS Trust
Joe Collier, Reader and Consultant in Clinical Pharmacology, St George's Hospital Medical School, London
Anthony D. Dayan, Director, DH Department of Toxicology, St Bartholomew's Hospital Medical College, University of London
Anthony J. Frew, University Medicine, Southampton General Hospital
Graham Harding, Professor, Clinical Neurophysiology Unit, Vision Sciences Department, Aston University
Bev Holt, Consultant Anaesthetist, Kendal, Cumbria
Ingrid Klingmann, G H Besselaar Associates S.A., Brussels, Belgium
Clive Marritt, Department of Health, London
Denis McDevitt, Professor of Clinical Pharmacology and Dean of Medicine, University of Dundee
David Morton, Professor, Department of Biomedical Research and Biomedical Ethics, University of Birmingham
Michael Orme, Professor of Pharmacology and Therapeutics, University of Liverpool
Naomi Pfeffer, CERES (Consumers for Ethics in Research), London
Fiona Reynolds, Unilever Environmental Safety Laboratory, Sharnbrook, Bedfordshire
Douglas Smith, Director, Institute of Naval Medicine, Gosport, Hampshire
Stephen Toon, Medeval Ltd, Manchester
Duncan Vere, Professor of Therapeutics, London Hospital Medical College
Kerr Wilson, Health and Safety Laboratories, Sheffield

Introduction

The World Medical Association's Declaration of Helsinki was adopted by the 18th World Medical Assembly in 1964. It has been amended several times. The Declaration gives recommendations guiding physicians in biomedical research involving the use of human subjects. This in turn has laid down the principles of Good Clinical Practice which is in effect an international ethical and scientific quality standard for conducting studies involving humans in medicinal and non-medicinal clinical investigations.

The risk benefit equation alters in balance for the two types of studies mentioned. For medicines, in general it can be seen that a degree of risk and discomfort may be acceptable if there is a high probability of gaining a real benefit in the improvement of treatment of disease or illness. Nevertheless, ethical considerations usually demand that the main purpose of human studies is for confirming safety. For non-medicines, there has been an increasing number of products which are currently tested in humans. These include skin care products, modified nutrients, genetically modified food, novel food, and agrochemicals. In some cases (e.g. skin care products) the degree of risk and discomfort is likely to be extremely low. Within this context, tests on humans are carried out in order to elucidate whether or not the application of these products can produce harmful effects such as allergy in humans. However, in other cases the potential of life improvement benefit is rather controversial and on occasions the degree of risk/benefit requires long-term assessment and may not turn out to be acceptable.

The Declaration of Helsinki (Appendix 1) states that it is the mission of the physician to safeguard the health of the population. His or her knowledge and conscience are dedicated to the fulfilment of this mission. It also goes on to quote the Declaration of Geneva. This binds the physician with the words: 'The health of the patient shall be my first consideration'. The

International Code of Medical Ethics is also cited in the Declaration by saying that a physician shall act only in the patient's interest when providing medical care which might have the effect of weakening the physical and mental condition of the patient. From this we can see that any research involving human subjects cannot be legitimately carried out unless the importance of the objective is in proportion to the inherent risk to the subject. Each volunteer entering a study must be fully informed of the trial protocol so that they are able to make a balanced judgement of their willingness to participate. They should be informed of the level of any discomfort they may be expected to undergo. They should also be informed of any anticipated benefits, or indeed any hazards and potential risks, associated with the trial. The volunteer must also be informed of his or her right to withdraw from the study at any time. The volunteer's written informed consent should be obtained prior to the study commencing. These issues and the issues of encouragement and protection are fully covered in the text.

A key point of the Declaration of Helsinki is the section on non-therapeutic biomedical research involving human subjects. Point 4 of this states in the research on man 'the interests of science and society should never take precedence over the considerations related to the well-being of the subject'.

In this context, subjects are usually volunteers. A volunteer may be defined as one who acts without either legal obligations to do so, or without any promise of remuneration; it is a person who gives his or her services of his or her own free will. In terms of the use of humans as volunteers in research and testing, a volunteer is someone who actually wants to help, someone who acts without any coercion and who is perhaps interested in what scientists are trying to do. It is also necessary to define 'research'. Research is investigation and enquiry in order to address a problem, test a hypothesis, gather new information or perhaps to collate what is already known about a subject, in terms of academic and practical pursuit. It can also be the information gathered during such a course of investigation or enquiry.

This book is derived from individual presentations given at The Volunteers in Research and Testing Conference held in Manchester, UK, in April 1995, where the benefits and limitations of human studies were assessed and discussed in relation to the possible subsequent reduction of requirements for animals in research and testing. The contents clearly demonstrated that there is considerable potential for applying newly developed technology for assessing the safety and biological activity of new consumer products and pharmaceuticals to provide data which are both informative and relevant.

Hopefully we have managed to put together a book that will provide something for everyone in this ever expanding field. It discusses in depth the volunteers, consumers, research, law, composition and operation of guidelines and the ethics committees.

If the text acts as a useful reference for all workers in the field of human volunteer testing and stimulates discussion about improved non-invasive methods, as well as the complex moral and ethical issues surrounding animal welfare and human experimentation, then we shall have achieved our principal objectives.

Bryony Close
Robert Combes
Anthony Hubbard
John Illingworth

1

The Volunteer Subject, Encouragement and Protection

ANTHONY DAYAN

This chapter is based on the personal views of the author. Interested parties can find more information in the reading list given at the end of this chapter.

Understanding ourselves, how the body and mind work in health, in disease and in organic and psychological disorders, can only come from integrating knowledge gained from many types of laboratory experiments and the study of man. To the scientist there are many powerful reasons for encouraging the investigation of human beings in order to focus research and testing on the target species and its specific structures and systems. For the sake of self-knowledge and better health, the philosopher-ethicist and the derivative lawyer should support the scientist and clinician in undertaking experiments on ourselves and our fellow beings. Of equal force to those experts, however, must be concern about certain fundamental rights of man, notably personal autonomy, respect of personal integrity and confidentiality and freedom from unacceptable risk, pain and suffering. These factors, plus normative forces in society and their effects on legal and medical practice, have been important in defining the boundaries of what risks or suffering it is reasonable to ask someone to accept as a subject in a research study. The risks of treatment of illness and their acceptability raise different issues, which will not be considered in this chapter.

Volunteers – What For?

Much altruistic and selfless interest has been shown by humans in their willingness to take part in experiments and trials on themselves and their families. The study of medicine and basic human biology contains many examples of bold scientists and clinicians who vigorously subjected themselves to experimental manoeuvres, including the risks and the reality of infection and poisoning, in the desire to learn more about physiological and pathological reactions and the causes of disease; consider, for example, Lavoisier exploring diet and metabolism, John Hunter deliberately giving himself gonorrhoea in the eighteenth century, the studies of Ross, Reed, Gaugas and their volunteers on malaria and yellow fever, of Head on nerve function, of the Haldanes on hypoxia and carbon monoxide, of Forssman on cardiac catheterisation, and many others up to the present day. These noble individuals were willing to risk their own health and lives in order to find out things that they felt could not be discovered in any other way, and some were willing to invite others to accept the same incompletely known risks.

Almost all of them were well-educated, knowledgeable scientists, who presumably were able to assess the dangers of the experiments or to explain them to technically competent people, and who considered that the value of the results outweighed the risks. Note that the value was intellectual and rarely, if ever, was there any material reward, not even much opportunity for professional advancement in those days of minimal academic careers.

At least in a historical sense, their actions may be contrasted with those, for example, of Jenner when he first vaccinated a young boy with cowpox, when Pasteur gave his first course of rabies immunisation or Morton in first using ether as an anaesthetic in a surgical operation. They involved others, who may not have been able to balance risk and benefit in an impartial and informed way, even if the proponent had an expectation of safety and success.

Numerous other examples could be cited derived from many countries and various times and from diverse cultures. They all show the desire for knowledge, at least a scientifically plausible question to ask (by the current standard of the time), and the willingness of the scientist himself usually to accept the danger and discomfort of the procedure (as far as they were understood), or sometimes to persuade others to accept them if the experiment required someone in a condition that the scientist could not produce in himself, or that needed a number of people to give a reasonably certain result.

Those subjects of experiments in times past were rarely ‘volunteers’, as we now understand the term, but the auto-experimenters were certainly willing subjects, and, in the nineteenth century and subsequently, other people involved in investigations are likely to have been given some explanation of what was to be done.

The principal features in common in these and similar examples are the urge to find out something new that could only be done in man (either because the question was unique to man, or because an alternative species or experimental system was not available) presumably the belief after reflection that there was little or no risk from the experiment, no less strong

Why experiment on Man?

Basic knowledge of	Health Mechanisms of disease Reactions to disease Population variables Psychological processes
Applied knowledge of	Cause of disease Reactions to disease Therapy Prophylaxis Psychological processes Population variables
Pragmatic reasons	Information not otherwise available No alternative
Legal reasons	Medicinal and other product development (Not strictly correct but sometimes believed)
Insurance	Product efficacy and producer's liability (Also incorrect but often believed)

Figure 1.1 Why experiment on man?

a view that the knowledge gained would be so valuable as to justify the risk, and the expectation of no more than minimal pain, discomfort or other interference with the subject's normal life. The main reasons for experimental investigations of man are listed in Figure 1.1 as a guide to the real purposes and the sometimes mistaken perceptions on which such studies are based.

The growth of experimental biology roughly from the early nineteenth century, and scientific and investigative medicine over much the same period, illustrate how development of scientific methodology and the Baconian analytical approach have increased the urgency of our desire for knowledge of the mechanisms underlying health and disease, and our realisation that some understanding can only come from experimenting on man.

Volunteers and Compulsion – What Not For!

Disregard the sometimes apocryphal and sometimes depressingly true historical accounts of what those in authority have been willing to do to people under their control. There still remains a long and savage tradition of human cruelty to humans for a variety of reasons, including religious and political sacrifices and punishment, during which scientific and clinical observations have been made on anatomy, physiology and toxicology.

With increasing sensibility, and as part of our hoped for enlightenment, these procedures have become less overt, less frequent and more institutionalised, and of vanishingly small scientific value. At least under the circumstances of more or less normal life, we can perhaps hope that the last incidents of barbaric cruelty mixed with scientific observation may have ended with the virtual abolition of electrocution as capital punishment, and poison gas as a weapon of war.

Medical science, like other forms of knowledge, is not immune to abuse by powerful authorities, so it should not be surprising that deliberate and knowingly harmful experiments were done on humans in the 1930s and 1940s, including the deliberate infection of people with syphilis and leaving them without treatment 'to study the course of the disease,' and the bestialities of the Nazi and Japanese concentration camp 'experiments' done for a mixture of racist and pseudo-medical purposes.

Those acts were so extreme that it now seems easy to distance them from the inherent beliefs and practices of science and medicine, and to see them as cruel and unnatural acts involving total compulsion and extreme suffering, and with the 'experimenter' as someone acting in complete disregard of humanity, and any belief about professional responsibilities and standards. However, they must still be remembered as an indication of the evil and suffering that misguided 'science' may engender.

The rapid development of experimental medical science and especially of new approaches to drug therapies in the 1930s–1940s, and their acceleration in the 1950s and 1960s, led to the much more frequent use of humans in formal studies, both experimenters themselves and increasingly other normal subjects, as well as many ill people, in studying the pathophysiology of diseases and in trials of new and old therapies.

Growing awareness of this use of man by man, and anxiety about increasing numbers of reports on the abuse of subjects by exposing them to dubious or frankly unacceptable conditions and risks, coupled with the thrusting liberation and individualism of more recent times, have resulted in a reflection on the need to control these uses of man. This has led to the imposition by official and professional bodies of legal, regulatory and practical constraints on the intentions and practices of physicians and scientists. The result has been a steady growth in statutory and other rules and professional codes.

Prior to this growth in guidance and restrictions relating to practices, there had been international agreement to try to prevent physicians from ever again behaving as they had done in Nazi and other prison camps, which influenced the ideas of legal and professional experts.

The combination of this essentially negative approach to the prevention of excesses in human experimentation with positive moves to define the acceptable and the growing prominence of the socio-political rights of the individual have culminated in statutory and administrative codes of professional practice and rules for the conduct of all sorts of experiments on man.

Together, these now comprise an extensive body of institutionalised ethics supported by clinicians, scientists, ethicists, lawyers and others. Individual rights and responsibilities have become respected, it is true, but proper understanding of what can and cannot be attempted is becoming embroiled in complex administrative procedures. They are intended to protect both the subject and the experimenter, but inevitably they may be felt to impinge on the freedom of both. Although rightly presented in the context of 'ethics', with its appeal as a set of universal principles, in practice they must be seen more as the expression of contemporary beliefs, liable to change as socio-political, cultural and religious views evolve.

Ethics, Rules, Rights and Responsibilities

Certain key principles are now held in developed societies to define the ethics of experiments on humans, whether done to gain basic knowledge from the healthy or the sick or to explore medical, surgical or psychological therapies in the ill. In alternative social systems and cultures, such as those in African and Eastern nations, where the familiar Western concepts of democracy, individual rights defining the role of the community and a Judaeo-Christian heritage may not apply, some of the principles and many of the practices differ from those common amongst us, even though there are still analogous inherent and imposed constraints on human experimentation.

For our purposes ethics may be taken as the philosophical and religious principles that generate the moral code by which we try to lead our lives. Laws and professional or social codes and customs come from those and more general roots with the same basic purpose – to guide personal and interpersonal conduct in diverse circumstances in such ways that each of us has as much freedom as that society considers appropriate.

There are many who will object to that statement who will introduce concepts of 'natural' law and religious precepts and other cherished ideals of the democratic society. These ideas, deliberately eschewed, are important in governing our idcals and practical behaviour, in order to evade partiality in presenting a view.

In keeping with the main theme of using volunteers in research and testing, most attention has been given to basic research rather than to therapeutic trials in people who are ill, and in whom either the efficacy and safety of a new therapy are to be tried, or the comparative value of different treatments is to be compared. The same general principles apply in both instances, but therapeutic research carries the additional burdens of avoiding negative (by omission of current, effective remedies) and positive (toxicity of the new treatment) sources of harm, and the considerable difficulty of explaining neutrally to an ill person why they may not receive any treatment at all, if they are in the placebo group of a controlled trial.

The key ethical principles governing experimentation on ourselves and each other have come to be accepted as the following:

1 **Beneficence or non-maleficence.** Whatever is proposed should first benefit the individual affected or at least not be likely to cause any harm; that knowledge gained should then somehow benefit the community.

This carries the burden of demonstrating the societal 'value' of information, something very dependent on the position of the inquirer; for example, contrast the general 'worth' of studying the genesis of cancer to everyone, and demonstrating that a particular deodorant does or does not cause itching. Yet, we all are likely to use the latter, whereas the majority of us fortunately do not suffer the former.

2 **Voluntariness.** The subject of the study, whether the experimenter, a colleague or other third party, including a patient, should have freely agreed to take part and be able to withdraw at any time without penalty.

The essence of this is that no one should be under any overt or covert pressure, nor be exposed to any inducement from excessive gain, in giving their consent to participation.

3 **Informed consent.** This has become encrusted with many legal overtones, but its essence is that the subject must have had as full and understandable an explanation as possible of what will be done, its purpose, any risks and their consequences.

Only on the basis of full understanding, which requires particularly careful translation of scientific ideas into popular language, can someone be considered to have willingly agreed to take part in an experiment.

This has particularly important implications for proposals to study those not generally considered to be independent, self-controlling individuals, such as children, those with defects of cognition and people who do not enjoy a free life, such as prisoners and members of the armed forces.

4 **Autonomy of the individual.** In our society, everyone should be respected as an autonomous individual, with reciprocal rights and responsibilities and guarantees of freedom and privacy, although any or all of them may differ in diverse societies and at different times.

The force of this is to require respect for the individual and his or her person, the avoidance of trivial or degrading procedures, and preservation of confidentiality.

From these principles, which have evolved from centuries of philosophical and religious reflection, latterly accelerated by the growing possibilities of science and the intrusive demands of medicine and industry, has come an increasingly formalised system of rules and controls to govern human experimentation. The formality may encourage comprehensiveness at the cost of rigidity, as well as rigour, but it does fit our society's burgeoning demand for codified principles intended to afford justice and equality.

The codification has given us powerful documents and an administrative machinery backed by professional discipline and statutory requirements. The details vary in different countries, but the essentials have so much in common that they can be considered together.

'Ethics' can be considered as the fundamental governing principles defining the limits of permissible purposes and practices. 'Rules' are the legal, professional or voluntary precepts stating how people are to be used in studies, and so defining what must or should not be done, and indicating how judgements are to be made. 'Rights' may be taken as the protection and the powers that the subject and the experimenter enjoy, as indicated by the rules. 'Responsibilities', again of the experimenter and, albeit often ignored, of the subject too, are what each is expected to do unless agreement has been specifically withheld or refused.

It is helpful to look at how these are applied in practice, although the 'principles' must not be confused with the process of assessing ethical acceptability, which may change with time and place.

Practice of Ethics

It has become difficult to distinguish the principles from the process in many instances, especially as the day-to-day decision making, which refines the principles by setting case law as precedent, tends to be done locally, with central collation and review only being done intermittently, and mostly to meet new needs rather than generally to analyse and review current beliefs and decisions.

The essential principles of beneficence, individual autonomy, informed consent and voluntariness have been developed into clear, universally accepted statements of principles, notably the 'Declaration of Helsinki' of the World Medical Association (Appendix 1) from which have come multinational and national documents. The latter have diverse legal status, depending on the constitution of each country, and thc lcgal position of the individual and the professional in the state.

All these documents seek to enshrine as ethical principles respect for man and the value for all of knowledge that can only be obtained from man – provided that obtaining it can be justified by setting its value against the risks and costs to the people involved.

Inevitably, the principles have become intermingled with specific legal institutions, professional standards and academic and industrial interests and it is the admixture of ethics and practices that has attracted more public attention and criticism than the key ideas on which the processes are based.

Rules in Practice

We live by rules, whether overt, statutory or customary, and we are both comforted by their support and chastened by their constraints. It must be realised, however, that rules are what we make and apply, and that few if any can be regarded as absolutes, even though our Western society seems increasingly to run on a thickening welter of regulations and rules.

In studies on humans, formal codes have been promulgated by national authorities, sometimes by professional associations and sometimes by governmental institutions, all backed at some remove by legal powers.

By now, in the closing years of the twentieth century, the rules generally state the following.

1 Research on humans is permissible and is to be encouraged subject to controls and safeguards

2 Any such studies, whether involving physical procedures (such as inserting a needle, swallowing a substance, exposing to a particular environment or taking an X-ray), psychological interventions, or gathering information or anonymous specimens from individuals (for example, epidemiological statistics) must be done in a way that is approved by an appropriate reviewing body. The latter, some form of Research Ethics Committee, is responsible for ensuring that the research is consistent with accepted ethical and professional principles, and sometimes that it follows appropriate legal codes

3 Compliance with the rules, statutory or otherwise, requires review of the plan of the study to ensure:

- acceptability of its objective;
- adequacy of the procedures to achieve the stated objectives, i.e. that appropriate investigations can be done, the results can be analysed and there will be sufficient numbers of subjects or data points to ensure that a valid answer will be obtained, thus justifying the investigation;
- sufficiency of the training of the experimenter, adequacy of the facilities for the work and to cope with foreseeable adverse events and failures;
- appropriate means to attract volunteers without undue pressure or inducement to accept risks;
- adequacy of the explanation of the objectives, procedures, outcomes and risks and any benefits to be given to volunteers;
- that there be available at all times a source of information for the involved individuals;
- proper precautions to maintain respect for the subjects and confidentiality of identifiable information about them;
- availability of help and compensation for anyone harmed by the study;
- that nothing be done in the study or prevented from being done by it, will contravene national and local rules by omission or commission;
- above all, that the predictable risks, harm and discomfort at the most are minor and readily tolerable.

From these come many special precautions about involving those whose capacity freely to give informed consent may be jeopardised, for example children, the mentally infirm, members of religious orders, the armed forces and prisoners.

The position of patients already suffering an illness, as opposed to healthy volunteers, requires particular care.

1 Studies of the mechanisms of their diseases must not subject them to further suffering, nor can effective treatment be withheld, or only for a short period and then if it does not harm the prognosis.
2 Investigations of therapies, whether new or current, must not materially interfere with current treatment if it has been proven to be effective. The development and proving of a new therapy must be based initially on studying its effects in patients resistant to conventional treatment, or as an addition to and gradual replacement of the present treatment or on a limited phase during which the current therapy can safely be withheld. For serious and chronic diseases it is particularly important not to suggest to sufferers a desired but unproven benefit of a new treatment as that may lead to an unrealisable and even an unrealistic expectation of benefit.
3 Certain groups of people raise special and changing concerns, notably women, particularly those of child-bearing age or who are pregnant, and children.

   The anxiety about the position of women in general comes from perceived inequalities in their social position and the additional risks posed to them and the unborn foetus if they are pregnant. It is possible to test for very early pregnancy before subjecting women to an investigation, but mistakes may occur, and even finding out that someone is pregnant may be a disadvantage to them, thus breaching the non-maleficence principle.

This area has recently been assaulted by the feminist movement, with the result that in order not to be perceived as disadvantaging women, they have increasingly become treated like men, but with some additional caution about the possibility of pregnancy.

For children, the problem is crystallised in questions about the validity of consent, whether obtained from the child, if he or she is old enough to understand, or from the parents or guardian or both.

Rights and Responsibilities in Practice

There are two main parties to any experiment – the investigator and the subject – and each has certain rights and responsibilities (Figures 1.2 and 1.3).

Responsibilities (duties) of the investigator

Clear objective
Skills and facilities for study: and for safety
Clear explanation
No inducement
Respect for the person
Compensation for damage
Honesty
Non-interference with valid treatment (in therapeutic trials)

Rights of the investigator

Full cooperation by the subject
Information about conditions or circumstances that may affect the subject's acceptability
Compliance with the procotol
General timeliness
Prompt and full reporting of effects

Figure 1.2 Responsibilities and rights of the investigator

Responsibilities of the subject

Frank account of health and behaviour
Conformity with the protocol
Cooperation with the investigator
Timeliness

Rights of the subject

Full information
No pressure
Respect of autonomy
Confidentiality

Figure 1.3 Responsibilities and rights of the subject

The subject's rights include equitable treatment, the maximum effort to ensure safety, a frank and honest account of the discomfort and risks as well as the benefits of the experiment, and respect for his privacy and autonomy.

The rights of the investigator include being allowed to advertise the need for volunteers and to explain the purpose of the study, and full cooperation by the subjects in describing their health, any other treatments or chemical exposures, and adherence to the experimental plan, including any restrictions it may place, for example, on normal behaviour and diet.

The responsibilities of each are the corresponding reciprocals of their rights, plus the continuing need for the investigator to ensure that skilled personnel and suitable facilities are available, to monitor safety and stop or modify the protocol as soon as there is a reasonable suspicion that harm may be occurring. The investigator also has the responsibility, sometimes ignored, to publish the results so that there is no need in future for anyone else to repeat the study and so to subject further humans to the same risks, no matter how minuscule they may be.

How Volunteer Studies are Controlled: The Role in Britain of the Local Research Ethics Committee (LREC)

The practicalities of the protection of the volunteer whilst ensuring that medicine and human biology can still make proper studies, have resulted in a number of powerful non-statutory administrative measures in the UK. There are considerable differences between what is done here and in other countries.

The medical and allied professions, with the Department of Health, the administrative systems in the NHS and the health care faculties of universities and other research centres are now required to adhere to a common control system for studies in healthy people or patients. It lacks statutory sanction but infraction may still result in criminal or civil legal action, as well as punishment by professional bodies.

The basis is a series of Local Research Ethics Committees (LRECs), established in each health authority's area, which must consider and approve in advance all protocols involving experiments in man (but not conventional therapy).

Their remit covers basic investigations into the mechanisms of health and disease, trials of any type of drug that is not already licensed for that condition, increasing trials of new operations, diagnostic investigations and devices, obtaining and collecting personal information or biological specimens, and psychological or other non-physical procedures.

In addition, certain central professional bodies such as the Royal Colleges of Physicians, General Practitioners and the British Medical Association, have analogous committees that may be able to aid the examination and approval of investigations involving centres in many areas. For the new and still experimental subject of gene therapy, the official Gene Therapy Advisory Committee (GTAC) was established in 1994 to act as a national ethical and advisory group because of the novelty and lack of general experience of the procedures.

The Medical Research Council and most medical charities have established their own equivalents of LRECs to provide internal assessment and guidance, and so have the armed forces to cover their human research procedures.

Pharmaceutical companies and contract clinical research companies usually have their own internal committees to cover in-house studies, as well as employing the relevant LREC to cover any extra-mural work. The independence of the intra-mural ethical review groups appears to be fiercely cherished, even though they are not strictly autonomous in the way that LRECs are, because of the enormous importance to the organisations of not permitting any mistakes.

There are allied ethical review systems in other developed countries and international bodies concerned with health.

The existence of the LREC system has provided answers to four fundamental questions about the control of human experimentation.

1 *What is controlled by these 'official' ethical review committees?* Virtually everything from basic research to therapeutic trials is covered by their remit. The sole exceptions to the 'official' system of which I am aware involve human studies in such non-therapeutic areas as food and food additives, cosmetics and personal hygiene products, industrial and agrochemicals. In practice, human studies in these areas appear to be covered by committees established by the manufacturer or other initiating body, and to do so according to similar precepts and with no less rigour than LRECs.

2 *What does an LREC comprise?* The Department of Health requirements specify a minimum size (8–12 people) and composition – an independent chairman, adequate representation of medical and allied professions, of lay people and of both sexes. It is common for local ethnic and cultural groups to be represented, for there to be at least one lawyer, and, if possible, one or more ministers of religion, and sometimes a professional ethicist.

   The intention is to ensure coverage of technical expertise, including ethics, lay perceptions and feelings and judgements, and representative creeds and beliefs.

3 *What does an LREC do?* Its job is to examine every proposal for experiments on humans, if sick or healthy, and if the proposal involves one (even the experimenter himself) or thousands of people.

   It has to decide the following.

- Is the objective sufficiently clearly defined and is it worth studying?
- Is the experimental plan capable of giving a clear answer?
- Do the investigator and supporting colleagues have the necessary skills and experience, and are their facilities adequate for this study? Correspondingly, can they properly deal with any reasonably foreseeable emergency?
- Is there sufficient and appropriate information to show the probable safety of whatever is to be done?
- Does the protocol provide an adequate and clear explanation in appropriate language for the subjects of the purpose, risks, procedures and consequences of the investigation?
- For trials of therapies is there an assurance that in all other ways the patient subjects will receive conventional treatment?

- How are confidentiality of data and privacy and respect of the person to be attained and maintained during and after the study?
- Is the method of informing potential subjects clear and neutral?
- Whilst the subjects' out-of-pocket expenses should be covered, it is essential that no reward offered is so high that it induces someone to accept an excessive risk.
- Is there an adequate, non-contentious means of compensating subjects injured by the study and, correspondingly, do the professionals involved carry appropriate liability and negligence insurance?

Finally, from consideration of all these factors and knowledge of the proponents and other facilities, the LREC must decide that the proposed study is feasible, reasonable and consistent with professional and societal standards. In other words, it is ethically acceptable, a major task indeed!

In the case of candidate medicines and therapeutic trials, this system and its decisions are independent of the requirements of the legislation governing medicines and the associated Good Clinical Practice (GCP) regulations. Its deliberations are also independent of the rules governing exposure to radioactive isotopes, X-rays and other forms of electromagnetic energy.

In principle this represents a formidable process of enquiry and judgement, which should ensure acceptability and the minimisation of risk. Some complain that it has slowed or even ossified certain types of research, and that it represents a considerable cost in time and money to the academic, clinical and industrial research communities. Perhaps we should be happy to pay this price for the possibility of continuing acceptable research, and for the refinement of protocols resulting from the review process. The LREC system has prevented either a more interventionist and dirigist system, or the anarchy of no controls and even cruel and illegal behaviour, as in the past.

Details of many of these aspects are covered by other chapters in this book.

The Benefits and Problems of being an Ethical Researcher

As noted above, there are opportunity and time costs of conforming with this system. It makes even small pilot projects, the 'what-ifs' of fertile researchers, into slow and sometimes ponderous projects, including even simple class demonstrations. The process, however, offers considerable support and protection by forcing the researcher to be clear about aims and means and his or her ability to achieve them. It has also legitimised acceptable research both directly and by preventing unacceptable experiments.

A further benefit is that communication between the scientist or clinician and the volunteer subjects will be clarified by interrogation by the reviewers.

The Benefits and Problems of the Subject

A person should be clear why he or she is volunteering, what for, what it entails and what limited reward is offered. In these ways enthusiastic altruism can be tempered by clear understanding of discomfort and risk, and knowledge that compensation will be available if there is unexpected harm.

Perhaps the major remaining problem is whether the lay volunteer has obtained a sufficiently clear understanding of what is entailed by the trial, after an often exhaustive explanation of sophisticated research in plain English. A further concern is whether the volunteer accepts the responsibilities of being a subject, especially the need to conform to the requirements of the protocol and to tell the investigator if he or she breaches it by behaviour, consumption of forbidden foods, beverages or drugs etc.

The only real benefit to the volunteer should be the satisfaction of helping, but one cannot avoid the suspicion sometimes that material reward has been an attraction. That may be pragmatically acceptable if the benefit is no more than some days of restriction in an hotel-like environment, or pocket money, always provided that there is no real risk from the experiment.

Some Problem Areas

Other contributors will cover these, but it must be accepted that our system is not perfect. Concerns include the following:

1 RECs have a local remit, which may make for different judgements of the same protocol by different centres, or at diverse times. How can decisions be equated?

2 What, if any, is the formal status of non-National Health Service RECs? What power do they have to prevent what they regard as non-ethical research?

3 As local bodies, do all LRECs now require the same extent and quality of information in making decisions?

4 Do all LRECs have sufficient access to the specialised knowledge required to evaluate very complex investigations?

5 As there can be no formal or absolute criteria for deciding whether a proposal is ethically acceptable, would LRECs come to comparable judgements on the same information about the same protocol?

6 In these days of formalisation, how should or could LREC members be trained? This may be a particular concern for lay members, who need to achieve a degree of technical understanding whilst maintaining a proper distance from the professionals.

7 Without unacceptable restriction of individual freedom and privacy, how

can the greedy or over-enthusiastic volunteer be prevented from taking part in too many studies, or from concealing his or her simultaneous participation in multiple potentially incompatible studies?

8 How can researchers demonstrate that their proposal does not unnecessarily duplicate work already completed?

9 The lack of any central collation of data on studies performed and volunteers used makes it impossible to be sure just how much work is being done and how many people are involved and whether there have been any instances of serious harm (with the exception in the UK of two unusual cases that resulted in serious illness and death).

10 Should the LREC system be given a direct legal basis?

Summary and Conclusions

There may seem to be a fundamental discord between our respect for each other and our need for knowledge that can be obtained only by experimenting on ourselves and each other. True, the balance between these principles continues to move, but the benefits of learning about health and disease are so important that the altruism of the volunteer must be respected and encouraged, provided that it does not enter into the cruelty of professional excess, or the pathology of wilful personal suffering. Ethics here is a shifting fulcrum that must be guarded.

Deliberately, nothing has been written about what is permissible, and thus what is the limit of the acceptable, in a study in human volunteers. That is because it is impossible to define except in general terms: Studies must not carry more than minimal risk, they must not be more than minimally painful or unpleasant, they should not cause any permanent change or notable scar, and they must not be degrading or offensive.

Perhaps the old truism can fairly be cited 'Do not do unto others what you would not do to yourself' plus 'But be aware that their sensitivities and understanding may not be the same as yours'!

Discussion

How are the members of the LRECs recruited?

Recruiting LREC members is a district health authority responsibility. There is a wide range of healthcare professionals who should be represented on those committees. There should also be two lay members, at least one of whom should not be in any way connected with the running of the NHS, although there are no hard-and-fast rules on how to evaluate that. Some of the guidance in the standards framework that has been circulated will help to guide people's thinking a little more about exactly what sort of competencies they need in people whom they select to serve on their local research ethics committees. Local district health authorities are left to determine precisely how they go about it. It is extremely arduous sitting on a research ethics committee; it is not something that anyone who is very busy will readily volunteer to do, because it takes a good day to go through all the papers, then the meeting may last another day. It is a tremendous responsibility and is something that cannot be taken lightly. Sometimes contact with the researchers can create certain difficulties and that can take up days of time as well. This has to be done on a voluntary basis together with other commitments and it is often very difficult to find people willing to do the work.

How are the committees trained in ethics and how long do they spend doing it?

Until recently there has not been any formal training and it has been a matter for the individual to take himself off to relevant books and texts to read and to discuss things with colleagues. McKenna and Co. have produced an interesting set of SOPs (standard operating procedures) and at the same time the Department of Health has produced a training manual for members of ethics committees which is being widely applied. Basically it has been a matter of discussion within the committee and, to an extent, with colleagues, both professional and lay. It has been like so many things in this country, a bit haphazard, but attempts are being made to improve this.

At the moment it appears that ethics committees are not actually trying to become knowledgeable about all aspects of the work that they consider. One of the grey areas is that investigators are being relied upon to ensure that the work they are doing is worth while and the ethics committees seem to be concentrating more on the risk assessment of the subject and the information provided.

There may be a danger of the above but it depends clearly on the different ethics committees. On the Barts ethics committee, with certain exceptions, it covers most of the medical and teaching hospital university areas and can give a reasonable technical opinion in its own right. The author sits on another ethics committee for a para-governmental organisation and they know an enormous amount about a very narrow area and have less concept of the general nature of what is being done in human experimentation. It is a patchy risk and differs between different committees.

References and Further Reading

There is a huge amount of diffuse literature on the ethics and practicalities of scientific (and pseudo-scientific) studies in man.

The following are a few key documents and reports as a guide and to avoid what would otherwise be an uncomfortably large catalogue.

1 There is a helpful discussion and citation of many core documents in:

BURLEY, D. M., CLARKE, J. M., and LASAGNA, L. 1993, *Pharmaceutical Medicine*. 2nd Edn. London: Edward Arnold, pp. 268–89.

MARSH, B. T., 1993, Ethics of clinical research, in Burley, D. M., Clarke, J. M., and Lasagna, L., *Pharmaceutical Medicine*. 2nd Edn. London: Edward Arnold, pp. 268–89. It includes the full text of the Declaration of Helsinki: Recommendations Guiding Physicians in Biomedical Research Involving Human Subjects. Adopted by the 41st World Medical Assembly, Hong Kong, September, 1989.

2 Accounts of real and alleged excesses by medical scientists, and broader ethical aspects are given in:

BEECHER, H. K. U., 1959, *Experimentation in Man*. Springfield, Ill.: C. C. Thomas.

MCNEILL, P., 1993, *The Ethics and Politics of Human Experimentation*. Cambridge: Cambridge University Press.

PAPWORTH, M., 1967, *Human Guinea Pigs: Experimentation on Man*. London: Routledge and Kegan Paul.

3 Generally helpful documents:

ROYAL COLLEGE OF PHYSICIANS, 1990, *Guidelines on the Practice of Ethics Committees in Research Involving Human Subjects*. 2nd Edn. London: Royal College of Physicians.

1990, *Research Involving Patients*. London: Royal College of Physicians.

ROYAL COLLEGE OF PHYSICIANS' WORKING PARTY, 1986, Research on healthy volunteers, *Journal of the Royal College of Physicians*, **20**, 243–7.

THE LORD SCARMAN, 1986, Consent, Communications and Responsibility, *Journal of the Royal Society of Medicine*, **22**, 697–9.

BRITISH PAEDIATRIC ASSOCIATION AND ROYAL COLLEGE OF OBSTETRICIANS AND GYNAECOLOGISTS, 1993, *A Checklist of Questions to Ask. When Evaluation, Proposed Research During Pregnancy and Following Birth*. London.

NHS Management Executive, 1991, Health Service Guidelines – Local Research Ethics Committees. *Health Service Guidelines*: (**91**) 5, HMSO, London.

4 Two principal specialist journals in this area are:

Journal of Medical Ethics, published in the UK, and *Biomedical Ethics*, published in the USA.

2

Consumers' Viewpoint

NAOMI PFEFFER

The Consumers for Ethics in Research (CERES) was set up seven years ago to publicise the views of the half a million people who every year in Britain take part in medical research. Modern medical research has many remarkable achievements. As a result hitherto irremediable conditions can now be alleviated and cured. CERES supports the testing of both new and widely used medical techniques to see if they are safe and effective. At the same time, they recognise that this means that still more research will be done on people. Research brings benefits but it can also cause harm.

Today, professionals working in law, economics, politics and ethics influence medical research. The voices of patients and research subjects are rarely heard. In general, almost nothing is known about the volunteers' reasons for participating in research, or what it feels like to be the subject in an experiment. Some studies require almost no active participation on the part of the research subject, for example, where tissue removed during an operation is examined for research purposes. Many studies require varying degrees of time, effort or discomfort. Being a research subject can be extremely arduous, even for healthy people. An investigation into the relationship between ovulation and breast-feeding used as subjects women who had recently given birth. Whilst looking after a new baby, subjects had to take and post to the investigators daily samples of urine and breast-milk, keep an events diary, visit the hospital fortnightly for blood tests, and have ultrasound to check on ovulation. Many patients undoubtedly find it difficult to cope with illness and the demands of participating in a clinical trial. A study which was recently reviewed by a research ethics committee required subjects to spend three weekends in a hospital bed, attached to machines, unable to get up except to go to the lavatory. The investigators acknowledged that the research would probably exacerbate subjects' symptoms and discomfort. The investigation was considered to be ethical by the ethics committee. Nevertheless, it does make you wonder under what circumstances would anyone consider taking part in such an arduous study.

Subjects are crucial to the research enterprise. Yet people who might be or who have been subjects of research are almost never asked about their motives or experiences. Research subjects are rendered invisible in a number of different ways. They are almost never invited to speak at conferences where medical research is being discussed. Most conferences are too expensive for them to attend without some form of sponsorship, which is almost never forthcoming. Subjects of medical research are rarely thanked for their contribution. In peer-reviewed publications, researchers often acknowledge their colleagues' assistance, by, for example, thanking them for allowing them access to patients under their care. However, this courtesy is almost never extended to the people who participated in the study (Roberts, 1992).

CERES works with patients' self-help groups to publicise their members' views and experience of medical research. Running self-help groups is very costly financially and personally; members who may be ill often feel like giving up the struggle. CERES public meetings always start with at least one research subject talking about his or her personal experiences of medical research. What does being a 'volunteer' in research and testing mean to them? 'Volunteer' suggests someone performing an action of his or her own free will, without external constraint, prompting or suggestion by another. In the context of medical research, it is an excellent concept. However, it requires a degree of autonomy which rarely exists. As the following examples show, there is a crucial difference between legal consent – 'getting the signature on a piece of paper' – and valid consent – people freely choosing to participate in medical research.

Today, political, economic and social problems diminish the capacity of many people to act autonomously in relation to many things, including medical research. Who, for example, would accept that homeless people are fully capable of acting of their own free will. Yet every copy of *The Big Issue*, the magazine written and distributed by homeless people, contains several advertisements inviting people to participate in medical research as healthy volunteers. The payment offered by researchers undoubtedly is extremely attractive to a homeless person. It is unlikely to entice many people in paid employment. Can women who are illegal immigrants, who work as prostitutes and are HIV positive, and who are worried about being deported back to countries with few health services, be considered to have voluntarily given consent to the recruitment of their children into a clinical trial of Azathioprine (AZT)?

Whether or not to take part in medical research may be only one of several important decisions which patients may be considering. A breast-care nurse involved in research described one woman for whom breast cancer was a non-event. 'She was so desperately worried about recently being made redundant. It took away all meaning and purpose from her life. We only dealt with her cancer and treatment very basically, and we talked a lot about her job. With others, it may be her husband or a constellation of events going on in her life' (Alderson, 1993).

Patients with chronic conditions may agree to take part in research because they fear they will have less good care if they refuse. A young man suffering from sickle cell disease told CERES that he felt under tremendous pressure to participate in a trial of a new drug said to reduce the incidence of sickling, and hence reduce the frequency of painful and dangerous crises, which sometimes prove fatal. The consultant/investigator had been treating him for over 10 years, prescribing morphine, on which he is now dependent, to control the severe pain associated with the disease. His brother had died of sickle cell disease, and like many people with chronic, incurable conditions, he was extremely well informed about it. He was not convinced that the risks inherent in the trial were outweighed by its possible benefits. The experimental drug is toxic; it suppresses bone marrow, and increases the risk of acute leukaemia. As he put it, 'it is my life, and it should be up to me to decide how I am going to die'.

Moral pressure is sometimes put on patients to participate in research. The decision point is often blurred. A speaker at a CERES meeting said she has been asked to think about participation, and on the next visit it was assumed she would. Nineteen women had already agreed to be participants. She was the last recruit into a study of 20 new mothers. Since the researchers had included only the minimal number to make the project viable, there was also moral pressure to continue in it. She did not consider herself a volunteer.

How can 'voluntary' participation in research and testing be achieved? By researchers recognising the importance of respecting informed refusal as much as informed consent. If good information reduces recruitment, it demonstrates that ethics are working, and that people are not being forced to help with research. Unfortunately, good information is not always provided by researchers. Few seem to be able to use plain English. Who can tell what is involved in participating in a double-blind randomised placebo controlled cross-over designed trial to compare the tolerability and efficacy of combinations of X-65490P with placebo in the treatment of people diagnosed with diabetes mellitus? Yet many information sheets are written in this type of language. CERES has published *Spreading the word on research* (CERES, 1994), which offers guidelines on how to provide clear information for people asked to take part in health research.

Some investigators fear that giving patients information might put them off the trial. Others argue that for people with a serious illness, too much information about research might be an added source of stress. It is difficult to say what kind of information people considering participating in research might want to have because almost no one bothers to ask them. Information sheets produced by professionals usually contain information the researchers and other authorities believe patients and research subjects should have. Yet a lack of appropriate information may discourage potential research subjects from agreeing to participate in a trial. One reason given by the young man with sickle cell disease for being reluctant to take the experimental drug hydroxyurea was that he associated it with urea, a drug which had been tested in sickle cell disease with disastrous results. None of the investigators had thought it necessary to explain the difference between the two compounds.

Most people do not have any idea of what being involved in medical research means. There is an enormous gap between what the public and researcher know and value. Take, for example, ideas about what constitutes a good outcome. Some researchers still seem to find merit in the old maxim, 'The operation was a success but the patient died'. The quantity and quality of side effects can be seriously underrated. One woman who had suffered extensive damage to her arm and shoulder after undergoing radiotherapy for breast cancer asked, 'What is success? My medical notes describe a "successful cancer treatment and effective radiotherapy". Yet I walked out of hospital feeling very ill, a wreck. My idea of success is to have a nice long disease-free time, to be able to look after myself, to work, to do all the things fully which I enjoy, and to put to the back of my mind the knowledge that I was a cancer sufferer. That is vastly different from the doctors' idea of success. Some doctors say, "You're alive, what else do you want?" But they too have higher expectations than simply to be alive.'

The concept of equipoise and the technique of randomisation are central to much medical research. Both turn upside down most people's ideas and values in relation to medicine. Equipoise is a crucial concept in medical research. Equipoise means that investigators are genuinely uncertain about which of the treatments being tested is best, and that people in each trial group have, as far as is known, an even chance of benefit or harm. Research starts from uncertainty. A question is being asked because no one knows the precise answer. Treatments are being tested or compared because no one knows which is the better one. Benefits are not certain but are unknown and hoped for. However, a patient who has just been confronted with the crisis of the diagnosis of a life-threatening disease wants to believe he or she is going to receive the 'best' treatment available for his or her condition. Patients want to hear a specific recommendation, not that their doctor does not have the answer. As one woman who had been invited to participate in a trial of different treatments of breast cancer put it, 'at that moment of being told I had breast cancer, I couldn't take it. I needed him to say that he knew the best treatment for *me*' (Alderson, 1993). Learning about medical uncertainty comes as an additional shock to patients who already feel trapped in terrifying uncertainties.

Randomisation is a very difficult technique for lay people to accept. It signifies that treatment will be decided as a matter of chance. Patients want treatment tailored to their specific requirements. Randomisation disregards their individual uniqueness. It depersonalises patients. Furthermore, it asks them to put aside their own concerns and consider the interests of unknown people who in the future may suffer from the same disease. As a breast cancer research nurse put it, 'randomisation, with its attendant depersonalisation, is a problem for women who feel threatened by the loss of their intrinsic selves anyway. Benefits for unknown women a generation away don't stand much chance against hanging on to something of self now' (Alderson, 1993).

It is almost impossible for subjects to obtain redress when research is found to be unethical. A good example is the now notorious investigation into the value of advice offered by the Bristol Cancer Help Centre. The Bristol Cancer Help Centre advised people with cancer to adopt an organic, vegetarian diet, and advocated complementary therapies such as relaxation. When the paper on the investigation was published in 1990 (Bagenal *et al.*, 1990), it was given enormous coverage in newspapers and on the radio and television (*Lancet*, 1990 and 1991). Women who had sought the advice of the Centre and had participated in the study were shocked and distressed to read that compared with women having only conventional treatment, they were twice as likely to die and three times as likely to suffer a relapse. However, follow-up investigations showed that the study was methodologically flawed. Yet when the authors of the paper withdrew some of the claims it made, their retraction received far less publicity that the original report. As a result, the myth prevails that women with breast cancer who go to the Bristol Cancer Help Centre are more likely to suffer a relapse and die. Many of the women who had participated in the study formed a support group and sought redress, which has still not been obtained.

The Research Ethics Committee which had approved the study of the Bristol Cancer Help Centre has not taken action against the researchers. However, if they chose to act, the only sanction available to a research ethics committee is to withdraw ethical approval and thereby nullify the investigators' indemnity. Without being specific, there is one instance where that sanction was used, and it highlights the importance of attending to the context in which research is conducted. A surgeon wrote to so-called 'long-waiters', that is, people who had been on a waiting-list for nearly two years, inviting them to participate in a drug trial. In return, they would undergo free surgery at a private hospital earlier than if they waited for NHS treatment. The ethics committee withdrew its approval of the study, and informed the pharmaceutical company that the investigator was no longer indemnified.

It is not known whether the research subjects recruited to the trial were told of the ethics committee's decision. There is no reason for them to have been informed. The Royal College of Physicians Report on Fraud and Misconduct in Medical Research, for example, makes no such recommendation. Almost no attention has been given to the rights of subjects who have participated in fraudulent or unethical research. The main concern has been to safeguard the reputation of the research community.

Summary and Conclusions

How can 'voluntary' participation in research and testing be achieved? CERES believes that six issues need to be considered. First, researchers must appreciate the virtue of respecting informed refusal as much as informed consent. This requires giving potential subjects the information that they want, and not information researchers and other authorities feel they should have. If researchers want the public to participate in research, they have to respect their ideas and values, and try to understand the dilemmas that research confronts them with.

Second, researchers must acknowledge that many potential research subjects feel ill, anxious, ignorant of medical knowledge, dependent and vulnerable. They have to recognise the ways in which differences in class, gender, race and income diminish people's capacity to act as volunteers. This might mean rejecting some people who seem to agree to be subjects, on the grounds that their participation is not voluntary.

Third, when they are healthy, people should be taught to understand medical uncertainty. A public which has been educated when healthy to appreciate uncertainty and realistically to assess the difficulties and dilemmas in treating disease efficiently, successfully and economically is in a much better position to evaluate the particular trial being proposed and discuss the options more intelligently (Thornton, 1994).

Fourth, the Department of Health and professional bodies should develop a system of redress for people recruited into unscientific and unethical research. Medical researchers should be encouraged to see themselves as accountable to research subjects.

Fifth, researchers should involve potential subjects in the design of research. In this way, they may give appropriate weight to outcomes, risks and benefits. This leads on to the sixth requirement.

Researchers must acknowledge the contribution people make to medical progress. Research subjects should be thanked in publications. When the research has been completed, it would be nice if they were told the results. Research subjects should receive reports on the findings of the research to which they have contributed, with an invitation to comment. The contribution each year of the half million or so research subjects to the development of modern medicine should be applauded.

Discussion

Most of this section is in relation to patients, but little is known about the personality of the people volunteering. Personality scales on normal volunteers have been constructed and it has been found that you are more likely to be extrovert if you volunteer for clinical trials than if you don't. This may also be true of patients.

In 20 years' experience of consumer product studies, it appears that money is the prime reason why people take part. Some social activities have come as a small second as they can socialise with their friends. One of the most important things is that study directors give adequate information in simple understandable English. It is important that volunteers do complete the trials. If only 50 per cent of the volunteer group that we require complete the study, then the study is invalid. They need clear information on the dates that will be required, the kinds of inconveniences that may happen, the effects on the skin that they are likely to have. Because of that we have very few people who drop out because they do not like what is happening. It is mainly dropping out for family reasons or illness on their part, unconnected with the study.

It is very difficult to produce clear information, and the researchers who are experts in their fields are not necessarily very good at producing information sheets in plain English. Such experts require sufficient support, encouragement or advice on it. It is not only up to the lay person on every committee to take on that role – everyone can contribute to that process. Not everyone on the committee has expertise in all fields considered by the committee.

Should volunteers and others who take part in experiments be able to be proactive in deciding in a community what kind of experiments should be undertaken? For example, at the moment, a lot of experiments are undertaken because a drug firm is interested in a particular drug, or medical professionals may be interested in a particular line of research. It may not be what the community wants. There may be thousands of people with chronic fatigue syndrome which they want researched and yet it is dismissed because it may have a low profile in the medical community or may not be something the drug firms want to investigate.

One of the aims of CERES is to try to encourage researchers to take on board the kinds of issues that patients want investigated and to include them into the design of the research. At the last meeting in sickle cell and thalassaemia, there were many examples of this aim. Some people were worried about the orphan drugs that no company felt were worthwhile developing because they did not feel there was a sufficiently large section of the population for it to be profitable. There was also discussion on ways to prevent sickling, such as keeping warm and generally looking after yourself that they wanted investigating. It is very difficult to get money for this kind of work.

One fears that sometimes a society like CERES attracts the people who want to complain. Within the fabric of doctor–patient relationships in medical research, very close bonds are often developed. Quite a lot of work in hypertension is conducted and far from producing disgruntled patients it is often found that people who come out of one study are wanting to know if

they can go into another one because they liked the special relationship that this gives them and the special access to identified care. Secondly, studies in patients with heart failure are conducted and doctors at one particular centre who do this came up with the idea of running an annual Christmas party for them, which has become a highlight of their social calendar. Patients attend and they know the staff well and obviously have good relationships with them. The danger is that if you just describe circumstances where relationships have broken down, you give the impression that these are the only types of relationships that exist. Specific instances related to circumstances where patients are facing life-threatening diseases were discussed. It was implied that this was a most inappropriate set of circumstances in which research should be done. If these people are not involved in research to try to identify which of several methods of treatment might help them to live longer it is very difficult to see what substitute there can be.

Most of the members of CERES are members of research ethics committees, voluntary organisations or community health councils. The CERES brief is to promote good research and good practices in research. Unfortunately it is the case that the people who will speak out in public are more often those who do have an axe to grind. It is very difficult to find research subjects and they are a hidden group. Modern medicine has achieved a great deal, particularly over the last few decades. However it is increasingly important to try to educate people about medical uncertainty.

Messages of health education that we are desperately trying to get across to the public have almost no impact at all.

There are examples in other countries, Denmark for example, where the authorities tried to bring the public along when they changed their definitions of death to stem death. It shows a willingness to involve the public and to invest in that.

Notes

This chapter is based on the experiences of the Consumers for Ethics in Research (CERES) group.

References

ALDERSON, P., 1993, *Women's views of breast cancer treatment and research: report of a pilot project*. London: Social Science Research Unit, Institute of Education.

BAGENAL, F. S., EASTON, D. F., HARRIS, E., CHILVERS, C. E. and MCELWAIN, T. J., 1990, Survival of patients with breast cancer attending Bristol Cancer Help Centre, *Lancet*, **336** (8715), 606–10.

CERES, 1994, *Spreading the word on research or patient information: how can we get it better?* London: CERES, PO Box 1365, London N16 0BW. £2.50.

Lancet, 1990, Comments: Sept. 15, **336** (8716) 636; Sept. 22, **336** (8717) 743–4; Nov. 10, **336** (8724) 1185–8.

1991, Comments: Nov. 30, **338** (8779) 1401–2.

ROBERTS, H., 1992, Answering back: the role of respondents on women's health research, in *Women's Health Matters*, London: Routledge, 176–92.

THORNTON, H., 1994, The dilemmas of randomisation and equipoise from the viewpoint of a patient invited to participate in a breast cancer trial, *CERES News*, **11**, 2.

3

Human Volunteers in Research: A Physician's Overview

DENIS McDEVITT

'Human Volunteers in Research and Testing' is a topic of some potential controversy. In the mid-1960s a book was published entitled *Human Guinea Pigs* (Papworth, 1967) which described much of the cutting edge of research over the previous 15–20 years and put it into a slightly different context. For example, in terms of the development of cardiac output it stated that volunteers were being held in the position of a cross while all kinds of terrible things were done to them. Although that was an overstatement it did draw attention to the fact that much of what had been done until that stage had been done without what we would now regard to be adequate controls. There have been many instances since then of things coming to light which society would be very unhappy about. Studies were done in the USA on the transmission of the hepatitis virus by releasing it into an institutional population; studies were done amongst the blacks in southern America looking at the epidemiology of syphilis to name just two. There have also been intermittent scandals raised in the press, some of which were possibly contrived; this area will be covered later.

In the last 10 years the death of two volunteers during research procedures again jogged the memory of the medical profession to review the whole process to make sure that it was adequate.

My first recollection of volunteers in research was when I was a medical student. One of the lecturers asked for volunteers to take part in a project within the department. Being young and somewhat foolish I was one of the people who said that I would help. There were no medicals, no information, certainly no consent and before I knew what was happening I had been given a drug and was sitting on a chair with sulphur dioxide being pumped into the air to see if the drug was an anti-tussive. Very rapidly I learned that if I did not breathe during the course of this experiment I did not cough and therefore no worthwhile results were obtained. It was retrospectively an illustration of many of the issues in research that ought now to be prevented.

In the late 1960s and the early 1970s whilst training as a clinical pharmacologist and physician, I was involved in student experiments as part of the process of teaching clinical pharmacology. Students were subjected to a series of things from which they were meant to learn. Again, there was no ethical approval, but there certainly was medical supervision. However, in some of these experiments in medical schools there was no medical supervision because the experiments were being done by physiologists and other people who would not have known what to do had anything gone wrong and would certainly not have had access to resuscitation equipment.

At that stage one of the things that researchers did was predominantly to use themselves as their own volunteers in research studies. There are positive aspects to this in that anyone who is going to run studies should know what it is like to be on the receiving end. However, there are also some difficulties; one being that in a relatively small pool of volunteers it means people will be used fairly frequently. Thus, if you are a clinical pharmacologist studying new drugs there may be problems with exposure to new chemical entities. Also, by definition if investigators are lying on couches as volunteers they cannot be working and therefore it is not a cost-effective method of doing research.

In the early to mid-1970s I went to the USA for further training. It was a revelation to me because there they were recruiting both normal volunteers and patient volunteers. They were recruiting the normal volunteers predominantly by the method of payment. We need to recognise that without some form of payment most volunteers will not volunteer. The *quid pro quo* for the patient volunteers was often that they got free treatment. This, by definition, recruited the people who did not have good insurance policies and therefore in the American system could not afford to pay for their treatment. I hope I learned the best of what was on offer at that stage and when I came back to the UK in the mid-1970s we started a process of trying to recruit volunteers by the method of using what in perjorative terms is called the payment of expenses, but which in fact enabled us to have a much larger pool of recruits, and therefore to be involved in a much wider area of research.

If you are going to operate such a system you need very good controls on the process. These controls are covered in this book. In terms of experience I can offer two other pointers. One is that, as a civil consultant in the Royal Air Force, I am actually on the ethics committee at the Institute of Aviation Medicine. There, they are doing studies which would not get passed by a normal ethics committee because there is a very huge element of risk involved even though it is very carefully controlled. You may say that these types of studies should never be done, but if we are going to have armed services and pilots flying aircraft at horrendous speeds subjected to forces of gravity which defy imagination, then we have to know both what happens and also how these physiological processes can be controlled. This is really the fringe of research but I think it illustrates the need for having really adequate controls. Finally, as a member of the Medicines Commission I was involved in the discussion process of advice to the Minister of Health on the question of normal volunteers and how some sort of control should be exacted in that area. Again this resulted from the deaths of two volunteers and the fear that perhaps we did not have adequate systems.

Therefore when I say that this is just a physician's view, it is clearly more than that: I have in fact been involved in research both as a volunteer, an investigator and in the discussion processes. I thought that by reviewing my own experience it would illustrate not only some of the issues but also the development that there has been in this process of using volunteers in research over a period of 20–25 years.

What is the justification for doing studies on volunteers? There are a number of things that should be considered. One is the advancement of medical knowledge which is very often linked to improvements in our understanding of the treatment of the disease. This is not necessarily directly drug related because we need to know about physiological processes in order to be able to unravel the way in which people respond to disease and how they are helped by drug treatment. In addition, we need to have a system for testing drugs as a preliminary to their introduction to patients, on the way to getting product licences. There really is no substitute to using man. It should be recognised that the best experimental animal for man is man himself and that the sooner we can begin to look at studies in diseased man, the more likely it is that important advances will be identified.

Risk/benefit assessments have already been referred to and this may be extremely variable. On the one hand there may be very little in the way of what can be called benefit and therefore no risk is acceptable. On the other hand in relation to disease, for example, looking for a treatment for cancer which is inevitably going to end patients' lives, then we clearly will accept risks in therapy which would not be acceptable in terms of treating self-limiting disease.

We need to recognise that there are patient and non-patient volunteers and consider that non-patient volunteers are not necessarily normal subjects as they may be people who are not going to get benefit themselves from the study and do not have a significant illness that is relevant to the proposed study. Certainly in the drug assessment process it is a requirement now that some information will be obtained in patients with compromised renal and hepatic function in relation to the metabolism of certain drugs.

Volunteer recruitment is an issue that should be focused on. The process should allow volunteers to offer their services of their own free will and there should be no process of coercion, or even implied coercion. Certainly within a medical school environment, a teacher asking a student if he or she would like to take part in an experiment, would, no matter how polite he or she is, always have the possibility of coercion being involved in relation to the examination process. Therefore, it is better that any attempt to recruit is done by some kind of general notice. The best way to do this may be to advertise in the local paper. This has been done by a contract drug company that runs on the premises of Ninewells Hospital who advertised for obese subjects to take part in a study. They were absolutely overwhelmed by the response of the public who wanted to get slim at someone else's expense. Payment is an issue, but it should not be mentioned in any attempt to recruit. Subjects need to be able to give legally valid consent, need to be fully and properly informed, and they must know that they have the opportunity to withdraw at any time for whatever reason.

Financial inducement is a fact of life, that of the society in which we now live. Most people are not governed by altruistic motives and if we wait for people to volunteer out of willingness to help medical science, many of the studies would never be done. If there is to be a reward, at the moment it is paid as expenses. It is said only to be a reasonable amount related to the nature and degree of inconvenience, but there is no doubt that the majority of people who are involved are either unemployed or students who are getting an increasingly diminishing grant from the government to support them. This is certainly a legitimate way in which they can supplement their grant. On the other hand, payment should not be inducement although there is no doubt that it is an inducement, however small the payments are. If they are too small then people will not volunteer. A mechanism is required within the research environment for making sure that the reward is considered only to be a reasonable inconvenience payment. It should be recognised that the actual financial reward plays a significant part in people volunteering. Nevertheless they should know that, if they have to withdraw for medical reasons, they will be fully recompensed.

Concerning safety, ethics committees have a very strategic role and the pharmaceutical companies themselves now contribute through good clinical practice, trying to make sure that studies are only done on premises which are adequately resourced in terms of staff and facility. The importance of making sure that the investigators are able to cope with an emergency, or have immediate access to somebody who can, must be stressed. There is no point in having a defibrillator standing in the department if, when the subject collapses with a cardiac arrhythmia, it turns out that no one knows how to use it or that it has not been serviced for six months and therefore does not work. That may sound funny but there is at least anecdotal evidence of some contract companies who were hiring rooms in hotels as a means of doing some of these studies. Discussions have taken place as to whether there should be a form of licensing and register for conducting studies on normal volunteers, comparable to what happens with animal experimentation. However, it would be very difficult to police properly. Therefore it has largely been left up to ethical committees and/or the code of practice of the Association of the British Pharmaceutical Industry (ABPI) who are themselves extremely concerned about volunteer usage and who would be implicated in any litigation if unnecessary risks occurred and patients were damaged.

Summary and Conclusions

All of the issues relating to experimentation on human volunteers need to be considered at the same time. There are some people against the use of animals in research. The same people are often against the use of people as normal volunteers and human experimentation as well but they almost certainly want all drugs to be 100 per cent safe. It is impossible to hold all these points of view at the same time and remain a rational being. If we are going to advance the process of finding new therapies for patients, and of understanding the disease processes better, then the system will depend on the use of volunteers, be they non-patient or patient volunteers, for the identifiable future. In the short term, the problems cannot be resolved in the tissue culture laboratory and will probably never be able to be. A system which will be functional but which will be very critically surveyed to make sure that it has the highest possible standards and is protecting the individuals involved, is definitely required. It is vital that public confidence is maintained and that volunteers continue to aid progress in medicine.

Discussion

The subject of researchers volunteering themselves for trials was raised. It was thought that if researchers did include themselves in the team to be experimented on, that it would not only provide built-in safeguards for the volunteers, but also greatly improve the public image of volunteering.

The problem is that researchers are often prepared to try things out on themselves that they would not do on volunteers and the same restrictions that apply to the use of volunteers should also apply to the experimenters themselves. Therefore this is not necessarily built-in safety. The safety resides in the inability to perform any study without the approval of the relevant ethics committee. It is strictly not true that researchers are no longer volunteering. What is happening is that they are being used as subjects for experiments much less frequently than previously. It is not cost effective to have highly trained research workers lying on benches just taking part as subjects in the experiment.

Where does the independent doctor for these trials come in? If the doctor who is responsible for the trial is the one responsible for the safety, there must be an element of coercion for the volunteer to continue with the study. It is impossible for the volunteer to give informed consent unless there is some independent doctor present at the trial.

The opportunity exists for any patient or subject to withdraw from any study at any time that they so wish.

Therefore they could go to the doctor conducting the study saying that they would like to withdraw – would this be easy for the volunteer to do?

This is done. Part of the process of recruiting the volunteer is that of giving informed consent and part of informed consent is the premise that at any stage they may cease to be a volunteer if they so wish without giving any reason.

Saying it is completely different to doing it in practice. A patient may feel reticent to withdraw as he has built up a relationship, with an element of trust, and the patient may feel he is letting the doctor down who is doing the study. This may be seen by some ethicists as being a coercive situation.

The relationship would apply whether there is an independent doctor or not.

A totally independent doctor with no interest in the study, would essentially be the patients' advocate, and therefore there would be no fear of breaching the trust or relationship with the researcher.

With normal volunteers, the coercion could be the wish to get to the end of the study to receive all the payment (as they may be doing it to get access to the volunteer payment). There is no other coercion and many simply do not turn up for the next part of the study. For patients it is a slightly different situation because the relationships are very important and many of these studies are run by the nurse as the person who is making the routine observations – therefore lacking the coercion factor involved that is suggested. Patients who are diseased are very keen to participate in these studies because they see that either themselves or other people with a comparable condition may actually ultimately get benefit.

Can the ethics committee that is set up to approve protocols be the appeal committee should any patient or volunteer wish to approach someone for independent advice? If so, can this be written into an agreement?

This could be written in but the average ethics committee is overwhelmed in terms of the business that it has participated in and therefore if you add another strand to their responsibilities it may be almost impossible to get people to serve on those committees. If an independent advice group is required it would be better to construct it independently. There is an implication that doctors are more interested in research than in their patients; it would be impossible to deny that this is never true, but doctors generally have the best interests of patients primarily at heart.

The issue of paying people is very difficult because what in effect you are doing is taking up a contract between the volunteer and the physician or researcher and it is quite clear that the value of that contract does vary considerably between people. A lot of the people that we do research on are students and people who are well aware that they will receive some payment (although it is not advertised) and indeed they expect that. Perhaps this should be more formalised and written down so that people know what they have to do and what they will receive if they withdraw from the study. The problem is not coercing people to take part in it, but persuading people that they are not suitable to take part in the study and turning people away, both in patient and volunteer studies.

Within an institution it is important that some scale of values is drawn up and it is not left to the individual department, and this is where the ethics committee comes in. They should know what payment is being offered as expenses and should feel comfortable that this is not a particular inducement even though we recognise that that is the reason why it is done. They should undermine any process by which one department increases its opportunity for recruiting volunteers by offering more money than others. Particularly where student populations are concerned within an institute some mechanism needs to be sought by which one can control the amount any one person will volunteer. That is actually quite difficult to do. Ideally we should have some kind of central registry but that depends on the volunteers. They will not always tell the truth because they want to get into yet another study because of the pay-off. It is potentially a difficult area.

Note

This chapter is based on the personal views of the author. One or two general observations are based on personal experience in the recognition that many of the subjects touched on will be covered in more detail elsewhere in the book.

Reference

PAPWORTH, M. (1967), *Human Guinea Pigs: Experimentation on Man*, London: Routledge and Kegan Paul, 320 pp.

4

Clinical Research – The Relationship between Law and Guidelines

CHRISTINE BENDALL

Clinical research activities have been a matter of public concern for many decades. The revelation of atrocities during World War II put the subject into sharp focus and prompted the first of a series of ethical statements relating to the proper or acceptable conduct of experimental activities on human beings. Clinical research today is regulated in a number of ways.

1 Professional practice standards for physicians lay down general and fundamental principles of proper conduct which can be applied in experimental as well as in purely therapeutic contexts.

2 Numerous bodies, professional associations and industry groups have published their versions of guidelines relating to the conduct of clinical research examining the role of ethics committees, the obligations of corporate sponsors, the problems of fraud, the special needs of certain types of volunteer populations, the financing of research (including the payment of investigators and volunteers) and, in particular, the provision of compensation for those who may be injured as a result of participation in a clinical study. The available published guidance is extensive and can be obtained from a number of different sources.

3 There is also, to a differing degree across Europe, a certain amount of legal provision relevant or relating to clinical research. Applicable law in this context may be in the form of legislation (whether general or specific to clinical research) and 'judge made' or case law, developed by the courts.

Legal Provisions addressing Clinical Research

1 *Europe*

At European Community level, there is virtually no legislation addressing the matter of clinical research. Pharmaceutical legislation in Europe (which dates back to 1965 and the 'First Pharmaceutical Directive' (Directive 65/65/EEC)) has concentrated upon the marketing, manufacture and wholesale distribution of products for the purposes of sale or supply on the open market. Products at a developmental stage have only more recently been given consideration with a view to producing legislation; this includes clinical research in medicinal products (and devices). The pharmaceutical sector is, however, one of the most highly regulated industrial sectors in Europe and it will be only a matter of time before the European Community introduces measures to harmonise the approach of its member states towards the clinical phase of product development. It is interesting to note that the European Community has already addressed the matter of the use of animals in research (Directive 86/609/EC on the protection of animals used for experimental and other scientific purposes) whilst human research has not yet been the subject of legislation.

As indicated, the Community has already paved the way towards detailed legislation on clinical research. In Directive 75/318/EEC (Annex, Part IV) provisions are set out stating the requirements for study data which must be lodged with the regulatory agencies in order to obtain a marketing authorisation for a medicinal product. Significantly, in order to be acceptable for the purposes of supporting an application, clinical research data must have been derived from trials designed, implemented and conducted *in accordance with good clinical research principles*. A failure to comply with this requirement may mean that the assessing regulatory authority will discount the relevant data when making its assessment of the safety, quality and efficacy of a product. This provision is, of course, only relevant and therefore, effective, in relation to studies intended to count towards a commercial venture, i.e. company-sponsored research in medicinal products. It should also be noted that the principles of 'good clinical practice' (GCP) mentioned in the legislation are not specified: only the general concept is identified.

The Commission has already mooted the question of adopting a directive dealing with the conduct of clinical research in the European Community. The idea was first raised in 1991 and the member states (then 12) were consulted on the proposal. The response received was mixed, with some Member States in favour and a number uncommitted. After the results of this preliminary consultation were published (a discussion paper on the need for a Directive on Clinical Trials 111/3044/91 23.1.91), the proposal was 'put on the back burner' whilst the European Commission concentrated upon progressing important measures to deal with the harmonisation and removal of trade barriers in relation to the registration and marketing of pharmaceuticals. However, it now appears that the proposal may be brought back for discussion in the relatively near future. It will be interesting to see the scope and level of detail attempted in any emerging draft proposals. With the European Community now consisting of 15 member states with different cultural attitudes and approaches to clinical research, the task of reaching agreement, particularly if any detailed provisions are contemplated, will not be an easy one.

2 *Member States*

At the level of individual member states, the approach to the regulation of clinical research is varied and this presents significant difficulty for anyone conducting (multi-centre) research across Europe. In each case, local requirements and practice must be ascertained and considered whilst the basic 'core' of the research must be preserved. Thus, the plethora of different regulatory/legal and administrative requirements poses notable logistical problems both in designing and administering such research. If one examines the different provisions made by member states, the approach varies from the enactment of detailed and specific legislation addressing research (such as can be found in France ('Loi Huriet': Law on the Protection of Persons Undergoing Biomedical Research, 1987, as amended and subordinate decrees) and Ireland (Control of Clinical Trials Act, 1987, Control of Clinical Trials and Drugs Act, 1990)) to the use of principles of general legislation (which can be seen in the UK) and/or to the application of legal principles derived from case law (again an approach which tends to be taken in the UK). Figure 4.1 indicates the basic approach in a number of Member States of the European Community to the enactment of specific legislation on clinical research (over and above product regulation) and/or reliance upon non-binding guidelines, to promote good practice. The approach is far from harmonised and the detail of the provisions can vary considerably in some respects.

The rules and practice relating to compensation of research subjects for injury are a good example, where the Nordic member states tend towards a 'no-fault' based system of compensation across the board, in contrast to other countries where the only available legal remedy involves proving negligence or a defect in the trial product.

Guidance relating to the Conduct of Clinical Research

As already mentioned, the role of guidelines in shaping the attitude and approach to the conduct of clinical research has been substantial. Beginning with the Nuremberg Code published in 1949 (Anon. 1949), international statements have been particularly important in developing ethical codes. In

Clinical research–regulation

Country	Specific legislation	Guidelines
Belgium		√
Denmark		√
Eire	√	
Finland		√
France	√	√
Germany	√	√
Italy	√*	√
Netherlands	√**	√
Portugal	√	
Spain	√	√
Sweden		√
UK		√

*Decree 27.4.92 No. 139 refers to GCP rules which reproduce CPMP Guidelines. No legal sanctions.
**Medical Discipline Act 2.7.28 as amended requires compliance with the Declaration of Helsinki. Act relating to insurance in clinical research and medical experiments.

Figure 4.1 Clinical research – regulation

1964, the Declaration of Helsinki was adopted. It has been amended several times since (most recently in 1989), most notably when it introduced a requirement for independent ethical review of research proposals involving human subjects. In 1992 the Council for International Organisations of Medical Sciences (CIOMS) revised earlier guidelines on research involving human subjects (CIOMS, 1993). In the European Community, the Committee for Proprietary Medicinal Products (CPMP) issued a Note for Guidance on good clinical practice for trials in medicinal products in the European Community in 1990 (111/3976/88-EN 1990). The issue of this CPMP Guidance document was the Community's first real foray into the subject of clinical research. When followed by an amendment to Directive 75/318/EEC setting out the requirements for clinical research included in an application for a marketing authorisation, the topic of 'good clinical practice' was pushed to the fore, at least in the minds of commercial sponsors. Whilst the legislation did not specify a particular set of good clinical research principles in its requirements for research conducted within, or for the purposes of submission to a European Community authority, the CPMP guidelines have become essential reading. However, the guidelines are not perfect and do give rise to a number of problems of interpretation.

Appendix 2 provides some examples of national guidelines relevant to research in selected European member states.

Guidelines are of course only guidelines. Unless specifically referenced in legislation, they are not legally binding. Moreover, guidelines are statements of ethical principle and, as such, are often declarations of desired objectives rather than descriptions of the means of attaining them. Whilst the fundamental principles tend to be held in common, the recommendations of guidelines, both national and international, differ to some degree and can give rise to problems for the researcher trying to determine which are the appropriate set of guidelines to adopt or to consider how to resolve differences in recommendation. As already indicated, these documents are not precisely drafted, so that the exact meaning may be open to interpretation.

An Examination of Law and Guidance in the UK

Having outlined the general pattern of 'controls' in other research within Europe, a more detailed consideration of how they operate may be achieved by considering Member States. However, for present purposes it is intended to focus upon the position in the UK. The picture is one of a mixture of basic legislation relating to medicinal products, general legislation relating to the manufacture and supply, of the protection of individuals, common law and guidelines addressing aspects of clinical research. Critics of the current UK position have highlighted the fact that: there is little (or no specific) legislation; there are few or no legal sanctions and too many 'toothless' guidelines; a lack of any specific case law relating to research and no legal basis for the establishment of ethics committees or for the ethical review of research proposals. Others could no doubt add further to this list. This said, the UK has been a very active location for research and the system of ethical review has been operative for some time compared with other European countries. The fact remains, however, that in the opinion of some sections of society, the present situation gives rise to shortcomings in the appropriate 'regulation' of clinical trials. This criticism leads to questions as to whether the human volunteers who are the subjects of clinical research projects are adequately protected by the systems currently in place: (there are other questions, but this issue is central to the performance of ethical research).

An assessment of the adequacy of the protection of human subjects of research protection in the UK necessarily involves examination of the collective impact of relevant law and guidance.

In practice, concerning the intervention of the law the following are true.

1 The law of tort (battery and negligence) is applicable.
2 The law looks to current guidelines for evidence of reasonable and appropriate standards of conduct when judging questions of negligence.
3 The law of product liability (Consumer Protection Act 1987) applies.
4 The law of contract applies to the conduct of healthy volunteer research.

5 The offences-against-the-person legislation (criminal law) is applicable.
6 The Medical Act of 1983 is relevant to the conduct of investigators.
7 Corporate sponsors may be penalised for 'non-GCP' studies as a result of EC legislation (75/318/EEC) applied in the UK.
8 The law addresses confidentiality issues and data protection, and medicines regulation ensures that the regulatory authorities are aware of all research from Phase II onwards carried out within its jurisdiction on medicinal products.
9 Case law in the treatment context addresses matters of consent, information and warning of risk.
10 The Family Reform Act 1967 and the Children Act 1989 are relevant to the ability of a legal minor to determine participation in research.

This appears to provide a substantial body of legal control over research activities. However, it is also necessary to point out that the law essentially requires proof of fault in order for a researcher or sponsor to be liable to pay compensation to a trial subject for personal injury arising as a result of participation in a trial and that legal claims are complex (particularly in the proof of causation), expensive and lengthy. Moreover, the law of contract is irrelevant in most patient volunteer trials where no such relationship exists between patient volunteer and doctor/investigator or is established between company sponsor and patient volunteer. The law also does not require ethical review and ethics committees have no legal powers. There is no law specific to the conduct of research and there are few legal sanctions for failure to adhere to GCP standards. The applicability of case law which has developed with regard to disputes over treatment has never been tested in the context of research, and case law can in any event only evolve when individuals are prepared to litigate a matter of dispute to trial. Research has never been the subject of judicial consideration. The application of legislation addressing the therapeutic context is not confirmed in the context of research. The Medicines Act 1968 does not apply to any Phase I research, regulating dealings in and use of 'medicinal products' only. It is still also true to say, despite all the publicity and indeed the many conferences relating to clinical research, that a number of intending researchers do not know, understand, seek to establish and/or apply the law in any event.

Guidelines in the UK have sought to address the 'gaps' which the law has left unfilled. But there are several and the list is long. (Appendix 3 contains a list of relevant UK guidelines.)

In general, these guidelines adopt very similar approaches to the fundamental issues arising in research, but there are divergences of view; for example on the subject of the use of prisoners and other vulnerable groups (ABPI Guidelines, 1988);[1] the payment of researchers for studies with regard to the basis of calculation;[2] the degree of information and warnings required to be given to subjects[3] and issues of compensation of 'healthy volunteers' and patients.[4]

In their favour, the guidelines are flexible in terms of updating and amendment and in the amount of explanatory detail they contain. Most importantly, because the law looks to current standards of good practice (embodied in such guidelines) they do have significant force and validity, although strictly not legally binding. Nonetheless, they have the drawbacks mentioned above, inherent in all non-legal guidance documents and they leave gaps of their own in terms of subject protection, which some would like to see 'plugged'.

It is possible to make a start in assessing the impact of the combination of guidelines and such legal provisions as exist in terms of providing adequate protection to research subjects, by focusing upon matters of information, consent, confidentiality, compensation and ethical review.

Information. Case law relating to patient treatment demonstrates that failure adequately to inform a patient, in particular about the risks of a given treatment, may give rise to liability in negligence. However, overall these decisions provide little practical help in determining which (if not all) risks should be mentioned to a patient and leave much to a doctor's discretion. Extrapolation from these principles therefore cannot assist directly in preparing an appropriate information sheet. The guidelines offer more practical help by referring to particular matters that should appear in any information sheet but, arguably, they too leave much to doctor/researcher discretion in the case of patient volunteers. Even the CPMP guidelines reveal inconsistency. Full disclosure is however generally advocated in healthy volunteer research on the basis that any risk or hazard will be significant to a healthy subject who stands to gain nothing personally from participation except the satisfaction of contributing to scientific knowledge.

Consent. Both the provisions of civil and criminal law underwrite the individual's right to choose whether or not to undergo any examination, procedure or treatment. Except in cases of clinical emergency where a procedure may be deemed to be in the best interests of a patient, non-consensual contact may amount to a criminal assault. Civil law rights give rise to remedies for damages arising following failure to obtain consent or where consent is obtained following the provision of inadequate (and misleading) information. The law also provides guidance on the ability or competence of individuals to give consent – although all such guidance arises in the therapeutic not a research context. Uncertainty still persists, however, in relation to the recruitment of minors (who are too young to decide for themselves) and incompetent adults to research which is unlikely to offer the participants any prospect of individual benefit. In fact, it is clearly established that legal proxy consent cannot be given on behalf of an adult and it is doubtful whether parents can consent on behalf of a child to non-therapeutic procedures. Lawyers have developed the unofficial 'not against his/her best interests test' in an attempt to justify their inclusion, but there is no certainty, even though such research may be vitally important to the class of subject concerned.

The general rule of all guidelines is that consent to participation in research is essential. However, in exceptional circumstances, the guidelines vary, with the CPMP guidelines seeming to rule out research in incompetent adults (and possibly children) and others seeing nothing unethical *per se* in the inclusion of such subjects where minimal risk is involved, a responsible member of the family/medical team agrees, the subjects themselves do not appear to disagree and an ethics committee has been satisfied in its review of the research proposal as to the provisions for the welfare and safeguarding of such subjects. What is strictly legal and what is ethical are not always synonymous.

Confidentiality. There is both legislation and common law relating to the matter of confidentiality. With limited specific exemptions in both branches of the law, personal information must be kept confidential and not disclosed without the subject's consent. Adherence to these rules should ensure that subject data and medical records are kept secure and subject consent is obtained for contact with a subject's GP, for discussion or exchange of information and to access, for example, by a trial sponsor or monitor to such records for purposes of audit and verification.

The guidelines, too, stress the need to safeguard confidentiality and preclude any publication of identifying data.

Compensation. This is an area where the law and ethical guidelines tend to diverge.

Legal liability for personal injury requires fault in general (arguably even in relation to a defective product and so-called strict liability); in the absence of settlement, redress is only available through the courts.

The guidelines, particularly those written by the ABPI and RCP, advocate the assumption of 'no fault' responsibility for any injury arising out of participation in a trial (drug or procedure) in the case of non-patient and Phase I studies. This can be achieved by entering into a legally enforceable contract with the subject. However, the ABPI recommendations effectively only affect corporate sponsors of research although arguably they should be good practice across the whole spectrum of research. There is a reluctance within the NHS to provide any such advance guarantees (see HSG 91(5)).

The guidelines differ in their approach to patient volunteers with regard to making voluntary arrangements to compensate in cases of injury. The Association of the British Pharmaceutical Industry (ABPI) guidelines advocate settlement where the injury arises out of trial participation, but do not advise the giving of a legal binding undertaking. Nonetheless, it must be said that in all cases of company sponsored research of which the writer is aware, these recommendations have been adhered to voluntarily. The ethical concern raised by the Royal College of Physicians (RCP) and others in the field of ethical review is that the law and guidelines leave open the possibility that a subject injured in research as a result of that research may not be compensated if he or she is a healthy volunteer in a non-company, sponsored study or a patient volunteer unless they can make a legal, that is, fault-based case for damages through legal action.

Ethical review. Despite all guidelines perpetuating the Helsinki Declaration requirement for ethical review, there is no legal underpinning of this function. The only reference in English Law appears in a statutory instrument made under the Medicines Act 1968 (SI 1981 No. 164 on Clinical Trial exemption from licensing) – where the fact that ethical approval is refused or withdrawn must be notified to the authorities who have issued a clinical trial exemption certificate for research. Anecdotal reports indicate that there is still research proceeding in the absence of any review. There is also still considerable doubt and debate about precisely what type of work constitutes research warranting review. The Department of Health guidelines of 1991 list reviewable projects, but the matter would clearly benefit from further clarification particularly in distinguishing audit from reviewable research.

It would be easy at this point to revert immediately to the question of whether in fact more law or more legal control and clarification in relation to clinical research in the UK would present the solution to the shortcomings and problems which are perceived as resulting from our current approach to research. However, before adopting such a conclusion, there are a number of factors about the nature of law and its method of control which should be considered. In the first instance, public opinion is not static, it evolves over time and it is often difficult for the law to keep up. Amendments to legislation are not automatically straightforward or speedy matters. In addition, ethical issues can be difficult to express in legislative terms, guidelines do benefit from the fact that their structure and content is not circumscribed and there is space and time for elaboration and explanation. It must be borne in mind that specific legislation, particularly where it seeks to limit conduct and method, allows researchers less flexibility. The problem with regard to precision in drafting cannot be satisfactorily avoided by using more general text: poorly drafted ambiguous legislation, unclear or vague court judgements, merely creates more uncertainty. On the other hand, it is difficult not to accept that the binding nature of legislation probably does provide a greater general incentive to those involved in research to comply with accepted principles of conduct. Whilst it should not be assumed that the law fails to support existing guidelines, because the courts would determine the existence of negligence, or failures in the presentation of an experimental product in any given case, by specific reference to those texts representing accepted standards of conduct, the process is more indirect.

Undertaking a programme of legislation may contribute to an improvement in the conduct of research. It is clear that we may be forced down that route to some degree in any event, by the advent of European legislation,[5] and there seems to be clear scope for arguing that some aspects of the regulation of clinical research in the UK might benefit from coverage in legislation. Comparison of the UK with other European systems may be helpful in providing food for thought – the French legislation is, it is said, working well. The requirement for ethical approval could, for example, be implemented into law, although this would naturally raise questions of accountability, responsibility and resourcing and place firmly in the spotlight the standards of performance of those who are charged with undertaking such review. It may also be appropriate for legislation to specify certain core matters which must be notified to all potential study volunteers, but it would seem impractical for the law to seek to set standard formats and content lists, since it would be extremely difficult, if not impossible, to consider all possible circumstances and contingencies. There would however inevitably be a 'knock on' effect in the field of therapeutic treatment arising out of any such initiative which would require careful consideration. In taking a pragmatic approach, there is foreseeable benefit in certain basic requirements, e.g. consent being stated in law, but the moment that the law strays into areas requiring an exercise of judgement or discretion, matters are likely to become complicated, and may be no more advanced. Requirements regarding insurance might be addressed – but this would force consideration of the double standard currently applied to corporate sponsors and NHS based research.

Developments in this area will arise as a result of changing views of researchers, sponsors and the force of public opinion. Change in the law in relation to compensation for injury in the absence of fault is a much wider issue than arises in the research context. No-fault compensation has already been considered and rejected by the government – but may yet reappear on its agenda depending upon the impact of public view.

Discussion

It has been stated that there is no specific law in the UK relating to clinical research. In this respect, reference to the situation in Brussels may be of help. There is a note for guidance of 1990 which does not have any legal force. There is also a 1991 Directive of the EC on good clinical practice, the objective of which is that the note of guidance will be incorporated in each national law of all the Member States. Three Member States, Spain, Italy and the Netherlands, have done that already. As a consequence, the total guidelines on good clinical practice are now part of Dutch law. The Dutch authorities have set up an inspectorate for good clinical practice and they inspect the clinical researchers.

If you look very closely at the Annex to 75(318) which was amended by 91(507) it simply says that these studies have to be done in accordance with good clinical practice with small letters and no definite cross-reference to the CPMP guidelines. They do not implement the CPMP guidelines. However, these guidelines are the obvious source of principles when you are looking as a company sponsor to the requirements that you need to meet in order to make your clinical research data acceptable to the authorities. Several of the Member States have decided to go one further and have reference to the CPMP guidelines as their good clinical practice, but it is not right to say that these guidelines were made law by 91(507)EEC. The Italians have also referenced the CPMP guidelines in their legislation. There is an understandable trend but it does cause and pose its own difficulties because they are not perfect in terms of drafting. They do have internal inconsistencies.

Postcript

Since this lecture was delivered, the proposal for a European Directive has been revived – a consultation document (111/5608/95) was issued by the Commission in October 1995. Draft proposals for a Directive in the form of proposed legal text are expected. SI 1981 No. 164 has been replaced by SIs 1995 No. 2808 and No. 2809, but the provisions are essentially the same.

Notes

1 Prisoners should never be used. Compare RCP which does not rule out any particular group.

2 The RCP has concerns not specified by other bodies over payments to researchers/establishments calculated on a per capita basis – may encourage inappropriate recruitment.

3 CPMP guidelines appear to suggest full disclosure is necessary. DoH HC(90)22 (on treatment) indicates the use of doctor discretion. RCP guidelines of ethics committees 1990 recognise 'impracticality' of giving full information. The lists of matters for disclosure vary to some degree. The disclosure of all or only material risks is unclear particularly in patient studies.

4 The ABPI guidelines applicable to company-sponsored research advise contract between healthy volunteer and sponsor for the payment of compensation in the event of trial-related injury and advise payment of compensation in Phase II–III trials in certain specified circumstances but without legal commitment. The RCP indicates a preference for a similar, no-fault approach to all categories of volunteer.

5 However, European legislation is predominantly concerned with the establishment and maintenance of a common market and although the protection of public health is an important element in its legislation in the field and its scope of interest in health matters was extended by the Maastricht Treaty, the Community addresses issues from a trade and free movement of goods standpoint. Its primary focus therefore will be upon clinical research related to marketing of medicinal products and so the scope of the provisions may be limited.

References

ANON., 1949, *Nuremberg Code reprinted from Trials of War Criminals before the Nuremberg Military Tribunals under Control Law*, No. 10, Vol. 2, Government Printing Office, Washington, DC.

CIOMS, 1993, *Guidelines for Biomedical Research involving Human Subjects*. ISBN 92 9036 0569, Geneva.

5

Local Research Ethics Committees: A View from the Department of Health

CLIVE MARRITT

The Department of Health (DoH) is responsible for the health of the nation. Health is defined in its broadest sense as a state of well-being, a state of ease rather than 'dis-ease'. People mainly come into contact with health services when they find themselves in a state of 'dis-ease'; they look to health services to return them, as far as possible (and sometimes further than possible) to their previous 'better' condition. Health services are therefore increasingly being evaluated in terms of the extent to which they contribute to their patients' *good clinical outcomes*.

Good clinical outcomes can be and are achieved through the delivery of established treatments to patients. Improvements in clinical outcomes can be achieved by improving the effectiveness of the delivery of established treatments (e.g. clinical audit) and new and better treatments. If audit committees are responsible for overseeing the reviews of the quality of (predominantly) established treatments, local research ethics committees arguably have a role in overseeing the scientific and ethical quality of proposed and ongoing research. Both contribute to the overall achievement of continuous quality improvement in health care.

There is no legislation as far as LRECs are concerned, so a subtitle for this chapter could be 'Ethical committee review and DoH guidelines'. Here the purpose of LRECs, the Department's guidelines, otherwise known as the *Red Book*, and some recent developments will be covered.

The purpose of LRECs is quite straightforward. It is a service to protect research subjects and patients, more generally. It does this in two ways: by preventing unethical exposure to risk or invasion of privacy and it approves ethical attempts to identify improved treatments. In both respects LRECs look at the quality of research. When one thinks of quality in England, it is very easy to think in terms of clinical audits as the review of how well treatment is currently delivered and how it can be done better. However, a lot of innovation and improvements in the health care that is delivered to patients is achieved through research and LRECs are, in many ways, complementary to the clinical audit initiative in that they are the mechanism that we have in England for monitoring the quality of clinical research. In doing that LRECs also provide a service to research workers and their sponsors. It must be emphasised that this is not the purpose of an LREC but a spin-off effect of an LREC doing its work competently. This is very important to remember because from the DoH's viewpoint the contribution of research in improving public health is what makes LRECs' work so valuable.

The Department's guidelines are referred to as the *Red Book* (Department of Health, 1991) because they are published in a red book! It is a book of guidelines – there is no statute underpinning what is written in there. The second chapter gives advice about the administration, establishment and operation of LRECs and it should be emphasised that this is a district health authority responsibility. NHS Trusts should not have their own ethics committees. Chapter Three considers research proposals, looking at issues such as consent, confidentiality, recruitment of volunteers (whether talking about healthy volunteers or patients, they should all be volunteers), finances (including inducements, and what should be paid to people who participate in research projects). Chapter Four looks at special considerations such as children, young women of childbearing age, prisoners and mentally disabled people. The Appendices include codes of practice on the use of foetuses and foetal material, which is a controversial issue. They also contain the World Medical Association's Declaration of Helsinki. A point made in an earlier chapter that should be emphasised is the wide range of research whose ethics LRECs are expected to review. It covers any research involving NHS patients, foetal material and *in vitro* fertilisation to do with NHS patients, the recently deceased on NHS premises, access to the records of past or present NHS patients, and the use of or potential access to NHS premises and facilities. It is important for researchers to try to understand that LRECs have to cover such a wide range of science and the researchers should try to be constructive in their approach. A good deal of understanding on both sides can help to ensure that the misunderstandings that sometimes arise can be resolved amicably and, importantly, quickly.

There are two big issues in research ethics at the moment in this country. One is training for research ethics committees and the other is the review of multicentre trials. Under the current system, if a trial is to be carried out in a large number of locations it has to be submitted to every LREC which is involved in that trial. All of the LRECs consider the proposal in full. The effect of this is that there are all kinds of requests for amendments, different requests from different places, which can have adverse effects on the protocol, making it impossible in some cases for the research to proceed. Sometimes the same research is given full approval by some LRECs and sometimes it is rejected out of hand. It is understandable from the point of view of those people who sponsor multicentre trials that this makes their life very difficult and it is understandable why they become concerned that something should be done to improve the current system as far as multicentre trials are concerned. This was an issue raised to the DoH by the pharmaceutical industry, the Medical Research Council, medical research charities and also the DoH itself. The DoH's guidelines actually make it very difficult for the administrators in the DoH and their professional colleagues.

The DoH was concerned about these two issues and consulted on these points, namely training and multicentre trials. One of the issues that is difficult to deal with in multicentre trials is to persuade LRECs, with their local focus, that there is actually a problem. One result of the consultation exercise was that people were far more concerned about training than about the multicentre trials. So it was decided that training would have to be addressed first, and hoped, through the training, to help to prepare the ground for subsequent work to improve the system on multicentre trials. The outcome was the idea of standards for LRECs. This was initiated in 1994, is an ongoing initiative, and is an overall DoH initiative which has been taken forward in partnership with the private sector. One very important part of the private sector partnership is the production of standard operating procedures (SOPs) for the LRECs (McKenna, 1994). There are three principal SOPs: the format of applications; the assessment of applications and the approval or refusal of applications. There is also within this document a sample constitution, standard terms of reference and a suggested common application form, something dear to the hearts of many people who are involved with sponsoring more multicentre research.

The DoH has also produced a document, 'Standards for LRECs – A Framework for Ethical Review' (Department of Health, 1991). This is known as a competence framework and is referred to as 'The Framework Document'. It is a competence approach to assessing training needs. It works in two ways. You can look at the various competencies which are spelt out for all the various aspects of LREC work. You can think about any management activity you can engage in to address some of the problems if you feel there are any shortcomings with your own LREC. This may involve liaison with the local district manager, for example, to get improved administrative backup. One quite common complaint the DoH gets from LRECs is that they cannot get enough staff to enable them to do their work as efficiently as they would like to. The other way is to enable committees to look at various parts of this framework and say that they can identify certain specific items which individuals need training in to function more effectively on the committees or, indeed, sometimes areas where committees can identify a whole area in which they need to be a little more proficient (see *Bulletin of Medical Ethics*, Sept. 1994, for reviews).

Concerning the definition of a volunteer, framework module 12, which is the most directly relevant to the question of volunteers, gives the DoH definition. It points out that LRECs do have a role in ensuring that people are not invited to volunteer for things which should never be allowed. It should be clearly explained to them what it is they are volunteering for. Within module 12 there are statements which are intended to look after the volunteers' interests, for example, 'the LREC should ensure that the status and safety of the proposed research procedures are reviewed and the degree of risk clearly identified', and 'the LREC should ensure that procedures for obtaining consent are assessed for approaches which may coerce or unreasonably induce the potential research subject into joining the study. Guidance materials to be made available to research subjects should be reviewed for accuracy and clarity.' These are just some of the key phrases in the standards for LRECs which should be applied and considered in this important work.

There are 17 modules in the framework document. Some address the issues of managing the process, some get to the part of actually making decisions, balancing ethical considerations, and others, the last eight modules, are devoted to ensuring good practice. They cover the whole range of activities that are described in the *Red Book*.

Finally, the question of multicentre trials. Having launched the standards, having had the opportunity to go out and talk to people on the LRECs in the process of promulgation of those standards and encouraging people to use them, the DoH now have a Department initiative going on to look at the issues of muticentre trials. This is being chaired by the Chief Medical Officer. The content of those discussions is at the moment private and confidential, but you can be reassured that this issue is now being taken very seriously indeed at the very highest levels.

Summary and Conclusions

This chapter has addressed the issues of training and management of LRECs with the view of producing overall consistency of operation. The framework document to assess training and other needs and the SOPs should serve as helpful illustrations of the relationship between process and outcome. It is hoped that, by utilising these products, the LRECs will, in time, acquire greater confidence in the abilty of others to offer a lead in clearly defined aspects of the consideration of the ethics of multicentre trials.

Discussion

What guidance is given to the LRECs for their composition because quite a number of ethics committees do not fulfil the criteria for good clinical practice composition, particularly when you look at the specific examples that are

quoted for the Food and Drugs Administration? This has happened so frequently that one particular hospital has refused to use them for any further research until they adapt their membership according to the guidelines.

Anything to do with the composition of the LRECs is the subject of guidelines, not of any formal legal requirements. A number of paragraphs in the *Red Book* refer to membership. This says, for example, 'an LREC should have 8–12 members. Members should be drawn from both sexes and from a wide range of age groups. They should include hospital medical staff, nursing staff, general practitioners, two or more lay persons. Despite being drawn from groups identified with particular interests or responsibilities in connection with health issues the LREC members are not in any way representatives of those groups. They are appointed in their own rights to participate in the work of the LREC as individuals of sound judgement and relevant experience.' The most important point about any LREC is not whether it has got the correct experience but whether or not that LREC actually delivers competent comments on the research which is submitted for its approval. The committee may not be set up precisely in accordance with these guidelines, however, these are only guidelines. If it is true that because of that, a particular ethics committee does not deliver competent ethical review, one would then be referring that particular district or committee to the standards framework and to the McKenna & Co. SOP and inviting it to consider whether, as it currently stands, it measures up to the requirements that have been issued as guidelines recently.

The composition and procedures have been covered, but are the DoH taking any steps to confront the dilemma of whether patients should be on a par with healthy volunteers for compensation purposes. Many ethics committees can work perfectly acceptably except that they find they have two classes of people they are assessing from the ethical point of view. Healthy volunteers are often covered by ABPI guidelines or other insurance schemes, patients are not. Is the Department doing anything to offer advice, particularly to new trusts because at the moment it is very confusing, and if they are, what are they doing?

The DoH's policy on compensation for clinical harm is in line with the legal position that compensation is available in the UK where negligence can be shown. There is no legal liability on any NHS body to pay compensation where negligence cannot be shown, particularly where it has not occurred. The ABPI have their form of indemnity for non-negligent harm, but under rules on the use of public funds, the DoH are not able to allow the NHS to offer a similar facility to people who participate in public-sector-sponsored clinical trials. This is a difference. In terms of the guidance that is available on when compensation can be paid, there is revised guidance on NHS indemnity in preparation, but it deals primarily with the issue of negligent harm. Non-negligent harm is touched on as an issue which relates to negligent harm in certain circumstances.

Notes

This chapter gives a view of Local Research Ethics Committees (LRECs) from the Department of Health's (DoH's) perspective.

References

Bulletin of Medical Ethics, 1994, **101**, 5–7.

DEPARTMENT OF HEALTH, 1991, *Local Research Ethics Committees*, Ref. HSG (91) 5.

MCKENNA & CO., 1994, *Standard Operating Procedures for Local Research Ethics Committees*: A Framework for Ethical Review. McKenna & Co., 160 Aldersgate Street, London EC1A 4DD.

DEPARTMENT OF HEALTH, 1994, *Standards for Local Research Ethics Committees – A Framework for Ethical Review.*

NHS TRAINING DIVISION, 1994, *Using Standards for Local Research Ethics Committees.*

6

Recruitment, Selection and Compensation of Volunteers for Phase I Studies

BEV HOLT

Phase I studies, especially in normal volunteers, differ in many respects from studies carried out later in the development of a new drug. Recruitment procedures differ. Normal volunteers do not usually just walk in 'off the street', satisfying study protocol criteria in quite the same way as often happens with studies in patients. In most cases, normal volunteers are compensated for their involvement in studies which is not usually the case for patients. This chapter considers these and many other issues involved in Phase I volunteer studies.

There is no definition of a normal volunteer. Indeed, the question could be 'Does a normal volunteer exist?' although this might seem simple as far as the physical and medical characteristics of an individual are concerned. There are tables identifying normality for weight and height. Insurance companies publish what they consider to be the ideal weight and height of individuals. A person can fit into those tables quite well and be only 1.4 m high and weigh less than 45 kg or 2 m high and weigh 90 kg. In addition, all haematological and biochemical parameters have 'normal' ranges. Those are based on percentiles such that 'normal' is defined as those who fall within the 90 per cent percentile are classified as normal (i.e. 5 per cent at each extreme are considered abnormal). However, in the volunteer groups that are very often used for Phase I studies, that is, normally young, fit males, you will sometimes find that what is normal for the general population is not necessarily normal for that group of fit young men. So it becomes a little more difficult to define 'normal' in terms of normal medical experience. This makes volunteer selection difficult because very often those setting up trials have such tables and ranges but they may not be totally applicable to healthy young male volunteers (who may, for example, have generally low serum cholesterol), but they are still perfectly acceptable. Often, we get very fit athletes in Phase I studies whose pulse rate may be very low compared with the average, but this could be considered abnormal. So should such individuals be excluded from studies? Obviously not.

There are enormous variations in normality within a population, such as variation due to ethnic origin or age, a lot of which have not been classified in the literature. It is only when you come to do clinical trials that you begin to realise how very difficult it is to see a normal. One of the worst things for categorising as normal or abnormal is the electrocardiogram (ECG). There are problems in trying to say what is a normal ECG because an ECG is really like your fingerprint – we have all got them but they are individual to every single person. To say anything like there is a normal ECG is extremely difficult and it is extremely difficult to define. Indeed, there is no such thing as normal and the normal volunteer is in fact a very rare creature.

It is very much easier to define 'normal' in animals. The laboratory rat has been bred over very many years. It has not actually been cloned yet but it will not be very long before we get genetically engineered animals, all of which will be absolutely identical and which would be absolutely ideal for pharmacokinetic trials. With animals you have much more uniformity.

The human situation is quite different. People often forget that human volunteers are both of these things – they are human and they are volunteers. You cannot alter those two facts. By being human they are susceptible to all human foibles. They are liable to fall ill (although animals are also liable to fall ill). When you have a group of young people living together in a closed community as you very often do during a clinical study they might infect each other or just one of them might get ill. Volunteers may have been to exotic places – it is not unknown to have people coming into volunteer studies and then suddenly develop an unknown fever – malaria has been diagnosed during a volunteer study. Volunteers can die – particularly if you are going to do Phase I studies in the elderly, you have to accept that volunteers could die from totally intercurrent causes and even in studies of young fit volunteers accidents may arise. A volunteer may be knocked down in the street and killed. This may seen straightforward but if the drug that the volunteer was taking altered CNS function in any way or was liable to make volunteers drowsy then there should be a warning to this effect (often studies restrict car driving or the operating of machinery in such circumstances). A similar problem could arise if the test drug is an antihypertensive which may cause postural hypotension. Such circumstances lead to the question, 'Was this death related to the drug?' It may not be possible to answer such a question.

Volunteers often have family problems which may affect the study conduct – for example, a wife who gets ill or a father dies or something similar. These problems may stop a volunteer from completing the study. Those individuals who design studies do not always appreciate that you can have these sorts of problems. Some volunteers will enter studies because they are unemployed, then when they find a job they feel that the new job is more important than completing the study. An example is a study that requires 16 volunteers. Entering 16 volunteers may cause no problem and go through the test. But if a couple of the volunteers drop out for whatever reason this may not be avoidable. However, those who designed the study often do not appreciate the real world and may say: 'You have totally ruined our latin square that we set up for the statistics because you have had to replace two volunteers. Couldn't you have anticipated that one of these volunteers was going to drop out and avoided recruiting him in the first place?'

This type of situation puts the unit running the study in a totally impossible situation and it shows a great lack of understanding on the people who set the study up in the first place.

Finally, of course, being human, some volunteers can be perverse and difficult and there is no point in saying much more about that except that when you have a group of people all living together in the confines of doing a clinical study, one person can be very disruptive and upset the whole status quo.

Volunteers are also just that, volunteers. In animal testing there is a lot of legislation setting limits and the reason for this is because the animal has no choice. In the human testing there is no legislation concerning the use of normal human volunteers in Phase I drug studies. Anyone can set up to do a drug study and use human volunteers. The reason for that is, it is considered that the volunteer has his or her own free will and is a volunteer who is free to change his or her mind. Unfortunately a lot of volunteers change their minds rather perversely. The reasons include not realising the time factor for the study being quite so demanding and they do not like the side effects of the drug. Some volunteers are more susceptible than others, some do not like venepuncture after 30–40 times, some might complain about the living conditions in the trial unit, they find they cannot live in close proximity to other people, and there may be outside pressures such as family not wanting them to continue for various reasons. There are other outside pressures for different reasons. There is a group that says people should not be used for drug trials, particularly students because they are doing it for the wrong reasons. It is used as a political lever by such people who say that because students often do not have enough money they are forced to go into drug studies. These groups put volunteering into the same bracket as prostitution.

With all these problems in mind how do Phase I units go about recruiting? First, there is advertising. How much can one advertise for human volunteers? It is easy enough to do it in a limited way. You can advertise in student halls of residence, certain student magazines or in the press generally. Advertising can even be put out on television. Studies have been advertised on supermarket trolleys and the back of buses. There are some ethical considerations here as to whether one should do this because people might volunteer for these clinical studies for the wrong reasons. Advertising at some point has probably got to have some cut-off from the ethical point of view. It is probably up to the ethics committees who sanction the trial initially to say to what extent and how public one should go about advertising for volunteers. Probably the better way of advertising is by word of mouth. If a unit is running clinical studies and it is running enough of them it eventually gets a critical mass of volunteers who by word of mouth through their friends and people they meet mention that there are clinical trials going on, that it really is not such a bad thing after all and that they may like to come along and take part. When a unit has enough people this method seems to work reasonably well. Then there are the special groups of patients or volunteers, people who, for example, have got renal failure or high blood pressure. Advertisements for these groups can be placed either in outpatient clinics in hospitals or in GP clinics.

Who responds to this type of advertising and how do people respond to it? Students mostly respond because they have the time, they have less money and they are normally in the vicinity of where many of these studies are carried out (around teaching hospitals or university centres). There are two types of centre involved in running Phase I studies – the undergraduate and postgraduate centres. As far as volunteering is concerned, the postgraduate student is by far the best individual, normally well motivated and with more time. There are also the unemployed. This can be a difficult group. Units must realise that there are several sorts of unemployed – those that are genuinely looking for a job and will take part in a clinical study as a fill-in and those who are unemployable, the drop-outs and so on; these people may only be coming on a study to feed their own drug or alcohol habits. One has got to be very careful when recruiting to make sure that you can differentiate between the two. There are also the employed who are taking a holiday from their employment in order to earn extra money. These are often very well-motivated people who are quite interested in getting on with the study. However, before recruiting these individuals, units have to make sure that they have the time and that the study is not going to interfere with their work in any way.

Why do people volunteer for Phase I studies? Altruism is normally the reason for the special groups (such as renal failure patients) because they realise that they have a chronic condition and that drug studies may be helping them and others with their condition very considerably. These groups are often very keen to participate in studies. One concern though when they take a new medication in a clinical study is that this may be upsetting their standard regime of drugs, and in some volunteers this may make their condition worse. At times such people have to be prevented from volunteering. There are also people who will volunteer for genuine interest, sometimes medical students fall into this category – volunteering just to see what it is all about. Often such people have a particular interest in certain drugs. However, by far the strongest reason for volunteering is money. Volunteers can make quite a lot of money from continually volunteering on drug studies.

Payment can be a problem since some volunteers are so motivated by payment that they effectively become 'the professional volunteer'.

Volunteer payments have to be approved by an ethics committee. A Phase I unit cannot just suddenly decide to pay an enormous sum of money if they are suddenly running short of volunteers in order to complete a study. The ethics committee have to decide on what a volunteer is going to be paid and will have to approve that the sum is reasonable. The way this is done, is that most organisations have a scoring system. This usually entails points being awarded for each blood sample given, the amount of time spent, for an intravenous cannula or any other study procedures. It can also include an inconvenience factor if, for example, a volunteer cannot drive for the study duration or cannot drink alcohol or eat certain food types. Each of these will score points which are totalled to give a score. Then this is put against a rating system such that for example, on a 1:1 rating system a volunteer would get £400 for 400 points. There are other rating systems as well. The scoring system can stay the same and the rating system increase as cost of living increases. Most ethics committees accept this type of system which is seen as a fair recompense for the time and discomfort that the volunteers spend on the study. The overriding rule is that payment should not, at any time, be seen as a payment for the risk involved. The ethics committee should ensure that there is no risk involved or that the risk is absolutely minimal in any drug study. It is a myth that volunteers are paid for taking a risk. The risk in nearly all drug studies is minimal but this is not always recognised and there are some volunteers who believe that they are being rewarded for the risk that they are taking.

There are some people who finance their way through university by volunteering on a number of drug studies – the so-called 'professional volunteer'. The only way that anything can be done about this is to limit the number of studies that a volunteer can take part in during a year. This is normally limited to three studies per year, with a wash-out period of at least three months between each study. This works for one centre. However, there is nothing to prevent that volunteer from going to another centre and volunteering for another study the moment that he has finished one study and starting on another. There have been cases of volunteers being on two studies at once which is obviously highly dangerous because there could be interactions between the two test drugs involved. There have been various suggestions put forward as to how this matter could be coped with, by having a central computer through which all volunteer information is processed. There are ongoing discussions about this but to date there has not been anything that looks feasible which is of a reasonable cost-effectiveness. This may be easy enough to do but is very expensive to set up if done correctly.

Unfortunately a large proportion of young people today, if they are not on hard drugs, may smoke cannabis. Cannabis is a very persistent drug which can be detected for several weeks after it has been used or inhaled and this shows up positive on drug screening. It is for this reason that all volunteers should be screened for drugs of abuse. It is often difficult to get a group of volunteers within the university environment who are totally free from traces of cannabis. Smoking and alcohol can cause similar problems. Occasionally if you ask someone if they are a smoker or a non-smoker, they reply by asking what you want. This immediately causes suspicion. Some companies will accept volunteers on drug studies if they smoke less than a certain number of cigarettes a day. This is difficult to monitor as is the intake of alcohol. It is possible to breathalyse volunteers every morning when they present for the drug study. However, this is difficult and one has to trust the volunteer to a certain extent on the smoking and alcohol problem. Obviously a heavy drinker, even if he abstains during the course of the trial, is going to have a liver that is more active than a non-drinker and his response to drugs may be different. It is very difficult sometimes to differentiate those sorts of people, although laboratory screening can detect the worst of these subjects.

A further issue is the problem of the volunteer's general practitioner and consent. Often units have problems when recruiting volunteers in deciding how to inform the volunteer's general practitioner (GP) and to get the GP to co-operate. The guidelines vary considerably between the UK and the continent. In the UK the guidelines state that before a volunteer can go on a clinical study, the volunteer's GP must be contacted and the GP must give his approval for the volunteer to participate. This is obviously in the volunteer's interest in case there is any underlying condition that the volunteer has which the GP feels might put him at risk in any way from being on a drug study. Indeed, the volunteer may not be aware of a problem that could be serious. There are certain conditions, for example, asthma, where certain drugs are absolutely contra-indicated such as the beta blockers. If a volunteer may have had mild asthma during his childhood, he may not have had any evidence of this for many years. However, it would be extremely foolish and it would be putting the person at risk if he or she were included in a drug study that included a drug from the beta-blocker class; there are many other more complex examples.

Finally, one should consider the mental status of volunteers. This is something that is often not tested for and which can obviously be a problem in some respects. There is nothing normally in the study protocol in the inclusion and exclusion criteria which is going to cover the mental status of the volunteer. It can be very difficult at times to ensure that you have a volunteer who is mentally healthy and well motivated to come on a study. However, such volunteers are usually quite easy to spot but often only after they have got on to the study; beforehand it is sometimes quite difficult. The problem is that there are an increasing number of central nervous system (CNS) drugs for the treatment of depression and psychotic conditions. Whereas when you do animal studies and have good animal models for organs like lungs, livers and hearts, when you come to the central nervous system it makes the human unique. Man has a CNS totally different from that of animals. You cannot go to an animal and say are you feeling more depressed today or more elated today? You have no indication from the animal studies as to how this drug is going to affect the human being. There have been a few disasters with CNS drugs in human volunteers because of this. There have been some strange results from using CNS drugs on groups of volunteers and sometimes the whole group of volunteers has been affected. It is a problem that is going to become increasingly important in the selection of volunteers and the recruiting of them. We have to look carefully at their mental status before taking on any studies for CNS drugs.

Summary and Conclusions

The identification of a normal volunteer is far from easy. Indeed the question 'Does a normal volunteer exist?' is not easy to answer. The very process of volunteering in some ways renders normal volunteers abnormal. Recruitment and selection of volunteers for Phase I studies have been discussed both identifying problems and some possible solutions.

The ethics of compensation for Phase I studies is at times a touchy subject. However, with the full co-operation of ethics committees this is no barrier to successful research studies.

Despite the problems discussed in this chapter most Phase I studies still run smoothly. The most striking fact is not that there are problems, all studies have problems (and most are surmountable), but that they are quite different from studies in patients in the later stages of drug development.

Discussion

Volunteers often come from abroad and they often do not have a GP. If a volunteer does have a GP, it is one way of policing the fact that they should not do more than three studies a year. The sooner a central system is available for monitoring volunteers the better. In the past this has been very informal and has relied too heavily on patients telling the truth. This is not the best way to find out if a patient is doing, for example, two studies simultaneously. Research nurses have even spotted volunteers 'two-timing'. Surely there is a real need for a formal network to be arranged to relegate such events to history.

This does happen already although only via an informal network. It is inevitable that we are going to see a formal network eventually emerge when it becomes cost effective to do so. At the moment computer systems that are available for this are either not very effective or they are cost prohibitive.

The fact that people volunteer for studies should really go into their medical records. This would enable information to be gleaned maybe in 20, 30, 40 years' time when there is a possibility that the study material may be carcinogenic. Can't such records be used as the database to find out what they have been on before you actually start giving them the drugs – you can go through their medical records and see what is happening.

The problem here is which medical records? Those that reside with the volunteer's GP, the ones which reside with the hospital or those with the organisation undertaking the drug study? Because none of these is legally public property. It is sometimes very difficult sometimes to cross-reference all these records.

If lawyers can get hold of them why can't study units?

Lawyers have a lot of difficulty getting hold of them.

I thought that had changed recently in the UK.

People are usually entitled to look at their own records now but nobody else is. It is very difficult sometimes to get access to medical records. There are the hospital records, the GP records and sometimes if people move GPs they do not move their records. There are also dental records and some hospital clinics also have their own set of records. It would be ideal if all this was carried around on a microchip. It would be the ideal solution.

Are you not losing information then, you may be missing long-term carcinogenicity, for instance.

You could, very easily, lose this information.

7

Volunteers: The Susceptible and the Disadvantaged

DUNCAN VERE

The use of minority groups in clinical trials has always provoked much discussion. They may have various disadvantages or special needs. There has been much research into this area recently and generally it has moved strongly towards research with subjects being drawn from such groups, removing the needless barriers. However, this has uncovered real problems, many still unresolved, and these will be discussed later. In addition, although not falling under the category of susceptible or disadvantaged, women in research and testing also have special needs and they will also be discussed.

The stuff of ethics is twofold. One should see who have real interests in a piece of proposed work and then see that none of them is short changed, wittingly or otherwise. This includes working out the potential balance of gains and losses for each party involved, seeing that they understand this and consent to it without misunderstanding or duress; that is informed consent. They should know not only what is known, but also which areas are uncertain; above all, there must be a clear grasp of what is pure therapy, what is pure research and what is therapy-with-research amongst all that may happen to them.

To look first at the general aspects of these problems, three may be considered.

First, consider the nature of the clinical research contract. An easy point from which to start is the consumer-supplier contract in everyday merchandising; one well-known retailer expresses this by the slogan 'never knowingly undersold' (Figure 7.1). Here the vendor is provider and has an ethical duty to the purchaser, who is autonomous; the purchaser is entirely free to decide whether or not to buy. This changes instructively in the clinical research contract; the vendor is now the 'provider' and the volunteer. The researcher becomes the 'purchaser'; but the ethical duty is now heavily upon the

'Never knowingly undersold'	Vendor = provider ethical duty: provider to purchaser	AUTONOMOUS
'Never knowingly or anticipatively) under- or over-bought'	Vendor = provider = self. Researcher is 'purchaser'. Ethical duty: purchaser to provider	PART PATERNALISTIC

Figure 7.1 The clinical research contract

purchaser, because it is the researcher who should know and understand the risks and gains of participation. Hence there must be a substantial aspect of paternalism involved, though 'informed consent' aims to minimise this by making as much information as possible open to the volunteer which has relevance to their choice; this maximises their autonomy.

The second aspect is the intriguing partition of responsibility between researcher and volunteer; each has a set of features which is purely within themselves. Only the researcher can take responsibility for information given, for considering the balance of profit and risk and the environment of the research. Features which shift the balance of risk and gain peculiar to the volunteer include sex, age, mental disorder or deficiency, disability and handicap and the nature of illness. However, there is an area of overlap in which researchers and volunteer interact to influence decisions (Figure 7.2).

This overlap area comprises the influences of money, employment and other interpersonal relationships. It is within this area that pressures can be brought to bear which change decisions; this is what the Americans, with their amazing knack of coining the apt but awkward phrase, call 'contextual duress'.

The third aspect is those factors amongst minority groups with special needs which can curtail effective information to the volunteer; for these, fully 'informed consent' cannot happen. They may have a reduced opportunity to ask questions, may not know what to ask because they do not know enough about what could happen (e.g. possible adverse events). Often they do not understand what they are told (possibly due to a failure to understand scientific language or concepts), think that they understand it when they have not or do understand it but make a biased decision because there is 'contextual duress'. There may also be simple internal limitations such as age, dementia, confusion, intoxication, injury, illness, disability or handicap which makes fully informed consent difficult, if not impossible.

Now, to turn to groups with special needs (Weijer and Fuks, 1994), these are first and foremost *women*, not a minority. Whereas women were excluded from clinical trials for many years, largely because they might become pregnant, this view has shifted dramatically, especially in the USA. The

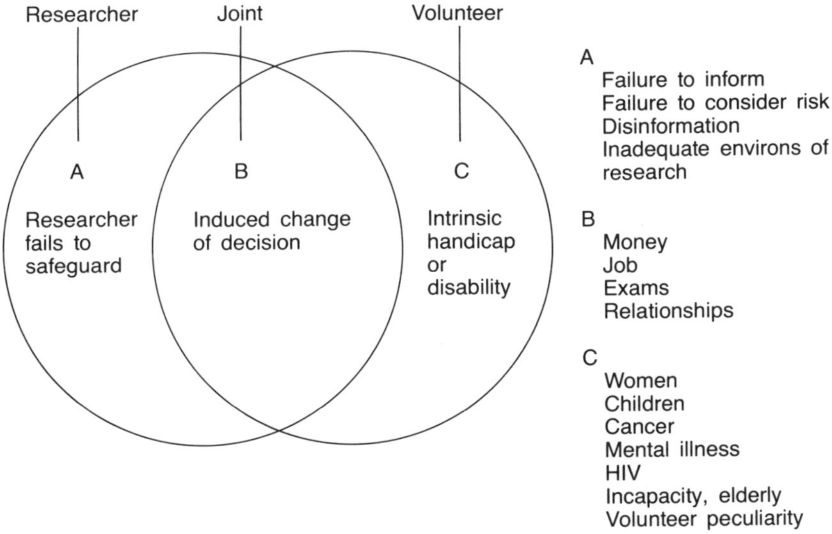

Figure 7.2 Responsibilities

reasons for this shift, and the safeguards now envisaged for female volunteers, are set out extremely well in the Georgetown Symposium of 1993. McCarthy (1994) set out the historical perspective for this; suspicions which arose from unethical trials in the past (Tuskegee, Willowbrook) had combined with the abortion debate to bias opinion and regulation heavily against the inclusion of women in trials. This view was enshrined in the report of the National Commission for the Protection of Human Subjects of Biomedical and Behavioural Research in 1975. The chief factor which McCarthy identified as shifting this opinion was the debate over testing remedies against HIV infections; there has been intense pressure to include females in those trials and it has been realised that similar arguments apply for treatments against many other disorders (Anderson, 1994). McCarthy argued strongly that in pivoting attitudes upon non-maleficence, the duty to consider beneficence has been over-ridden. Not surprisingly, this argument has been strongly amplified by that against gender discrimination.

There are, however, problems to face if women of childbearing age are included in trials; these were considered in an outstandingly helpful paper by Bush (1994). The problems are the high rate of spontaneous teratogenesis (about 5 per cent), the fact that some drugs are foetotoxic after the first trimester (e.g. warfarin, anticholinesterases) and that the risk of cyesis increases in longer trials which are thereby disadvantaged, though much needed if useful drug surveillance is to take place. There are the problems of home pregnancy testing and diary cards, their cost and the timing of animal studies in relation to that of human studies if women are to be included.

There is certainly a time-order problem for animal tests too. Above all there is the abortion issue: should there be a 'consent to pregnancy' exclusion instead of 'potential for pregnancy'; should tests for cyesis be *required* and should there be prior 'consent to abortion'? Lastly, there are legal problems. In no less than 40 states in the USA legal suits are allowed on behalf of the foetus (Sandomire, 1993), but firms can also be held to be accountable for what they 'should have known' about a drug's actions in females if they decide to exclude them from trials. The draft Federal Drugs Administration (FDA) guideline of 1993 proposed that the former restriction on female volunteers be removed, and that gender-related analyses (including pharmacokinetic) be included for each investigated new drug (IND). Bush ended her paper (1994) with some clear and carefully balanced suggestions for a strategy to include female subjects in trials, with graded safeguards for each of the vulnerable subgroups who might volunteer, whether they be pre- or post-menopausal, taking oral contraception or not.

There has also been strong debate about *children* in clinical trials. Historically, this goes back to a ruling given by Druitt, a Treasury Solicitor, who advised that research in children could only take place if it were devoid of risk and of direct therapeutic benefit to the child. These conditions obstructed all non-therapeutic work, however risk free and generally useful. They were conditions which were impossible to fulfil since no therapy is risk free, and the ruling involved no consideration of the ethical duty of beneficence in relation to other factors. The other legal imposition in England has been the exemption of parents from 'therapeutic privilege', the option to avoid giving information which might harm the recipient. Doctors have a duty to tell parents all the potential risks of a procedure which their child may undergo (Kennedy, 1991).

Bender (1994) reviewed the essential elements for ethical paediatric research. These, he stated, are medical competence controlled by self-criticism, recognition that understanding is age limited and parental informed consent which is as precise and conclusive as possible. It seems strange that he did not discuss the shift in risk–benefit balance to the right for children as opposed to adult volunteers. Kauffman (1994) considered both legal and ethical issues, concluding that exception of children from clinical trials is now indefensible ethically. He also discussed the problem, which arises particularly in the USA, of surrogacy; a surrogate's operations may not be in a child's best interests. Susman *et al.* (1992) studied how 44 people aged from 7 to 20 viewed consent to research, and showed that most knew and understood the concrete aspects (e.g. freedom to ask questions, times of studies, benefits of therapy) but were significantly less clear about abstract elements (e.g. the scientific purpose of studies, choices amongst therapies). Most significantly, they showed that chronological age is not related to elements of informed consent, and that reasoning about trials parallels very closely reasoning power for physical phenomena in general.

Koren *et al.* (1993), a group of authors from a very international background, considered the maturity of children to consent. The Helsinki

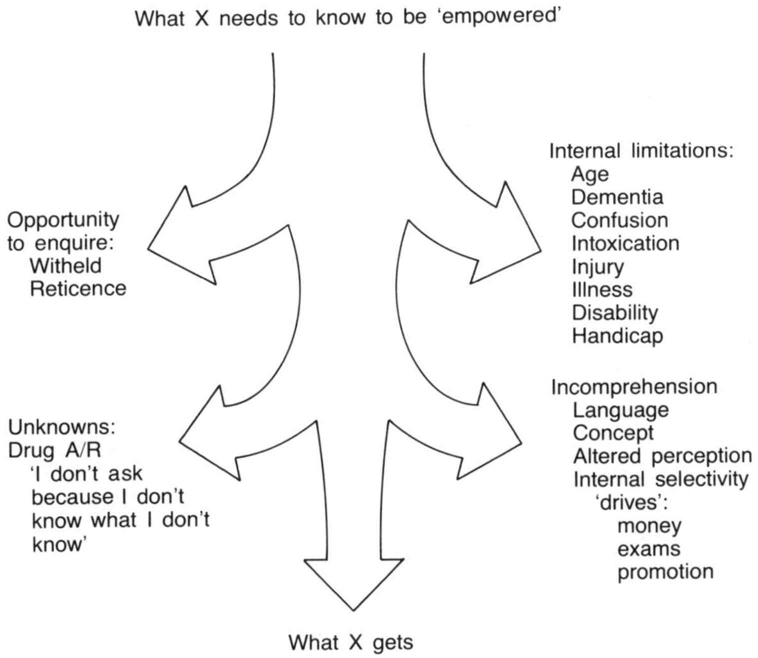

Figure 7.3 Fully informed consent cannot exist

Declaration (World Medical Association, 1964 (see Appendix 1)) allows surrogate consent by parent or guardian, but it is now generally agreed that the consent of the child should, where possible, be added. If not legally capable of consent, a child should assent. Though the American Academy of Paediatrics gives 7 years of age as the cut-off point for assent, and 13 for consent, there is a 'minimal risk' perspective; risk is held to include fear of procedure, pain or separation, and an ethics committee can waive informed consent if it thinks high stress will be imposed upon the child, given high beneficence for the proposed procedures. These authors review the literature on paediatric trial consent and comprehension; some authors had found that children aged 7 to 9 years could comprehend and refuse participation, and at 14 years were comparable with adults in comprehension power. Their conclusion was that whereas children are in general deemed to be minors who cannot competently consent, societies across the world are guilty of ethical discord since the same children are expected and allowed to babysit, even being given courses and examinations to fit them for this; since babysitting involves a level of skill and ethical comprehension that is comparable with that needed to consent to clinical trial, they proposed the 'babysitter test' to compare the two situations; people expect children to undertake responsibilities in the interests of adults which they are not allowed (by adults) to take for themselves. In the UK, the Medical Research Council adopts 12 years for competence.

English law now poses major uncertainties upon child consent (Shield and Baum, 1994), and there are special problems over institutionalised children; Kauffman (1994) discussed the direct benefit rule in relation to HIV cases particularly. There is a real question whether those who adopt high-risk lifestyles for themselves should stand as surrogates for a child. The difficulties of informed consent in children, especially those in intensive care, were debated in correspondence by Chinnery *et al.* (1993), Kanis and Bergmann (1993) and Modi (1993).

With regard to *mental illness and incapacity*, the main issues are who can consent and to what and what degree of selective protection should be given to those who are mentally impaired in relation to clinical trials. Geiselmann and Helmchen (1994) reported from the Berlin Ageing Study, a community-based non-therapeutic study with minimal risk, that though 76 per cent of the aged would be excluded from consent procedures on the grounds of their measured mental functional capacity, the remainder would be included and would be those with mild or moderate dementia who might benefit most from effective therapies.

Cournos (1993) discussed the issue of 'protecting' the mentally impaired from trials, but showed that general medical patients suffer similar degrees of impairment of perception for other reasons and no one suggests excluding them; and there is in any case the principle of beneficence with its ethical onus not to omit needy groups who might be helped.

Neubauer *et al.* (1994) discussed the German procedures about consent to treatments of any kind; patients must be able to understand the kind of therapy, its aims and consequences, as well as to consent. If they cannot, a guardian can be installed by a court. Becker and Kahana (1993) questioned the long-term validity of ongoing authorisation for a trial which continued into the long-term in demented subjects.

In a prize-winning, detailed study of the ethics of trials in dementia, Sachs *et al.* (1994), at the Windermere Senior Health Center in Chicago, Illinois, USA, found substantial problems with proxy consent. Others had already shown in literature reviewed by Sachs *et al.* (1994) that proxies gave consent believing that the subject would have refused it; though Sachs and his co-workers found this to be untrue of most, nevertheless a considerable proportion of subjects, having accepted proxies, refused to let them decide for them. It was helpful, they showed, when the patient chose their proxy and where both were involved together in the consent procedure.

In *mental retardation*, Morris *et al.* (1993) studied the ability of clinicians to determine capacity for informed consent. They found high reliability ratings across clinicians, a high relationship between being found capable and intellectual rating scores, but most importantly showed that it was possible to educate the subjects about therapy situations. Similar findings for *dementia* were obtained by Markson *et al.* (1994) when physicians were presented with a paper scenario; although they knew the standard for mental incapacity, they applied it wrongly under test.

In *mental illness*, Delano and Zucker (1994a and b) describe the procedures allowed for surrogacy by the New York State Office. Surrogates could be used only if needed by the subject, if knowledge about therapy was of overriding importance to the subject and if therapy could directly benefit the patient. If risk was more than minimal, the patient's therapy team should also be consulted. The patient could choose a surrogate or have a committee, and either patient or surrogate could object to a treatment proposal.

Milliken (1993) discussed the situation of surrogates in Canada, showing that though therapeutic research is needed, it must be clearly defined, submitted to independent review and that surrogacy is needed for informed consent. There is a right on the part of the incapacitated to take part in trials. However, adequate criteria for surrogates had not yet been established, nor were procedures for fair and adequate compensation should injury occur.

Another important group with special needs are *unconscious* patients, especially when accident or injury has occurred which makes it impossible to contact relatives when they enter hospital. There are impressive possibilities for 'scavenge' therapy under test at present, and these patients should not be denied access to remedies with minimal potential risks and the promise of real benefit. Kim and Spivey (1994) noted the frequent omission of investigational review board (IRB) consent procedures in such trials, indeed in the UK there have been a number of instances where they were not brought to the ethics committee because people thought that since no one could consent there was no need to do so. In the UK there is often misunderstanding about this; a patient's relatives cannot consent to such a trial. However, they should be given the same information as in any other such situation and invited to assent; they have a natural right to know that which is proposed and what may be done, and why. The balance of risk to benefit is shifted across to the far right whenever informed consent is impossible; this may justify what is proposed, but in no way does it exempt such studies from ethics committee review. There is also a particular need for detailed care by the investigator in such studies; for example, some of the novel 'scavenge' drugs proposed for use after stroke or head injuries, though almost devoid of direct toxicity, do prolong the Q–T interval on the electrocardiogram. If so, they might well interact hazardously with other similar agents which are likely to be given to such patients, e.g. local anaesthetics, anticonvulsants. The investigator must try to anticipate all such eventualities, taking steps to avert them.

Minority groups of susceptible people are sometimes created by medical activity; for example, it is patients who have been frequently exposed to radiation or who may well be so exposed, who are most likely to enter therapeutic trials involving radiation. It is very rare for patients to be asked about past radiation or for investigators to anticipate future radiation nor do patients keep radiation inventories. Triallists often fail to add the body doses from sealed and unsealed source radiation when assessing immediate exposure, let alone summarise dose over a large period.

Perhaps the other group which has attracted most debate is *oncology patients*. Discussion has centred upon the large numbers who for some reason are excluded from trials, and upon the difficulty of explaining cancer trials well in the 'form of words' given to patients. Joseph (1994) showed that only a small minority of patients with cancer enter trials, and reviews the reasons. Schain (1994) did the same, finding that less than 3 per cent enter trials. Individuals who need a high level of personal control, who want to feel that they have a high priority with their physician or who need frequent feedback of results, are unlikely to be good trial candidates.

Other significant minorities are *drug dependents*, who pose immense ethical difficulties for trials. This was reviewed by Ostini *et al.* (1993), and those with HIV infections, have stimulated a large literature, mostly letters to journals exposing a variety of difficult situations regarding confidentiality and the ethical duties of carers.

Many factors may influence consent, but these will not be discussed in any detail since others have contributed material at length about the chief factors: information and money.

Weijer and Fuks (1994) stressed that the duty to exclude subjects at undue risk rests with the clinical investigator, who should screen each subject personally. The response of physicians to good clinical practice (GCP) guidelines has been discussed in several ways. Idanpään-Heikkela (1994), explaining the World Health Organisation (WHO) guidelines, pointed out that some countries still have no drug investigation regulation, whereas others have some but need more. Dal-Re (1993) found that while a large majority of guidelines are kept by physicians, there are exceptions; patients are often not told about the reasons for the design of a trial, the specific experimental procedures to be used and the number of participants. The European guidelines on GCP were reviewed by Morice (1991) and Allen and Vandenburg (1992); these guidelines allow only therapeutic research (Kennedy, 1991) for incompetent subjects, hence non-therapeutic research in children cannot be consented to by their parents.

An interesting point is evidenced by the work of Peiters *et al.* (1992); volunteers are themselves a minority group. Their personality features differ significantly from those who do not volunteer (Chapter 6).

Payment undoubtedly influences volunteering, and varies surprisingly between countries. Chaput de Saintonge *et al.* (1988) found that pre-clinical students think that payment is for risk taking, whereas clinical medical students, though perceiving the risks as greater than their pre-clinical colleagues, thought that the time spent in the experiments was the main determinant of payment. Vere (1991) reviewed work in Spain and England on this topic. Experience of trials changes attitude to payment, payment changes attitudes to volunteering and perceived risk affects both. Thus the two myths which are conventionally predicated of ethical payments, i.e. that they must not be for risk and that they should not be such as to induce volunteering, are both found to be incorrect in the real world.

Shimm and Spece (1991) discussed the ethics of reimbursing volunteers by the drug industry arguing strongly that payments should never be to individual investigators, but put into a pool within their institution governed by the dean and open to application by any member of staff.

Information given to minority groups has been studied by several authors. Lynoe *et al.* (1991) identified worryingly large groups of subjects in gynaecological trials who had misunderstood ethically significant information. The readability of the information given to subjects has been carefully assessed by several groups; Murphy *et al.* (1994) in New Zealand found that the reading difficulty was around form 5 level at secondary school for newspaper editorials, form 1 for popular magazine articles and that the consenting information for trials lay between these two. This was better than the findings of Grossman *et al.* 1994 (for oncology patients in USA), who found that their readability indices were much less than for Hemingway, less than for Lincoln's Gettysburg address, and roughly similar to those for a life insurance policy. Meade and Howser (1992) discussed ways to improve and determine the reliability of consent forms in oncology.

The retention of information was studied in The Netherlands by Uddens *et al.* (1992). Their work showed a correlation to the level of education of the subjects; certainly in terms of readability and that the information sheet needed a higher education level than the investigators had intended. In France, Gerard *et al.* (1992) studied the impact of written consent (under Huriet's Law) upon the doctor–patient relationship, and found no significant loss of faith in the doctor, with written information providing a real aid to comprehension. Dal-Re (1992) in Spain found ethically significant omissions from the information given by physicians to volunteers. He also examined the effects of various levels of adverse drug reaction information on volunteering, showing that higher levels of information did significantly discourage volunteering (Dal-Re, 1991).

Similar work by Mazur and Hickam (1994) examined the effects of physicians' explanations on patient preference, especially comparing information about long-term as against short-term treatment outcomes; patient responses differed significantly with regard to long-term (five-year) survival. It is very satisfactory to see that ideological statements are gradually being supplanted by experimental findings in many countries, but it is disturbing to see that non-therapeutic research in incompetent subjects is still forbidden in major areas, even though such research is often highly beneficial in its results to those subjects; the onus of non-maleficence still overrides the duty of beneficence too often.

Summary and Conclusions

Thus, the role not only of the susceptible and disadvantaged, but also women in clinical trials is changing. It is important that by inclusion of such groups the potential benefits of new treatments are not denied to any particular group. However, as with all patients, *all* possible disadvantages should be discussed together with possible benefits as part of the consent/assent procedure which remains as important as ever before.

Discussion

The mark of society is how it can deal with the disadvantaged and how it looks after the sick in the community. Medicine should take a hard look at itself and its direction because there is a huge dilemma in pharmacologically based medicine.

Confucius said 'Those who conform with nature survive and those who go against nature perish'. Shouldn't we be aware that drugs act on the target sites of illness, but perhaps 90 per cent of an individual may not be ill? Drugs should be natural enough not to disadvantage the individual or cause side effects and should conform more with nature. Shouldn't medicine look more at lifestyles and natural medicines rather than those drugs which can actually cause disadvantage?

Major reduction in disease impact in societies across the world has resulted from finding out the causes of disease. Finding out how to live in harmony with the natural environment is to antagonise those causes of disease. In the UK this has resulted from, from example, clean water, good housing and the avoidance of infection transmission which have had a major impact on the incidence of disease. It is only 30 to 40 years ago that the majority of people who were in a hospital were there because they had all sorts of infections or horrible accidents and that is now not the case. Many of those infections have virtually disappeared.

Nature is also extremely cruel and many diseases are due in fact to perfectly natural processes. Dementia is one such area where failure of the mind, often quite early in life, in certain groups of people, is very much a natural phenomenon. Potentially there are groups of drugs which have an enormous amount to offer in that area. The important point about clinical trial design is that people who might be benefiting from those treatments, should not be denied that advantage. There is not a simplistic way of looking at this. Where there have been advances against disease in terms of living in balance with nature it has happened because people have understood the natural process and have learnt to live with it. There are many groups in very primitive communities throughout the world who do just exactly that, who have learnt how not to overfish, not to overfarm, not to poison crops with artificial chemicals but how to live with nature and grow productive crops with adequate field rotation and so on. All of that is true and we need to learn lessons from those.

In France, there is a problem in obtaining consent from the unconscious patient. The French have a legal procedure whereby, if the patient recovers you then have to get retrospective consent. What would happen if, in a study environment, the patient refused consent?

If you need consent to treat the unconscious patient, you can go to the immediate relatives and get assent, but you cannot get consent. You can also ask the relatives for their view on the patient's wishes concerning treatment if he or she was capable of giving consent. You can only do that by going through the patient's relatives. When it comes to research in the unconscious patient, it has now reached a stage where there is no other better treatment than the experimental one. That has to be explained to the relatives very carefully. Then I think you can go ahead with it, but this may still cause problems in the French situation.

There are situations where the patient may not have any relatives around at the time you need to treat. There is also the situation of deliberate suicidal intent.

Patients have been treated for attempted suicide in intensive care units, especially in the USA. It is not unknown that such patients, when they recover, take legal action against the treating physician for interference.

This whole area is ethically sensitive. The situation in France is well known and one has to work with that system. In the USA and in Germany there is surrogacy involved. In the UK you have to look for the relatives and achieve assent if you can, but they may not consent for their relatives. In France you have Huriet's Law where there must be a written signed consent form and if you cannot get it at the time you must get it afterwards.

There is a helicopter service that serves the accident and emergency departments of London hospitals. In this situation, there are unconscious people admitted to hospital and their relatives may not even know they have had an accident. Under the forthcoming European guidelines there will be a number of requirements which are quite contradictory in this respect. One is the requirement for written consent and another is the requirement for an opportunity to reflect. Unconscious patients certainly do not reflect about what is happening to them. The European guidelines will allow only therapeutic research, no other kind of research and so you would only be able to do your research if it involved a drug which might be a direct benefit to the person involved. There is a group of drugs in development now which have minimal toxicity in all the animal tests and human volunteer exposures in conscious persons. These are the scavenge drugs and there is a very strong expectation that they may be of direct benefit in limiting the damage following an accident or a stroke. There could be ethical grounds for withholding such treatment which might be of very strong direct benefit to those people even though the evidence suggests that the likely toxicity is zero or very minimal. There is currently no law or guideline throughout the world that copes with these types of situations. Laws, rules, guidelines and regulations really do very little to help in such ethical dilemmas.

References

ALLEN, M. E., and VANDENBURG, M. J., 1992, Good clinical practice: rules, regulations and their impact on the investigator, *British Journal of Clinical Pharmacology*, **33**, 463–6.

ANDERSON, C., 1994, Panel backs pregnant women in trials, *Science*, **263**, 1216.

BECKER, D., and KAHANA, Z., 1993, Informed consent in demented patients; a question of hours, *Medicine and Law*, **12**, 271–6.

BENDER, S. W., 1994, Remarks of a paediatrician on informed consent in children, *Acta Paediatrica (Supplement)*, **83**, 58–61.

BUSH, J. K., 1994, The industry perspective on the inclusion of women in clinical trials, *Academic Medicine*, **69**, (a) 708–15.

CHAPUT DE SAINTONGE, D. M., CRANE, G. J., RUST, N. D., KARADIA, S. and WHITTAM, L. R., 1988, Modelling determinants of expected rewards in healthy volunteers, *Pharmaceutical Medicine*, **3**, 45–54.

CHINNERY, P., ASIMAKOPOULOS, G. and KENNY, R. A., 1993, Informed consent in clinical trials. Consent may not be possible, *British Medical Journal*, **307**, 1496–7.

COURNOS, F., 1993, Do psychiatric patients need greater protection than medical patients when they consent to treatment, *Psychiatric Quarterly*, **64**, 319–29.

DAL-RE, R., 1991, Clinical Trial of Drugs, a study of information on adverse reactions on the obtaining of informed consent, *Medicina Clinica*, **96**, 566–9.

1992, Elements of informed consent in clinical research with drugs: a survey of Spanish clinical investigators, *Journal of Internal Medicine*, **231**, 375–9.

1993, Good clinical practice in clinical trial: the responsibilities of the investigator. A survey of 827 hospital physicians, *Medicina Clinica*, **100**, 423–7.

DELANO, S. J., and ZUCKER, J. L., 1994a, *Fortschritte der Neuro-Psychiatric*, **62**, 306–12.

1994b, Protecting mental health research subjects without prohibiting progress, *Hospital and Community Psychiatry*, **45**, 601–3.

GEISELMANN, B. and HELMCHEN, H., 1994, Demented subjects' competence to consent to participate in field studies: the Berlin Ageing Study, *Medicine and Law*, **13**, 177–84.

GERARD, J. P., ROMESTAING, P., MARQUIS, I., WAGNER, J. P., MAILLOT, M. H., BUATOIS, F. and BOHAS, C., 1992, Evaluation of the consequences of signing a written consent on physician-patient relations, *Bulletin du Cancer*, **79**, 667–74.

GROSSMAN, S. A., PIANTADOSI, S. and COVAHEY, C., 1994, Are informed consent forms that describe clinical oncology research protocols readable by most patients and their families? *Journal of Clinical Oncology*, **12**, 2211–95.

IDANPÄÄN-HEIKKELA, J. E., 1994, WHO guidelines for GCP for trials of pharmaceutical products: responsibilities of the investigator, *Annals of Medicine*, **26**, 89–94.

JOSEPH, R. R., 1994, Viewpoints and concerns of a clinical trial participant, *Cancer*, **74** (9 suppl.), 2692–3.

KANIS, J. A. and BERGMANN, J. F., 1993, Informed consent in clinical trials. Full consent may bias outcome of trials. Editorial and letters, *British Medical Journal*, **1307**, 1497; **1308**, 1182–3.

KAUFFMAN, R. E., 1994, Drug trials in children: ethical, legal and practical issues, *Journal of Clinical Pharmacology*, **34**, 296–9.

KENNEDY, I., 1991, Consent and Information: Research on healthy volunteers and patients, in Goldberg, Sir A. and Dodds-Smith, I. Ed. *Pharmaceutical Medicine and the Law*, London: Royal College of Physicians, pp. 33–43.

KIM, D. T. and SPIVEY, W. H., 1994, A retrospective analysis of IRB and informed consent procedures in emergency medical services research, *Annals of Emergency Medicine*, **23**, 70–4.

KOREN, G., CARMELI, D. B., CARMELI, Y. S. and HASLAM, R., 1993, Maturity of children to consent to medical research: the babysitter test, *Journal of Medical Ethics*, **19**, 142–7.

LYNOE, N., SANDLUND, M., DAHLQVIST, G. and JACOBSSON, L., 1991, Informed consent: a study of quality of information given to participants in a clinical trial, *British Medical Journal*, **303**, 610–13.

MCCARTHY, C. R., 1994, Historical background of clinical trials involving women and minorities, *Academic Medicine*, **69**, 695–8.

MARKSON, L. J., KERN, D. C., ANNAS, G. J. and GLANTZ, L. H., 1994, Physician assessment of patient competence, *Journal of the American Geriatric Society*, **42**, 1074–80.

MAZUR, D. J. and HICKAM, D. H., 1994, The effect of physicians' explanations on patients' treatment 'preferences', *Medical Decision Making*, **14**, 255–8.

MEADE, C. D. and HOWSER, D. M., 1992, Consent forms: How to determine and improve their reliability, *Oncology Nursing Forum*, **19**, 1523–8.

MILLIKEN, A. D., 1993, The need for research and ethical safeguards in special populations, *Canadian Journal of Psychology*, **38**, 681–90.

MODI, N., 1993, Informed consent in clinical trials, *British Medical Journal*, **307**, 1495.

MORICE, A., 1991, Good clinical practice and the clinical pharmacologist, *British Journal Clinical Pharmacology*, **32**, 529–30.

MORRIS, C. D., NEIDERBUHL, J. M. and MAHR, J. M., 1993, Determining the capability of individuals with mental retardation to give informed consent, *American Journal of Mental Retardation*, **98**, 263–72.

MURPHY, J., GAMBLE, G. and SHARPE, N., 1994, Readability of subject information leaflets for medical research, *New Zealand Medical Journal*, **107**, 509–10.

NEUBAUER, H., WETTERLING, T. and NEUBAUER, W., 1994, Willingness to give informed consent in elderly demented and confused (delirious) patients (German), *Fortschritte der Neuro-Psychiatry*, **62** (8), 306–12.

OSTINI, R., BAMMER, G., DANCE, P. R. and GOODWIN, R. E., 1993, The ethics of experimental heroin maintenance, *Journal of Medical Ethics*, **19**, 175–82.

PEITERS, M. S. M., JENNEKEUS-SCHINKEL, A., SCHOEMAKER, H. C. and COHEN, A. R., 1992, Self-selection for personality variables among 'healthy volunteers', *British Journal of Clinical Pharmacology*, **33**, 101–6.

SACHS, G. A., STOCKING, C. B., STERN, R., COX, D. M., HAUGHAM, G. and SACHS, R. S., 1994, Ethical aspects of dementia research: informed consent and proxy consent, *Clinical Research*, **42**, 403–12.

Sandomire, H., 1993, Women in clinical trials: are sponsors liable for fetal injury? *Journal of Law, Medicine and Ethics*, **21**, 217–30.

Schain, W. S., 1994, Barriers to clinical trials. Part II. Knowledge and attitudes of potential participants, *Cancer*, **74**, 2666–71.

Shield, J. P. H. and Baum, J. D., 1994. Children's consent to treatment, *British Medical Journal*, **308**, 1182–3.

Shimm, D. S. and Spece, R. G. Jr, 1991, Industry reimbursement for entering patients into clinical trials: legal and ethical issues, *Annals of Internal Medicine*, **115**, 148–51.

Susman, E. J., Dorn, L. D. and Fletcher, J. C., 1992, Participation in biomedical research: the consent process as viewed by children, adolescents, young adults and physicians, *Journal of Paediatrics*, **121**, 547–52.

Uddens, B. J., Algra, A. and Van Gijn, J., 1992, How much information is retained by participants in clinical trials? *Nederlands Tijdschrift voor Geneeskunde*, **126**, 2272–6.

Vere, D. W., 1991, Payments to healthy volunteers – ethical problems, *British Journal of Clinical Pharmacology*, **32**, 141–2.

Weijer, C. and Fuks, A., 1994, The duty to exclude: excluding people at undue risk from research, *Clinical and Investigative Medicine*, **17**, 115–22.

World Medical Association, 1964, Declaration of Helsinki. Adopted by the World Medical Assembly, Helsinki, 1964, and amended by the 29th World Medical Assembly, Tokyo, Japan, October 1975, the 35th World Medical Assembly, Venice, Italy, October 1983, and the 41st World Medical Assembly, Hong Kong, September 1989.

8

The Use of Surrogate End-points in Volunteer Studies

ANTHONY J. FREW

Developing new drugs is a very expensive business. Many compounds that are tested in the laboratory turn out to be ineffective or dangerous, while others fail to live up to their initial promise when they are used in real patients. At present it takes about 10 years to move an effective anti-asthmatic agent from the drawing-board to the clinic and the development costs are in the region of US$200 million. Before giving a new drug to patients in clinical trials, pharmaceutical companies need to gain some idea of potential efficacy. It is for this reason that a number of surrogate models have been developed which may predict efficacy in patients. Asthma will be taken as a model to demonstrate the usefulness of surrogate end-points in volunteer studies.

Bronchial asthma is a chronic inflammatory condition of human airways which is characterised by episodic narrowing of the airways. Asthmatic individuals often experience acute episodes of wheeze on exposure to non-specific irritants such as cold air, inorganic dusts, cigarette smoke, perfumes and paint. These are not allergic responses but are exaggerated responses of the airways to a non-specific irritant. This phenomenon is termed non-specific bronchial hyperresponsiveness. As well as increased non-specific responsiveness, many asthmatic patients have specific sensitivities to airborne allergens such as pollens, house dust, mites and animal danders. These specific responses are due to the presence of sensitising IgE antibodies directed against the relevant allergen. If present, these antibodies arm mast cells which line the airways. On subsequent exposure to allergens the mast cell releases chemical mediators (e.g. histamine, leukotrienes) which cause bronchoconstriction. When sensitised asthmatic subjects are exposed to allergen in the laboratory, they show a characteristic pattern of physiological response. Bronchoconstriction begins to develop within 5–10 minutes, and peaks between 15–20 minutes after allergen exposure before resolving over

1–2 hours. This is termed the early asthmatic response (EAR). Some but not all asthmatics will go on to develop a secondary or 'late-phase' asthmatic response (LAR) with recurrence of their bronchoconstriction between 3 and 9 hours after exposure. Subjects who experience LARs often find that their asthma destabilises following allergen challenge and they will have increased *non-specific* bronchial responsiveness (NSBR) for up to two weeks after challenge, even though their lung function has apparently returned to baseline (Cockcroft *et al.*, 1977; Durham *et al.*, 1987). Patients who experience an isolated EAR do not usually show alterations in NSBR or destabilisation of their asthma.

Use of Bronchial Provocation Tests to Predict Drug Efficacy in Asthma

Since the discovery of the EAR and LAR to allergen, there has been considerable interest in the possible use of inhalation challenge tests to predict drug activity against clinical asthma. Initial studies in the late 1960s and early 1970s were aimed at dissecting the pathophysiological mechanisms of asthma by using drugs which were already established in clinical practice. More recently, efficacy in bronchoprovocation tests has become one of the essential milestones in development of new anti-asthmatic drugs. Few drugs that are ineffective in bronchoprovocation tests are likely to undergo further development.

The central question is whether efficacy in bronchoprovocation tests is a reliable predictor of efficacy in clinical disease. In addition, do particular patterns of response in bronchoprovocation tests predict efficacy in a selected subset of asthmatic patients?

Three distinct types of challenge test have been used.

1 Specific mediator challenge (histamine, leukotriene, methacholine)
2 Indirect challenge (e.g. exercise, cold air, SO_2, distilled water, hypertonic saline, adenosine)
3 Allergen challenge.

Specific mediator challenges are generally used to determine the known activity of a drug (e.g. the efficacy of a leukotriene antagonist against inhaled leukotrienes or of an antihistamine against inhaled histamine). Sometimes the question at issue is the efficacy of a new drug preparation (e.g. a powdered aerosol) against a standardised challenge. Such challenges are useful parts of drug development in firmly demonstrating that the pharmacological responses shown in pre-clinical studies can be reproduced in normal or asthmatic humans at the doses selected and by the specific route chosen for administration.

Indirect challenges have received considerable attention because they can

Table 8.1 Pattern of activity of drugs against various types of bronchial challenge

	Non-specific provocants				Allergen challenge			
Drug class	Histamine	Methacholine	Exercise	Adenosine	SO_2	EAR	LAR	↑NSBR
Sodium cromoglycate	–	–	++	+	±	+++	+++	+++
Nedocromil	–	–	++	++	++	+++	+++	+++
Corticosteroids	–	–	–	–	–	–	++++	++++
,, ,, (longer term)			+++	+++	+	+	++++	++++
β2-agonists	++	++	+++	+++		+++	++/±	–
Antihistamines	++++	–	++	++		++	±/+	–
Leukotriene antagonists	–	–	++++	?		+/±	++	variable
Frusemide	–	–		?++		++	++	–

? = not clear
± = equivocal responses

be standardised more easily than allergen challenges and remove the variability due to differential sensitisation to allergens. Some of these act by neural reflexes and are independent of mast cell numbers while others act by triggering mast cells and thus offer an integrated measure of mast cell responsiveness to the challenge agent and pre-existing NSBR. Differential activity in these tests can thus be a useful indicator of site and mode of drug action. In general, drugs which are active in indirect challenge models are likely to work well in exercise-induced asthma but will not necessarily work in more severe forms of asthma.

Allergen challenge is considered to be the model that is closest to clinical asthma. As one would expect, good activity against allergen challenge is associated with efficacy in patients with a prominent allergic component to their disease. However, not all drugs which are effective against allergen challenge are equally effective in clinical disease.

Pharmacology of the Early and Late Asthmatic Response (Table 8.1)

Sodium cromoglycate (SCG) consistently inhibits the development of the early and late asthmatic responses when administered prior to allergen inhalation (Booij-Noord *et al.*, 1971). However, SCG does not influence the magnitude of the LAR if given after the EAR has developed (Booij-Noord *et al.*, 1972). Pretreatment with SCG prevents allergen-induced increases in NSBR (Cockcroft and Murdock, 1987) and the recruitment of eosinophils (Diaz *et al.*, 1984). Nedocromil sodium also attenuates the allergen-induced EAR and LAR when administered before allergen exposure and like SCG, nedocromil sodium prevents the subsequent increase in non-specific bronchial responsiveness (Aalbers *et al.*, 1991). The precise mechanism(s) through which SCG and nedocromil sodium exert their effects on the EAR and LAR is not known. However, nedocromil sodium is significantly superior to SCG in conferring protection against other non-specific bronchoconstrictor stimuli such as sulphur dioxide, adenosine and neurokinin A (Dixon *et al.*, 1987; Joos *et al.*, 1987; Richards *et al.*, 1989).

Corticosteroids are the most effective anti-asthma drugs available at present, although their use is limited by their potential side effects. When given as a single dose before allergen exposure, corticosteroids have little effect on the EAR, although they do attenuate the EAR when given over several weeks prior to challenge (Burge *et al.*, 1982), probably by depleting mast cell numbers (Djukanovic *et al.*, 1992). In contrast, corticosteroids are extremely effective against the LAR (Booij-Noord *et al.*, 1972). As with SCG, successful abolition of the LAR prevents the rise in NSBR that usually follows the LAR (Cockcroft and Murdock, 1987). Corticosteroids have no direct effect on mast cell mediator release (Schleimer, 1990) and it is likely that their effect on the LAR is due to a combination of direct effects on vascular endothelium and cellular recruitment (Schleimer, 1990) and indirect effects on cellular activation by inhibition of phospholipase A_2 (Blackwell *et al.*, 1981). Longer-term steroid treatment (e.g. 14 days treatment with inhaled budesonide) decreases airway response to methacholine, sodium metabisulphite and adenosine, with a greater effect against adenosine than the other two stimuli (O'Connor *et al.*, 1992), which is probably due to the effect of long-term steroid therapy in reducing mast cell numbers as well as airways inflammation (Holgate *et al.*, 1991).

β_2-adrenergic agonists

β_2-adrenergic agonists (salbutamol, terbutaline, for example) are widely used to treat asthma and act rapidly to relieve bronchospasm. When administered prior to allergen challenge, salbutamol attenuates the immediate response to allergen and the associated rise in plasma histamine (Howarth *et al.*, 1985) but has no effect on the subsequent development of the late-phase response or the subsequent increase in NSBR (Cockcroft and Murdock, 1987). If given after allergen challenge, some reversal of the LAR is observed (Malo *et al.*, 1990). In addition to its bronchodilator properties, salbutamol is a very potent mast cell stabiliser, being about 1000 times more potent than SCG in inhibiting degranulation of human pulmonary mast cells (Church and Young, 1983). This suggests that prevention of the LAR by other drugs cannot simply be attributed to prevention of mast cell degranulation.

Antihistamines

Despite the clear role of histamine in acute responses to allergen, antihistamines have not generally proved effective in treating clinical asthma nor do they alter bronchial responsiveness over a four-week period (Ruffin and Latimer, 1991). When used in challenge studies, antihistamines given by mouth or by inhalation prevent the response to histamine but not to methacholine (Brik *et al.*, 1987; Patel, 1987). Antihistamines also prevent bronchoconstriction induced by exercise, hyperventilation, or inhalation of hypotonic or hypertonic saline (Patel, 1984; Badier *et al.*, 1988; Rodwell *et al.*, 1991). This emphasises the importance of histamine as a mediator of these indirect bronchial responses, but also illustrates how these surrogate models can be deceptive in terms of predicting efficacy in the real disease.

The diuretic agent frusemide has never been used to treat asthma but has interesting effects on the bronchoconstrictor responses to different agents. Inhalation of nebulised frusemide almost completely abolishes the airway responses to exercise and to hypotonic 'fog' (nebulised distilled water) (Bianco *et al.*, 1988). Pretreatment with frusemide blocked the EAR and LAR to allergen (Bianco *et al.*, 1989; Robuschi *et al.*, 1990). However, frusemide did not affect the development of increased NSBR after allergen challenge, nor did it have any direct bronchodilator effect in patients with reversible airflow obstruction (Bianco *et al.*, 1989). *In vitro*, frusemide has no effect on contraction of bronchial smooth muscle to a range of spasmogens, suggesting that its effect *in vivo* may be due to an effect on mast cells or on nerve endings.

Summary and Conclusions

Bronchoprovocation tests are valuable tools for dissecting the pathophysiological mechanisms of asthma and for determining the activity and mode of action of new drugs. Such tests are a useful indicator of activity against some forms of asthma, and are a good model of the way in which surrogate end points may be used in volunteer studies. Nevertheless, whenever such tests prove positive, efficacy in the clinical disease then has to be confirmed by carefully controlled studies in patients with the active disease.

References

Aalbers, R., Kauffman, H. F., Groen, H., Koeter, G. H. and de Monchy, J. G. R., 1991, The effect of nedocromil sodium on the early and late reaction and allergen-induced bronchial hyperresponsiveness, *Journal of Allergy and Clinical Immunology*, **87**, 993–1001.

Badier, M., Beaumont, D. and Orehek, J., 1988, Attenuation of hyperventilation-induced bronchospasm by terenadine, *Journal of Allergy and Clinical Immunology*, **81**, 437–40.

Bianco, S., Vaghi, A., Robuschi, M. and Pasargiklian, M., 1988, Prevention of exercise-induced bronchoconstriction by inhaled frusemide, *Lancet*, **ii**, 252–5.

BIANCO, S., PIERONI, M. G., REFINI, R. M., ROTTOLI, L. and SESTINI, P., 1989, Protective effect of inhaled frusemide on allergen-induced early and late asthmatic reactions, *New England Journal of Medicine*, **321**, 1069–73.

BLACKWELL, G. J., CARNUCCIO, R., DI ROSA, M., FLOWER, R. J., PARENTE, L. and PERSICO, P., 1981, Macrocortin a polypeptide causing the anti-phospholipase effect of glucocorticoids, *Nature*, **287**, 147–9.

BOOIJ-NOORD, H., ORIE, N. G. M. and DEVRIES, K., 1971, Immediate and late bronchial obstructive reactions to inhalation of house dust and protective effects of disodium cromoglycate and prednisolone, *Journal of Allergy and Clinical Immunology*, **48**, 344–54.

BOOIJ-NOORD, H., DEVRIES, K., SLUITER, H. J. and ORIE , N. G. M., 1972, Late bronchial obstructive reaction to experimental inhalation of house dust extract, *Clinical Allergy*, **2**, 43–61.

BRIK, A., TASKIN, D. P., GONG, H., DAUPHINEE, B. and LEE, E., 1987, Effect of cetirizine, a new histamine H1 antagonist on airway dynamics and responsiveness to histamine in mild asthma, *Journal of Allergy and Clinical Immunology*, **80**, 51–6.

BURGE, P. S., EFTHIMIOU, J., TURNER-WARWICK, M. and NELMES, P. T. J., 1982, Double blind trials with inhaled beclomethasone diproprionate and fluocortin butyl ester in allergen- induced immediate and late asthmatic reactions, *Clinical Allergy*, **12**, 523–31.

CHURCH, M. K. and YOUNG, K. D., 1983, The characteristics of inhibition of histamine release from human lung fragments by sodium cromoglycate, salbutamol and chlorpromazine, *British Journal of Pharmacology*, **78**, 671–9.

COCKCROFT, D. W. and MURDOCK, K. Y., 1987, Comparative effects of inhaled salbutamol, sodium cromoglycate, and beclomethasone diproprionate on allergen-induced early asthmatic responses and increased bronchial responsiveness to histamine, *Journal of Allergy and Clinical Immunology*, **79**, 734–40.

COCKCROFT, D. W., RUFFIN, R. E., DOLOVICH, J., and HARGREAVE, F. E., 1977, Allergen-induced increase in non-allergic bronchial reactivity, *Clinical Allergy*, **7**, 503–13.

DIAZ, P., GALLEGUILLOS, F. R., GONZALEZ, M. C., PANTIN, C. F. A. and KAY, A. B., 1984, Bronchoalveolar lavage in asthma – the effect of disodium cromoglycate on leukocyte counts, immunoglobulins and complement, *Journal of Allergy and Clinical Immunology*, **74**, 41–8.

DIXON, C. M. S., FULLER, R. W. and BARNES, P. J., 1987, Effect of nedocromil sodium on sulphur dioxide-induced bronchoconstriction, *Thorax*, **42**, 462–5.

DJUKANOVIC, R., WILSON, J. W., BRITTEN, K. M., WILSON, S. J., WALLS, A. F., ROCHE, W. R., HOWARTH, P. H. and HOLGATE, S. T. 1992, The effect of inhaled corticosteroids on airway inflammation and symptoms of asthma, *American Review of Respiratory Diseases*, **145**, 669–74.

DURHAM, S. R., GRANEEK, B. J., HAWKINS, R. and NEWMAN-TAYLOR, A. J., 1987, The temporal relationship between increases in airway responsiveness to histamine and late asthmatic responses induced by occupational agents, *Journal of Allergy and Clinical Immunology*, **79**, 398–406.

HOLGATE, S. T., DJUKANOVIC, R., WILSON, J. W., ROCHE, W. R., BRITTEN, K. and HOWARTH, P. H., 1991, Allergic inflammation and its pharmacologic modulation in asthma, *International Archives of Allergy and Applied Immunology*, **94**, 210–17.

Howarth, P. H., Durham, S. R., Lee, T. H., Kay, A. B., Church, M. K. and Holgate, S. T., 1985, Influence of albuterol, cromolyn sodium and ipratropium bromide on the airway and circulating mediator responses to allergen bronchial provocation in asthma, *American Review of Respiratory Diseases*, **132**, 986–92.

Joos, G. F., Pauwels, R. A. and van der Straeten, M. E., 1987, The protective effect of nedocromil sodium on neurokinin A-induced bronchoconstriction, *Bulletin of European Physiopathology and Respiration*, **23**, 312S.

Malo, J. L., Ghezzo, H., L'Archeveque, R. T., and Cartier, A., 1990, Late asthmatic reactions to occupational sensitising agents: frequency of changes in nonspecific bronchial responsiveness and of response to inhaled β2-adrenergic agents, *Journal of Allergy and Clinical Immunology*, **85**, 834–42.

O'Connor, B., Ridge, S. M., Barnes, P. J. and Fuller, R. W., 1992, Greater effect of inhaled budesonide on adenosine monophosphate-induced than on sodium metabisulphite-induced bronchoconstriction in asthma, *American Review of Respiratory Diseases*, **146**, 560–4.

Patel, K. R., 1984, Terfenadine in exercise-induced asthma, *British Medical Journal*, **288**, 1496–7.

1987, Effect of terfenadine on methacholine-induced bronchoconstriction in asthma, *Journal of Allergy and Clinical Immunology*, **79**, 355–8.

Richards, R., Phillips, G. D. and Holgate, S. T., 1989, Nedocromil sodium is more potent than sodium cromoglycate against AMP-induced bronchoconstriction in atopic asthmatic subjects, *Clinical and Experimental Allergy*, **19**, 285–91.

Robuschi, M., Pieroni, M., Refini, M., Bianco, S., Rossoni, G., Magni, F. and Berti, F., 1990, Prevention of antigen-induced early obstructive reaction by inhaled frusemide in atopic subjects with asthma and actively sensitised guinea pigs, *Journal of Allergy and Clinical Immunology*, **85**, 10–16.

Rodwell, L. T., Anderson, S. D. and Seale, J .P., 1991, Inhaled clemastine, an H1 antihistamine inhibits airway narrowing caused by aerosols of non-isotonic saline, *European Respiratory Journal*, **4**, 1126–34.

Ruffin, R. E. and Latimer, K. M., 1991, Lack of effect of four weeks treatment of oral H1 histamine receptor antagonist on bronchial responsiveness, *European Respiratory Journal*, **4**, 575–9.

Schleimer, R. P., 1990, Effects of glucocorticosteroids on inflammatory cells relevant to their therapeutic applications in asthma, *American Review of Respiratory Diseases*, **141** (2 pt 2), S59–S69.

9

Whatever happened to Plain English? The Gobbledygook Smokescreen that baffles Research Subjects

STANLEY BLENKINSOP[1]

The importance of patient information in clinical trials cannot be overestimated. In this chapter patient information leaflets used in the consent procedure are discussed. Useful examples are given of how such information may be simplified – a procedure that researchers often find difficult and time consuming when trying to break away from their usual scientific style.

Words – around-the-clock Niagara of them – are the raw material of journalists. Sometimes a news editor will come across reports that have to be drastically rewritten to make them clear and understandable, often to millions of readers. However, on an ethics committee, there is often more confused, confusing and incomprehensible language than one would ever see as a news editor.

The last paragraph refers, of course, to the written information given to potential research subjects about what is involved if they decide to take part in clinical trials. In the UK over 500 000 people a year – around 1 in 100 of the population – volunteer for some form of medical research (CERES, 1994b).

Information that can be clearly understood is a key factor in research but how many of that annual 500 000 fully understand what they have agreed to and what pressures influence them to agree?

Experience would show that there is a real risk that, all too often, gobbledygook makes a most effective mask. Gobbledygook, a colourful import from American slang, is defined by the *Oxford English Dictionary* as 'pretentious and unintelligible jargon'.

There must be some suspicions that those unable to organise a clear, effective written explanation are equally unable to organise a clear, effective research programme. How much of that pretentious and unintelligible jargon is produced in ignorance – and how much is a deliberate smokescreen?

There are those who claim that it is the spoken explanation from the researcher, doctor or physician that matters. Invariably, information sheets list those who can answer any questions, but is there a danger of over-persuasion here? Quite naturally, researchers are enthusiastic and hopeful about their work. So they should be. Obviously they want people to volunteer. They are presumably deeply committed to their research programmes. However, they do usually have a financial interest too. That may be how they earn a living.

So how often does a researcher's function become one of deliberately quelling doubts, rather than giving unbiased information? How often does such 'salesmanship' persuade potential subjects into a quick decision to volunteer with the praiseworthy motives of helping others as well as themselves?

The Alzheimer's Disease Society have been sufficiently worried over the risk of such pressures that they highlight a warning that people should seek advice from their general practitioner (GP) or hospital consultant before committing themselves or their relatives as research subjects (Alzheimer's Disease Society, 1993). They say of researchers:

> It is almost certain that they will be very enthusiastic and optimistic about their research and will want you to become involved. Don't let this lead you into a quick decision. Go away. Think about the answers you have been given. Tell your GP or hospital consultant. Finally, having taken time to think about it, make up your mind.

What splendid advice, but even with GPs there could be pressures against completely dispassionate opinions. Some get considerable sums for each patient taking part in a research project.

Again, if researchers cannot offer a properly considered and adequate explanation in writing, why should they fare better when giving spoken replies 'off the cuff'? From the outset, subjects need clear written information that they can talk over with friends, relatives and advisers before deciding. Unless someone has a precise recollection of what they are told verbally the risks of misunderstanding can be considerable. All too often people hear what they want to hear.

The Patients Charter of 1991 clearly states:

> Every citizen has the right:
>
> To be given a clear explanation of any treatment proposed including risks and any alternatives, before you decide whether you will agree to the treatment.
>
> To choose whether you wish to take part in medical research.

In 1947, a war crimes tribunal at Nuremberg laid down standards for physicians to conform to when carrying out experiments involving humans – the so-called Nuremberg Code. These standards stipulated that clear information should be given to enable anyone asked to participate in medical research so they could make an enlightened and understanding decision. In 1964 the World Medical Association extended guidance on the ethics of such research in a statement which became known as the Declaration of Helsinki (World Medical Association, 1964 (see Appendix 1)). The Royal College of Physicians has been equally clear: 'Obtaining true or informed or understanding consent is central to the ethical conduct for clinical investigation'.

So why then do we have gobbledygook like the following examples in which the names have been changed to protect the guilty?

The following was addressed to parents of babies under 28 days old undergoing surgery for various birth defects.

> Dear Parents,
>
> *Study of Cytokine response in Neonates undergoing Surgery*
>
> We are asking you if you would help us with a study which involves your son/daughter who is going to have surgery performed to correct his/her congenital anomaly. Serial blood sampling will be carried out in the pre-operative and post-operative 24-hour period which amount (sic) to a total of 5 ml. This would minimally affect the patients' haemoglobin level.
>
> The blood samples will be assayed for the levels of cytokines. The purpose of this is to evaluate the prognostic value of the changes in cytokine level in the early post-operative period.
>
> You are under no obligation to commit your son/daughter in this study and you are free to withdraw at any time without it affecting the normal care of him/her (sic) in any way.

How could any layman or woman understand this pretentious and unintelligible jargon, especially those no doubt dreadfully worried about defects to their baby with some mothers also experiencing post-natal depression. What an air of uncaring, bureaucratic indifference about the son/daughter and him/her alternatives. Of course parents could ask for a fuller explanation but surely that could have been done in the letter, thereby avoiding more time being used to give information or clarification which should have been there from the start.

Now a letter to patients facing replacement of a diseased or artificial heart valve:

> *Freestyle Aortic Root Bioprosthesis*
>
> The Fordbridge Heart Centre is fortunate to participate in the assessment of a new heart valve which we feel conveys distinct advantages over previous models. The Freestyle heart valve is a tissue valve which does not require anticoagulation after an initial three-month period. The advantage of this valve is that it is not mounted on a frame which might impinge on the area for flow. The valve resembles a normal human valve but as for other types of tissue valve it is obtained from the pig. Extensive laboratory on animal testing (sic) has been

> undertaken in the USA and after consultation with the American Food and Drug Administration the valve is now available for use in humans.
>
> We have obtained this valve as part of a worldwide study with other centres in Europe and the USA. If you choose to receive this valve we would like to follow its progress carefully with regular check-ups. We will answer any questions that you have about your operation and would point out that you are not obliged in any way to choose this valve.

Again there is clumsy, sloppy English. Could people responsible for clumsy, sloppy language be equally responsible for clumsy, sloppy research?

Now a few examples of information sheets involving less serious studies.

> You have been selected by your doctor as an appropriate candidate for participation in a feasibility study to evaluate the functionality and acceptability of a combination of two standard devices intended to reduce the occurrence of asthmatic attacks.

Why not simplify it to:

> Will you help test two types of inhaler designed to stop asthma attacks? We want to know which is better and why.

Another classic:

> Those who are unable to adhere to the regime as a consequence of malfunctioning or adverse effects or who feel unable to continue to support the objective of the protocol before the trial is accomplished may terminate their participation and shall be assured that despite declining to participate, their routine clinical treatment will in no way be affected and that they will not be interrogated about their motives.

Why not:

> You are free to leave the trial at any time. You do not have to give a reason. If you opt out, you will continue to get the best care we can give.

Another:

> It is now well established that the substance currently under investigation is effective for the duration of a minimum of four hours.

Translation:

> The tablets work for at least four hours.

And again:

> The study involves adolescents aged 13 to 19 years but excludes all females of child-bearing age.

Translation:

> Only boys and young men aged 13 to 19 will take part.

Finally:

> After commencement of oral administration the patient's progress will be assessed and he or she will be frequently investigated to verify the occurrence of adverse reactions at ambulatory monitoring sessions to suit his or her convenience while lengthier interval monitoring will be accepted if he or she has not previously displayed any tendency to be predisposed to toxicity.

Translation:

> When you first take the medicine/tablets, you'll be asked to an outpatient clinic about once a fortnight. If there are no problems these visits will be reduced to once a month. We will arrange times to suit you.

Perhaps the best guide to preparing proper patient information is the 24-page booklet published by CERES – an acronym for Consumers for Ethics in Research. CERES claims to be the first such forum for those who believe that health service users – both in the public and private sector – should be closely involved at every stage of research affecting them. CERES stresses that everyone asked to take part in research or, in the case of young research subjects, their parents – should be able to make an informed free choice as to whether they agree. CERES holds open meetings and publishes newsletters and reports. To quote one of their pamphlets (CERES, 1994a):

> CERES was set up to help consumers of health services to develop and publicise their views on health research and on new treatments. CERES is also for members of research ethics committees, community health councils, health authorities and NHS trusts, voluntary organisations and for anyone who wishes to share information on consumer views of health research. 'Consumers' implies those who take an active part in medical decisions. They are not just the passive patients. Yet many users of health services feel ill, anxious, ignorant of medical knowledge, dependent and vulnerable. Differences in class, gender and race create problems. . . . CERES is concerned about how these differences can affect people taking part in research.

CERES, who hold open meetings and publish newsletters and reports, also publish a most helpful leaflet called 'Medical Research and You' (CERES, 1994b). Again it is clear and straightforward.

Research reveals that a large proportion of the British public has a low reading age and that the so-called 'tabloid' press, bought by the majority of the newspaper-reading public, pitches its reading level at the ability of the average 8–10-year-old (Hughes and Foster, 1992). Around 25 million people in the British Isles read a tabloid newspaper most days – although the umbrella term 'tabloid' takes in a wide spectrum from the *Daily Mail* with its high-professional-class readership to the *Daily Sport* where the all too obvious attractions are pictures rather than words.

According to scientific methods of checking written information, some tabloids have a 'reading score' of under 10. Many research information leaflets and consent letters have a reading score of 19 or more. That is university level. CERES says that such material is likely to confuse, worry or distress many of those for whom it is designed. Research often affects those already very worried about their health. As CERES says:

> Poorly written 'information' is likely to make them feel more worried. It gives a bad image to the project and to health research, an image of researcher not caring what patients think or need.

Using two different scientific formulae to measure readability the following passage can be assessed:

> If you were to agree to participate in this study we would allocate you to one of two treatment plans. All the participants in the study would be divided into two groups. Half would receive the medication and the other half would be treated the way we normally treat people in our unit. Our normal way is to watch carefully for signs of the disease worsening. Because we do not know which approach is best, half the participants will be allocated to receive each of half of the treatments, but in order to exclude any bias, it is important that the allocation is randomised using a computerised process similar to tossing a coin.

Using the Flesch formula, this passage has a 'fairly difficult' readability level. According to Gunning's Fog formula it requires a reading age of 18.6.

Here is a simpler version of the above text:

> If you were to agree to take part in the study you would be put in one of two groups. One group would be given the new medicines and the other group would be treated the way we normally treat patients in our unit. Our normal way is to watch for signs of the disease getting worse. At the moment we only know that the new treatment is as good as the normal treatment. We do not know if it is better. So we are asking you to have either one or the other treatment. In order to avoid influencing the results we need to randomise the choice of treatments. This is like tossing a coin to decide which group you go into. This means that neither we nor you choose the treatment.

This time the Flesch formula yields an 'easy' readability level and Gunning's Fog formula a reading age of 11.8.

These two formulae, together with other readability measures, can be calculated by the software program Microsoft Windows Word 2.0 (Manual for Research Ethics Committees, 1994).

Of course, it is not easy for highly educated people to understand the problems of poor readers. Some writers obviously think that writing grand prose – why use four short words when eight long ones will do – inspires confidence, respect, even awe. Yet simple, straightforward language is often much more difficult and with patient information leaflets it is very much more efficient. CERES stresses the point that:

> Academic and scientific language has great strengths such as precision. Yet it

> can prevent knowledge and control from being shared more fairly through society.

In general, ethics committees are critical in varying degrees of around a third of the information sheets and consent letters submitted. The most common grounds for asking applicants to re-think are that the reading level is too high; the material is coercive; the predictions seem too optimistic and over-positive and the impression given towards research subjects is cold and unfeeling.

How often do those writing information leaflets and consent forms talk to those they are writing for? What questions do potential volunteers have? The first draft should be checked with medical colleagues, other researchers, nurses and – most important of all – the sort of lay people who may be asked to take part in the study. It may be necessary to call in other people to help – even someone with experience of tabloid journalism! Do a small pilot with the new text and layout and try it on potential subjects before completing the final version. Almost every organisation within the NHS has access to professional public relations departments. Use them. The vast majority of drug companies also have their own public relations officers. Use them.

After an ethics committee had difficulties with a drug company on one of their patient information leaflets they were asked what exactly would be acceptable to them. This was rewritten by the chairman and sent to the company only to receive the reply that it was written in such simple language that it seemed like the sort of thing that appeared in a tabloid newspaper. This comment was probably not meant as a compliment – but it certainly should have been.

Sadly, that attitude is typical of too many drug companies towards ethics committees in general and to the lay sectors of those committees in particular. I believe it is all part of a growing trend of: 'If your committee doesn't like the way we want to do things we'll find a committee somewhere else who will.'

Here is an example involving the clinical research ethics committee at St James' University Hospital, Leeds. After they raised several points on a protocol, they received a reply from the drug company which included the following:

> I note your committee's comments on our protocol with considerable interest. Fortunately there are sufficient local research ethics committees elsewhere in the country without the participation of Dr . . . as a triallist. I understand that the Department of Health is currently engaged in drawing up new guidelines for local ethics committees in relation to their role in multi-centre studies. When this happens we will hopefully see less of the failures of communication that have occurred during your consideration of this protocol.
>
> (Dear, 1995).

Interesting, is it not, to hear a drug company talking of 'failure of communication' when we have seen the earlier examples of their information material?

The manner in which information is offered can also leave much to be desired. Remember that people are used to glossy leaflets. Material photocopied from a poor third-hand copy gives the impression of a slipshod casual project. Large dark print on white matt paper helps people with poor eyesight as well as those who are poor readers. Instead of long, dense paragraphs, material must be split into short blocks as easy to read as the paragraphs in a tabloid newspaper.

Consent to participation in medical research is a voluntary agreement based on adequate information. Research ethics committees must do everything possible to make certain that the researcher achieves this. It is not just a matter of obeying rules. There must be genuine communication if consent is to be valid.

Everyone should remember the power of short words and short sentences. Whether or not you are religious one of the most fascinating stories ever told forms the first sentence of the Bible:

> In the beginning God created the Heaven and the Earth.

Not really a lot of pretentious and unintelligible jargon there.

Summary and Conclusions

Patient information leaflets are, and for the foreseeable future will remain, the most important way of informing patients about research studies. Since this is the case, the use of plain, easy-to-use language should be a logical way to write such leaflets. Clearly this is not currently the case with all researchers. In some cases researchers have real difficulties in using simple, easy-to-understand language. Often a change in attitude for the researcher is needed. However, often by allowing more time to prepare such information leaflets and getting advice not just from medical colleagues but also from patient groups, gobbledygook can be avoided.

Discussion

When doing the preparatory work to produce a leaflet, I was in touch with the Plain English Campaign who said that the biggest area of complaints they received was on consent forms, not just consent forms around research but consent forms to treatment. People have said that they do not understand what they are signing agreement to. The Plain English Campaign were very concerned about not just the language used in consent forms for research but in general the ones people sign when they go into hospital for any form of treatment. I think this is a general problem that is far more common than we can possibly imagine.

It seems that less and less people are reading and maybe the way forward

is to start making videos. At least two London units use videos to show patients and relatives the sort of treatment that will be used. This may be more acceptable if somewhat expensive.

This seems a very sensible idea, especially for children. It will be interesting when someone submits that sort of material to an ethics committee because presumably that would be mentioned on the application and in the protocol. I think it would be a very good idea.

At this point, the importance should be stressed of not just short words but also accurate meanings. Some of the best examples that I can remember coming were for an earoximeter – you will be given a small clip on the ear! Another: 'your thigh will be fixed to a wheel'! The words were short but the meaning not clear!

Pharmaceutical companies certainly have problems in getting consent forms passed by ethics committees at times. It is very difficult to find somebody who is not of a university reading level suitable to be writing in the company. Information leaflets may be given to secretaries and others but even they are used to medical terminology. It would be good if there was a mechanism whereby the industry could give these sorts of documents to somebody who can give them assistance with that sort of writing and to give it to them quickly because time is always of the essence. Given that sometimes these documents are thrown back after ethical review it may be worth while spending extra time working on these.

This is a very valid point. All ethics committees must have had problems about the wording of some information leaflets.

Note

1 Stanley J. Blenkinsop, a former news editor of the *Daily Express*, is lay chairman of the Macclesfield local research ethics committee and vice-chairman of the East Cheshire NHS Trust. The opinions expressed above are his own and not necessarily those of the bodies on which he serves.

References

ALZHEIMER'S DISEASE SOCIETY, 1993, Information Sheet 14, *Volunteering for Research*, London.

DEAR, R. T. F., 1995, Local research ethics committees and multi-centre drug trials, *British Medical Journal*, March 18, 1995, **310**, 735.

CERES, 1994a, *Spreading the word on research or patient information; how can we get it better?,* London: Consumers for Ethics in Research.

1994b, *Medical Research and You*, London: Consumers for Ethics in Research.

HUGHES, T. and FOSTER, C., 1992, Communicating with the potential research subject. King's College, London.

Manual for Research Ethics Committees, 1994, Section II, p. 23.
WORLD MEDICAL ASSOCIATION, 1964. Declaration of Helsinki. Adopted by the World Medical Assembly, Helsinki, 1964, and amended by the 29th World Medical Assembly, Tokyo, Japan, October 1975, the 35th World Medical Assembly, Venice, Italy, October 1983, and the 41st World Medical Assembly, Hong Kong, September 1989.

10

The Risks of Studies in Healthy Volunteers

MICHAEL ORME

Volunteer studies may be performed in either healthy or patient volunteers. The risks involved in healthy volunteer studies are quite different to those studies involving individuals already suffering from a disease or illness. It is for this reason that this chapter will concentrate, almost exclusively, on the risks involved in healthy volunteer studies.

The importance of risk in healthy volunteer studies was highlighted about 10 years ago when two healthy volunteers, one in Cardiff and one in Dublin, died shortly after taking a drug in clinical studies as healthy volunteers. As a result, the Royal College of Physicians and the Medicines Commission both produced reports which dealt with the conduct of healthy volunteer studies although there was no information about the relative risks involved with healthy volunteer studies at that time.

It was initially assumed that the risks involved in healthy volunteer studies were very small but after these two deaths the insurance companies reacted and the premium for their insurance increased markedly. Insurance companies assumed that the risks were high and their response was not unreasonable. It was therefore very important to find out what the risks really were and it was therefore decided to look at the work done by all the members of the Clinical Section of the British Pharmacological Society over a one-year period (October 1986 to September 1987). A further study was done over the period 1990–1991 with very similar results to the earlier study. All members were sent a questionnaire to look at their work in healthy volunteers. They were asked a number of questions in four areas of concern.

First, class demonstrations – usually meaning medical or science students, who, as part of their course, were often taking a relatively simple drug in order to demonstrate to them the effect of the drug. The question here was

'What are the risks of taking these drugs?'

Second, the survey was interested in the research studies that were done in healthy volunteers to try to come to some measure of the risk of the adverse effects.

The survey also asked about Ethics Committee matters and facilities that were available for clinical trials. The survey asked if clinical trial protocols were reviewed by an external Ethics Committee.

The questions concerning research studies in healthy volunteers were the most important part of this survey. In terms of such studies the survey asked how many volunteers were involved in each study, did the study involve specialist groups (e.g. elderly patients, children); how were volunteers recruited and where they came from (e.g. did the triallists advertise or did they rely on word of mouth); were any trial screens done before volunteers either entered the study or before they left it in order to assess whether they were really healthy or not.

The adverse events related to these areas were categorised into three kinds: mild, moderate and severe. The definitions were, in essence, arbitrary. However, it was decided that a severe adverse event was one that was potentially life threatening. Moderate events were those that needed medical (either nursing or doctor) attention. Those that did not fall into those two categories were then categorised as mild.

The survey attempted to find out whether consent forms were used and a little about their nature. Finally, the survey asked whether the organisers of the trial had a central register of volunteers. Other questions were asked concerning trial organisation but were not of direct relevance to the risks of the study (for full information readers are referred to the original publication by Orme *et al.*, 1989).

Results

A total of 608 questionnaires were sent out with one going to every member of the Clinical Section of the British Pharmacological Society. The section has 149 members overseas, so because of the difference in the legal systems the information from overseas members was recorded for information only. Of the remaining 459 returns, 285 respondents gave no drugs to healthy volunteers and therefore they were excluded. We had 114 positive returns, and in order to get an overall response rate as high as possible we followed up 59 individuals who did not return the questionnaire after a reminder letter. Evidence from their work published in the literature suggested that they were very unlikely to be involved in healthy volunteer studies. The overall response rate was 87 per cent (good for a survey of this type).

As far as the class demonstrations were concerned, many units gave drugs to students as part of class demonstrations. Table 10.1 shows that during that year there were 7607 students who had participated in such a demonstration

Table 10.1 Drugs used in student demonstrations

Drug	Route of administration	Number of students receiving drug (n)
Lignocaine	Intradermal injection	920
Aspirin	Oral	560
Frusemide	Oral	403
Propranolol	Oral	390
Dihydrocodeine	Oral	297
Nitrous Oxide	Inhalation	280
Prilocaine	Intradermal injection	270
Glyceryl Trinitrate	Sublingual	241
Pilocarpine	Eyedrops	240
Acetazolamide	Oral	225
Phenylephrine	Eyedrops	224
Salbutamol	Inhalation	223
Total number of students given demonstration drugs		7607

Minor side effects were seen in 6.0 per cent of students ($n > 200$)

during the one-year period covered by the survey. There were 25 different drugs involved and the more commonly used ones are shown in Table 10.1. No severe adverse effects were reported, but about 6% of the group recorded minor adverse effects. A number of students complained of headaches and/or dizziness and had to lie down, but in all cases the symptoms resolved quickly and spontaneously.

In the clinical research studies, there were 1377 single-dose studies reported, that is where a single dose of a drug was given and the individual volunteer was studied afterwards, either with blood samples or with measures of the effect of the drug. There were also 375 multiple-dose studies, where the volunteer was given drugs for anything up to three weeks. The single- and multiple-dose studies combined involved 8163 volunteers. Of these volunteers, 28 per cent were students, 25 per cent were staff in the unit concerned, 19 per cent were staff in the institution but not in the unit concerned and 28 per cent were from elsewhere. The large majority of volunteers were given written information about the study concened and virtually all volunteers (98 per cent) had signed a consent form. A general health check was performed before and after the study in 80 per cent of the volunteers, but only 20 per cent of volunteers were screened for drugs of abuse. Only half the respondents knew of or used a central register of volunteers in their institution. This is now recommended practice to dissuade volunteers from undertaking too many studies in any defined period. Some of these responses are considered in Table 10.2.

Table 10.2 Arrangements for research studies in healthy volunteers

	% ($n = 85$) Yes	No
Provision of written information to volunteer	89.4	10.6
Pre-trial health screen of volunteers	81.0	19.0
Pre-trial screen for drugs of abuse	21.2	78.8
Presence of central register of volunteers	49.4	50.6
General practitioner routinely informed?	52.9	47.1
Signing of consent form by volunteer	97.6	2.4
Countersigning consent form by witness	81.1	18.9

Table 10.3 Moderate and severe adverse events in clinical research studies in healthy volunteers

Moderate adverse events	*Number*
Postural hypotension	12
Abdominal pain	10
Nausea and vomiting	7
Palpitations	6
Bronchoconstriction	5
Drowsiness or headache	4
Severe adverse events	*Outcome*
Severe skin irritation and rash requiring hospitalisation	Full recovery
Anaphylactic shock after oral vaccine	Full recovery
Perforation of duodenal ulcer after multiple dose NSAID study	Full recovery after surgery

In the clinical research studies minor adverse events were noted in 565 of those 8163 individuals (6.9 per cent overall). Moderate adverse events were seen in 45 individuals (< 1 per cent, Table 10.3). There were three individuals with severe adverse events, a potentially life-threatening situation (Table 10.3). The first had a severe anaphylactic shock following an oral vaccine and since that volunteer was in a unit where full resuscitation was available, made a full recovery and went home the same day. Another individual had severe skin irritation and a skin rash which required hospital admission for about a week and again made a full recovery. The most severe adverse event was in an individual in a multiple-dose three-week study with a non-steroidal anti-inflammatory drug (NSAID) who developed a duodenal ulcer which perforated. Following emergency surgery the volunteer made a full recovery. Clearly, the outcome could have been different had not full medical care been readily available.

This survey suggests that the risks involved in healthy volunteer studies in which drugs are administered are measurable, but very small. The figures reported here are very similar to the figures reported by Royle and Snell (1986) who found a serious adverse reaction rate of 0.91 per 1000. Most of the adverse effects of the drugs were of the type that are predictable from the known pharmacology of the drug (Type A reactions). A similar survey to this one was performed in patients and reported by Spiers and Griffin (1983). They found a serious adverse reaction rate of 13 per 1000, but a higher reaction rate would be expected in individuals who were suffering from an illness.

The outcome of this study has been to improve the quality of healthy volunteer studies. Most units doing this sort of work now keep a central register of volunteers and the individuals are only allowed to undertake a maximum of three to four studies each year. Ethics Committee approval and informed consent are now mandatory and the quality of the information sheets has improved very much in the last five years.

It is important that all those involved with clinical trials, particularly those involving healthy volunteers, should conduct their affairs with the greatest care in order to minimise the risks to the healthy volunteers.

Summary and Conclusions

There has, in the past, been much public concern over the apparent risk of research studies involving healthy volunteers. The data presented here on serious adverse events is very similar to the data of Royle and Snell (1986). This summary suggests that the risk involved in these studies is very small, with only 40 moderate and 3 severe adverse events in over 8000 subject exposures to drugs. In addition, the large majority of the moderate adverse events were of Type A (or predictable), being in many cases an extension of the pharmacological action of the drug. The three severe adverse events were, however, of the Type B or unpredictable variety. Nevertheless, in no individual were there any lasting sequelae to the drug exposure. Whilst there will always be risks involved in volunteer studies, this data is welcome and put such risks into perspective.

Discussion

The one death in Dublin mentioned earlier was an alcoholic and this was not known by the research unit. It must be very difficult to know when a healthy volunteer is healthy. For example, the researcher may not know the full medical history or the patient may withhold information because they want to continue on the drug study. There must also be the possibility of side effects in the study which do not become evident until some time later. These could all render them unhealthy volunteers.

Certainly any adverse effects that were considered were those that occurred during the course of the studies. If drugs are, for example, teratogens or carcinogens, then clearly this system would not identify these effects. One of the lessons that was learnt, particularly from the Dublin experience, was that since that individual was not only an alcoholic but was also on drug therapy at the time, if the unit had consulted his GP they would have known this and probably excluded him from the trial. Now the recommendation is that the regular GP of any volunteer is contacted. The GP should be asked to confirm that they are happy that this individual participates in any clinical study (to opt in and not opt out). Most units would not go ahead unless the GP says that he knows that individual, and is not aware of any health reasons why they should be excluded from participation.

There is some concern about the payment for doctors taking part in these studies. Is this the remit of the ethics committee to look into?

Many would entirely agree with you. The fact that many GPs receive direct payment for studies into personal accounts is of some concern. However, GPs are funded totally differently from hospitals. Funding for any study in the hospital setting should not go to individual doctors, it should go into a research account. The money largely pays for an individual researcher to do the research work. It should, however, not go into the individual doctor's bank account. It could easily go into the practice account to provide library services, for example, and improve services for patients. Concerning the ethics committees, many are just starting to ask such questions and it is understood that new European guidelines are being worked on at the moment to cover this issue.

There are lots of people, other than clinical pharmacologists, doing research tests in volunteers and you may have had an optimistic view from the group included in this survey. I have certainly been a volunteer for my colleagues, and have had drugs to make me hypoglycaemic in a corner of a laboratory with no suggestion of any resuscitation equipment. There may be other people in other fields not included in this survey who would not have had such an optimistic view.

The difficulty is trying to find what is going on. There are many other research studies going on that do not involve drugs. The survey did not touch these. Those conducting the survey did consult with the body that had then just been set up for contract houses in drug research and they were doing their own survey at the same time. Again, that would also have been selective. Those individuals who choose not to take part in that sort of study are probably the ones you are talking about.

The worst instances have been in some academic departments, trying to do studies without a budget. Since there is no budget they cannot afford to screen

the volunteers and do ECGs, blood tests and other tests. The contrast with contract houses where they have got to be seen to be correct is enormous.

This is certainly the case, but we should not accept that sort of situation. The way forward is to try, through ethics committees and others, to ensure that standards continually improve. The second survey would confirm that this is indeed the case, but again it is a pre-selected group.

I was interested in the 19 per cent of people within the institution taking part and the people in the unit (25 per cent). There is quite a lot of evidence that people handling drugs can be exposed to them in the sense that they absorb them while using them, in terms of administering them and so on. Does this compromise the study when you use these individuals? Has anyone looked at that? They may well have their metabolising enzymes induced already, you are not going to be able to know the exact accurate doses.

The amount to be absorbed across the skin is likely to be very tiny and one of the criteria that most units use would be that they would take a blood sample before the drug was given and if any drug was present, not just the drug under question, then that individual would not be included.

Would it be ethically acceptable to have spouses involved in trials? Often volunteers are spouses since they are keen to participate because of the possible beneficial effects for their own families.

There should be no reason why a spouse should be excluded. However, there should be a careful look at the reasons why they are volunteering and one would still need to check that they fit into all the other protocol criteria. In addition, one of the concerns with most new drugs is that they should not be given to anyone of childbearing potential and this may of course come into the spouse situation.

Are class demonstrations now being discouraged? Surely the more familiar medical students are with the drugs they are using, the better?

Most would accept the latter premise very much, but the question is how you make them familiar. There is a whole variety of new ways of educating medical students about drugs such as using computer techniques. Many would view giving a student a drug as part of a class experiment as unjustified. There are others who would disagree. There are many anecdotal but frightening stories of individuals who have been given drugs in just this situation. A typical one concerns sulphonamide to which some individuals are sensitive and have an anaphylactic reaction. If this occurs in a class laboratory the chances of having adequate facilities to resuscitate the individual are remote. That is a risk many would not be prepared to take.

Isn't that a case for having the studies conducted in a better place, rather than not doing them at all?

If you have a class of 150 medical students and you have to take them all off to hospital, the hospital would have to stop work all day in order to do it. The principle is fine but the practicalities are difficult.

Is it really difficult to get no-fault compensation for healthy volunteer studies or are people simply not prepared to pay for it?

It is probably more a case of not being able to pay for it. At the time of this survey a number of enquiries were made through Lloyd's and the best quotation that resulted was £50 000 for £1 million cover per volunteer. If you had 20 volunteers, that is £1 million insurance costs. That has since fallen. The pharmaceutical industry is able to get very cheap cover. The most recent one obtained through the Committee of Vice-Chancellors and Principals has fallen to about £3000 per volunteer. Equivalent cover is available in Sweden for about £30 per volunteer. It is therefore simply that the insurance companies in this country are just not aware of the risk. That was the purpose of this study – to show that the risks are not that horrendous.

The Association of Independent Clinical Research Contractors (AICRC) has been around for some years now and they have an adverse events committee which collect all the adverse events that have been found by their members every year. So they have an ongoing flow of information on adverse events. The ABPI wishes to join with the AICRC so the companies involved in research will be putting all their adverse events into the same system. This should eventually give a very good pool of information. If academic departments were to enter the same system then that would probably include all adverse events from all sources.

That would be extremely useful and a great step forward from the current approach which is very fragmented.

In screening volunteers, surely there is no difference between HIV and hepatitis testing? If a unit is going to test for one then they should also test for the other.

Most would agree on that but an emphasis should also be put on the necessary counselling before people are tested – that is absolutely vital.

The ethical situation over HIV testing is a morass and often it is totally self-contradictory. Counsellors have insisted that you must not advise someone who is HIV positive to give up work for the sake of the patient's psychological well-being, when in fact it was acceptable to advise a person to give up work because he or she might catch something from someone who is HIV positive. Sort that one ethically if you can. There have also been a number of husbands with HIV who have refused to talk to their wives about their infection even though it was clearly in their direct human interest to know. It is an appalling problem. Testing volunteers for HIV means counselling must take place and this makes people face the problem. Hepatitis should be treated in the same way. Our society has made a major difference between them on largely irrational grounds.

Many pharmaceutical companies treat Hepatitis B and C and HIV in exactly the same way. The wording that is often put in protocols is that 'patients should not be known to be Hepatitis B or C surface antigen or HIV positive (active testing not required)'. The reason that active testing not required is used (although usually only in patients, not normal volunteers), is quite simply because ethical committees would probably not allow routine testing. Otherwise pharmaceutical companies would be doing these tests all the time. There is usually a large number of people handling the blood all along the line, everyone, including the postman at times. It is surely a moral duty to try to protect those people.

References

EDITORIAL, 1986, Research on healthy volunteers: A report of the Royal College of Physicians, *Journal of the Royal College of Physicians*, **20**, 243–57.

ORME, M., HARRY, J., ROUTLEDGE, P. and HOBSON, S., 1989, Healthy volunteer studies in Great Britain: the results of a survey into 12 months activity in the field, *British Journal of Clinical Pharmacology*, **27**, 125–33.

ROYLE, J. M. and SNELL, E. S., 1986, Medical research on normal volunteers, *British Journal of Clinical Pharmacology*, **21**, 548–9.

SPIERS, C. J. and GRIFFIN, J. P., 1983, A survey of the first year of the operation of the new procedure affecting the conduct of the clinical trials in the United Kingdom, *British Journal of Clinical Pharmacology*, **15**, 649–55.

11

A Comparison of the Controls Regarding the Ethical Judgements on Animal and Human Research

DAVID MORTON

In this brief introduction to the chapter, I wish to compare the controls on some aspects of human and animal research; the bulk of the chapter will address animal matters.

World-wide legal controls on the use of animals in research normally encompass the 'Three Rs', first put forward by Russell and Burch in 1959. They are replacement, reduction and refinement, i.e., if there is an alternative way of achieving the scientific objective without the use of animals then that should be used, but if animals have to be used then the number should be reduced to the minimum, and the scientific procedures should be refined so as to cause as little suffering as possible. Interestingly, this approach does not seem to have been so overtly adopted in human research, possibly because humans normally consent to the procedures being carried out – whether that consent is valid in terms of being fully informed, voluntary, etc., is another matter. However, when comparing laws controlling research in humans and animals it often seems that animals get better protection in many ways, but this is nothing new because the first humane societies set up in the early part of the nineteenth century protected animals as well as children, and in some countries there are still no laws controlling research on animals (or humans – and they are not necessarily the same countries).

There are two strategies for controlling research: by the use of local 'ethics' committees (given various names) or by a national inspectorate sometimes with a national committee. Occasionally, both mechanisms operate side by side. It is worth looking at the strengths and weaknesses of each approach and their relevance to the control of human and animal research. In the UK there is a good deal of experience in the national inspectorate approach for animal research.

National Inspectorate and National Committees

A national inspectorate and national committee system applies to animal research in the UK and The Netherlands. These national inspectorates help to ensure best practice and a small number of inspectors look carefully at the means by which the scientific objectives are attained. The advantage of having a small number looking at all the research protocols is that they should develop experience in many different areas which will enable them to decide what constitutes 'best practice', which in turn will reduce any animal suffering to the minimum severity. It should be predisposed to consistent judgements on a national scale if the inspectors communicate between themselves.

Public accountability with a national inspectorate operates at parliamentary level through the Secretary of State. This system is less satisfactory for making ethical judgements, i.e., when the harms done are weighed against the potential benefits of the research, because these judgements are left to the local inspector who, even with advice from their colleagues, may not necessarily represent the norm in society. However, general guidance may be given by a national committee. Under this system multicentre human trials might not encounter so many problems because decision making involves fewer people rather than at present where judgements are made by many persons on many ethics committees with varying membership.

Local Committees

Local committees controlling animal research are given a variety of titles world-wide such as Animal Care and Use Committees, Institutional Animal Care and Use Committees, and Animal Research Ethics Committees. They review research protocols to implement the three Rs, but they may also act as a research review committee and pass comment on the quality of the research as it would be unethical to support research that is badly designed. Interestingly, the use of the world 'ethics' has caused many problems as it appears to set up a hostile reaction in scientists suspicious of anything that cannot be 'precisely' measured; scientists view ethics as *imprecise* and a matter of opinion. Many scientists do not try seriously to understand the subject when it involves the animal rights movement, so that reinforces their hostility and prejudice. However, this is slowly changing and the training that is now required for all those working with research animals should lead to a greater understanding in the long term.

Membership

Local ethics committees, as well as having those members with appropriate expertise such as scientists, veterinarians, laboratory animal scientists, animal technicians, lawyers and professional animal welfarists, should also include lay people who can represent public opinion. Not all committees have this range of membership and the greatest contention is the interpretation of 'lay' member. It should not be simply someone who is not practising science at the present time (e.g., retired scientist) but should be someone carefully chosen to reflect the views of the public and who would complement the skills of the other members. Statisticians would also be useful but they are not often represented. With new statistical analyses available, it may be possible to increase the power of the experimental design and also to reduce the number of animals or humans that are being studied. It is paradoxical that ethics committees often lack anyone who is experienced in making ethical judgements. In one sense this situation is analogous to a football team not having any footballers, or a medical audit team lacking auditors. If the local committee is called an ethics committee, surely it should have someone who is experienced in making ethical decisions?

Decision Making

Local ethics committees can come to different decisions, just as with a national inspectorate, but this not not necessarily a bad thing. However, if decision making is standardised, it may hinder scientific progress and the accommodation of changes and harmonisation in terms of ethical values and best practise. Variation in approach allows for progress but only if the system is flexible and open to scrutiny and audit.

Is public accountability facilitated by having lay people present to reflect public views? It is important that there is always open and frank discussion so that all members on a local committee can educate each other. The ethical judgements are then more likely to be made on a broader basis simply because of the number of persons involved and the variety of their background compared with a national inspectorate and committee. In the UK the inspectors make these ethical decisions under the Animals (Scientific Procedures) Act 1986 and the inspectors are either veterinarians or doctors. Their views might, therefore, tend to reflect their background and this does not necessarily mean they reflect public opinion. These ethical judgements determine what on balance is right and reasonable to do.

Regardless of how and who makes these decisions it is very important for a research project to be monitored to ensure that the appropriate actions have been taken and that no significant changes have been made to the approved protocol (Bohaychuck, 1993).

Subject Protection

In animal research two independent persons (Named Veterinary Surgeon and the Named Person in Day-to-Day Care) have a duty to act on an animal's behalf should the need arise (e.g., suffering over the permitted severity limit set out in the licence, animals not under experiment that are in pain, etc.). However, who is the professional person standing up for the human volunteer or volunteer patient in human research? Perhaps there should be a doctor to make clinical judgements independently of the researcher about whether the volunteer should take part in or continue on a trial. Sometimes researchers can become oblivious as to what is happening because they have so much involvement and investment in the research. This is not necessarily deliberate – scientists are not malicious but they are human and genuinely fail to see all aspects of a study.

No Controls

In some countries there are no controls on either human or animal research and there might not even be any guidelines. In human and animal research there is no statutory requirement for local research ethics committees or any scrutinising of projects in the UK or in many other European countries, although controls are slowly being introduced though not by means of an inspectorate.

UK Controls on Animal Experiments

The number of animals used in research in the UK is about 3 million a year (Anon., 1995) and this figure has decreased by about 5% per year since 1972. The Animals (Scientific Procedures) Act 1986 controls animal experimentation through an inspectorate which oversees about 12,000 researchers and about 5000 research projects. A research project is a programme of research work that would include several experiments. In law the secretary of state has to decide whether the likely adverse effects on the animals in a research project are balanced by the benefit likely to accrue as a result of that research. Obviously s/he does not do it in person but with assistance from the Home Office Inspectorate who are qualified in either veterinary medicine or medicine (Straughan, 1995). This harm (cost)–benefit analysis is carried out with the help of a standard application form and can be followed by information-seeking visits from the attending inspector. The form requires information on the background to the project, what is known and what is not known scientifically, what are the specific objectives of the work and what are the potential benefits of the work. Some of the standard questions about the study include the following:

- Is it going to provide advancement in terms of knowledge about a disease or treatment for a disease?
- Is it going to further our understanding of science, i.e., a gain in fundamental knowledge?

- Is it going to tell us about the environment or is it for forensic enquiries?
- Is it for educational purposes?

Also, how is the project going to be carried out, particularly regarding animal usage and the three Rs? Simply put, the three Rs state that animals should be replaced in experiments wherever possible by using non-sentient alternatives such as cell or organ culture, or computer modelling; the numbers of animals used in an experiment should be reduced to the minimum consistent with attaining the scientific objective; and the experiment should be refined so that as little animal suffering as possible is caused. This approach is extremely useful and could apply equally well to human research, in addition to the other normal ethical considerations of consent, confidentiality, etc.

Alternatives

The applicant is asked why alternative non-animal approaches cannot be used and why animals have to be used at all? The applicant has to make a legal declaration stating that alternatives have been considered and that use of other methods would not achieve the objective of the project. In this way applicants are encouraged to investigate alternatives to the use of animals.

Animal Suffering

How is refinement addressed? In the standard application form for an animal licence the use of cats, dogs, primates and equines requires special justification. The neurological development of primates probably does warrant greater concern, but are cats, dogs and horses really different from rats and mice which also feel pain and various other unpleasant emotional experiences (fear, terror, anxiety, etc.). It can be argued that this greater protection for 'companion' species is misplaced when the concern is about animal suffering. Any adverse effects should be minimised and so it is very important to set out end-points before the study is started so that everyone is absolutely clear when the adverse effects are out of balance with the benefits. Unless this is done, the ethical judgement of balancing benefit against harm done can be by-passed, for example, if the harm side of the equation increases, then the whole project should be reassessed. In order that the harm side is maintained at an acceptable level, the amount of harm is graded, as 'mild', 'moderate' and 'substantial'. In the UK there is a further category of 'severe' that is unacceptable as it is argued that it is a level of suffering which can never be justified.

There are guidelines on how to recognise when animals reach those end-points (Morton and Townsend, 1995) and the Home Office form requires a *description* of the possible adverse effects to the animals (HMSO, 1990). Harms have first to be recognised before anything can be done about them, i.e., it is important to recognise when an animal is in any discomfort or pain, because otherwise nothing can be done to avoid or alleviate the situation or see whether the proposed pain prevention regime is effective or not. Recognition of end-points is extremely important, and a typical pain/adverse effect score sheet lists signs that an animal will show. Humane end-points are applicable to all vertebrates including birds, reptiles, amphibia and fish.

Reduction

The final 'R' relates to how the proposed number of animals for a study has been minimised, together with a detailed justification of the number that may be used. Information is required on the statistical methods and controls to be used with a description of the control groups. Control groups should be looked at very carefully, e.g., a study of the effectiveness of a new form of pancreas transplantation would not require a control simply to show that an animal without a pancreas develops diabetes.

Facilities

There is a Home Office Code of Practice (HMSO, 1989) detailing what facilities for animal studies should be available and the standards that have to be met. Animals often spend most of their time in cages before being experimented on, but they have to be looked after throughout the whole of their life, not just during that short period of time when they are on the experiment.

Training

Finally, laboratory personnel in the UK have to be trained by attending a training programme. In The Netherlands training courses last about three weeks whereas in the UK it is a four-day course. Participants have to sit an exam at the end of the course. A study director would also have to be trained in experimental design, literature searching, the law, ethical issues, etc. Those carrying out the research would have to show they are competent in performing procedures such as giving injections, dosing the animals, and carrying out surgery.

Conclusions

The UK system for controlling animal research is by no means perfect, and there are very difficult ethical judgements to be made. Even if the harms have been minimised and the benefits maximised there is still the dilemma of whether a study should go ahead. The UK Home Office Inspectors are still having to face this dilemma, as are all researchers. Strategies are in place to minimise animal suffering wherever possible and it can be seen that animals are frequently better protected in some countries than human research subjects.

Discussion

Regarding the applicability of 'replacement' to human studies, is the end goal the need to end the use of humans in clinical studies or is it just to refine them to such a point where they are just a last-minute check to support the preclinical studies?

We should try to make sure that humans are only used when necessary, i.e., when validated alternative techniques are available, they should be used. For example, in the USA animals are used to train surgeons, but in the UK this has not been done for some time as there are other approaches. Virtual reality is now being used to train surgeons. Perhaps there are other alternative techniques which will avoid the use of animals and humans without jeopardising the safety of patients and this has to be a major objective.

There appears to be little communication between the sides of animal research and human research. One of the alternatives for using animals may be using humans. The question of when we need to use animals before we start with humans, or when we could go into humans after only a short stage in animals, needs to be asked. How could we proceed with this? Most of the animal research is for human medicine.

The strength of the local research review committee could be its broader base for these discussions. The attraction of an ethics committee is that it has flexibility of composition and Home Office Inspectors might make a valuable contribution on a human ethics committee. We may then be better able to define when animal experiments become limited and when humans can be used safely.

References

ANON. (1995) Scientific procedures on living animals in Great Britain in 1993, *ATLA*, **23**(2), 184–186.

BOHAYCHUK, W. P. and BALL, G. J. (1993) Good Clinical Practices Standard Operating Procedures for Investigators, 2nd Edn. Headley Down: Good Clinical Research Practices. p. 186.

HMSO (1989) *Code of Practice for the Housing and Care of Animals Used in Scientific Procedures*. London: HMSO 107.

HMSO (1990) *Home Office Guidance on the Operation of the Animals (Scientific Procedures) Act, 1986.* London: HMSO 182.

MORTON, D. B. and TOWNSEND, P. (1995) Dealing with adverse effects and suffering during animal research. In: revised version of *Laboratory Animals – An Introduction for Experimenters*, pp. 215–231, Ed. A. A. Tuffery. Chichester: John Wiley & Sons Ltd.

RUSSELL, W. M. S. and BURCH, R. L. (1959) *The Principles of Humane Experimental Technique.* London: Methuen.

STRAUGHAN, D. W. (1995) The role of the Home Office Inspector. *ATLA*, **23**(1), 39–50.

12

The use of Human Volunteers for Hazard and Risk Assessment of Skin Irritation

DAVID BASKETTER AND FIONA REYNOLDS

In toxicological safety evaluation processes, one of the ever-present problems is that presented by the need to extrapolate from information derived from non-human models in order to make judgements on human safety. Whilst professionals in this field have many sources of support for such extrapolations, nevertheless the most fundamental of these often arises from those occasions when, however unfortunately, there is detailed human experience of adverse toxic effects. However, there are certain areas in a toxicologist's safety evaluation work where it is possible to generate data in human volunteers which provides valuable, if not essential, information effectively using the species of concern and the end-point of concern. One of these end-points is skin irritation and it is this which forms the central theme of this chapter. However, it is also possible actively to generate human data which have direct relevance for safety evaluation processes concerning eye irritation, skin sensitisation and skin penetration/metabolism.

In this chapter, the safety and ethical considerations which are applied to studies on both hazard identification and risk assessment processes conducted in the area of skin irritation are discussed, emphasising the safety controls that are necessary but also demonstrating the value of the data generated.

Ethical Considerations

The work done in this area meets the internationally recognised Declaration of Helsinki guidelines covering the use of human volunteers (World Medical Association, 1964, updated to 1993).

The main principles however, (at least in the context of the sort of studies discussed here), are that the volunteers give fully informed written consent, do not suffer irreversible effects and have the benefit of no-fault compensation. All studies conducted undergo ethical review prior to initiation, although very routine investigations may be conducted under a generic ethical approval. A typical example of the latter would be the conduct of a skin irritation patch test using a toxicologically approved formulation intended for prolonged skin contact and which was not fundamentally dissimilar to other marketed products with a history of safe marketing.

Skin Irritation – Hazard Identification

The hazard associated with either a single chemical substance or a combination of two or more substances (i.e. a preparation or formulation) refers to the intrinsic propensity to cause a particular effect, in this case, skin irritation. No account is taken of risk factors such as anticipated exposure. Thus, in order to identify the skin irritation hazard, there is no option but to generate irritant responses. Consequently, this is the most difficult of the human study types we will discuss. As referred to above, a main concern is to avoid the production of unacceptable and/or irreversible effects. The methodology we have adopted to enable this to be achieved is that of a progressive protocol (Basketter *et al.*, 1994). In other words, initial exposure is strictly limited to ensure safety, but then exposure is increased incrementally to an end-point of minor, but definite, skin irritation. To make this clear, the detail of this approach is outlined below.

The strategy and protocol for the use of human volunteers for the identification of skin irritation hazard potential has been described previously (Basketter, 1994; Basketter *et al.*, 1994). In principle, and with full ethical support, the view was adopted that, if skin corrosive and other toxicologically unacceptable data are known not to exist, then it is possible to conduct a human equivalent to the Draize skin irritation test (Draize *et al.*, 1944; Draize, 1959). The protocol involves the use of occluded patch testing of undiluted substances for a period of up to 4 hours. In any individual panellist, the level of skin irritation is kept to a minimum by progressively increasing the duration of the patch test, up to a maximum application time of 4 hours. In other words the key stop point is the stage when the substance produces minor, reversible, skin irritation. This stepwise protocol is summarised in Figure 12.1.

Every panel is calibrated by a positive control, 20 per cent sodium dodecyl sulphate (SDS). Experience shows that, on average, about 60 per cent of the volunteers give a mild skin irritation reaction to this control. The degree of irritation is limited by the strict controls applied to the duration of application and thus the reaction typically is a mild erythema which fades in no more than a few days.

How is the data from this protocol interpreted? In terms of skin irritation

- 30 volunteers
- Occluded patch (25 mm Hill Top chambers)
- Progressive exposure: initial patch applied for 1 hour, each succeeding patch applied to a new site with exposure time increased by 1 hour (up to a maximum of four hours)
- Undiluted test substance
- Concurrent positive control (20 per cent sodium dodecyl sulphate)
- Patches sited on upper outer arm
- Scoring at 24, 48 and 72 hours
- Grades of reaction:

0	No reaction
+	Weakly positive reaction (usually characterised by mild erythema across most of the site)
++	Moderately positive reaction (usually distinct erythema possibly spreading beyond the treatment site)
+++	Strongly positive reaction (strong spreading erythema with oedema)

A reaction score of + or greater at 24, 48- or 72-hour assessment in an individual subject is taken as evidence of a positive irritant response to the test material. Panellists who demonstrate this level of response with any test material are not exposed further to that material.

Figure 12.1 Summary of 4-hour patch test protocol

hazard potential, notably in the European Union (EC, 1988 and 1991), the primary piece of information that is required is to determine the proportion of individuals who would have had a skin irritation reaction following 4 hours' occluded exposure.

This information is then compared with the level of reaction to the standard positive, but minimally irritant control, which is tested in each panel (York *et al.*, 1996). It is most important to note that there is no need to test substances past the point at which they produce a minimal irritant response. For example, if a substance produces an irritant response after 1 or 2 hours' occluded patch test treatment, then it is reasonable to assume that an irritant (and probably unacceptably severe) response would be elicited by longer application times. Figure 12.2 shows an example of the test results.

Test material	Exposure time/positive responses						
	15 min	30 min	1 hour	2 hour	3 hour	4 hour	Total positives
CocoTAC	0/33	0/33	0/33	0/33	1/32	7/31	8/32
Alcohol C12-C15/E3	0/33	0/33	0/33	0/33	0/32	0/32	0/32
SDS (20%)	0/33	0/33	1/33	3/32	14/28	6/14	24/32

Figure 12.2 Patch test results for cocotrimethylammonium chloride (CocoTAc), alcohol C12-C15/E3 with SDS (20 per cent) tested as the positive control

In this test an extremely cautious approach was taken and the first two exposures were for periods of 15 and 30 minutes. In this and subsequent tests it was found that both 15- and 30-minute exposures did not give rise to positive responses, and exposures of this length are no longer routinely used. A panel of 33 volunteers was recruited and at the 1-hour exposure there was only one positive response (+ reaction) which was to the positive control, SDS (20 per cent). This individual was therefore not re-exposed to SDS and at the next exposure (2 hour) a further three individuals produced positive responses (+ reactions) to the SDS. However, there were still no positive reactions to the other two test materials.

At the three-hour exposure a panellist dropped out for reasons unrelated to treatment, therefore 32 panellists were exposed to CocoTAC and Alcohol C12-C15/E3 and 28 to SDS (20 per cent). Of these, one produced a positive response to CocoTAC (+ reaction) and a further 14 to the SDS (3 ++ or +++ reactions and 11 + reactions). In order to prevent panellists producing ++ or +++ reactions they are advised to return for early removal of their patch if they experience sensory effects (e.g. itchiness, soreness, warm/burning sensations). However, infrequently ++ or, even more rarely, +++ may still be obtained. For the final 4-hour exposure, 31 panellists were exposed to CocoTAC, 32 to the Alcohol C12-C15/E3 and only 14 were exposed to SDS. Of these seven gave positive reactions to CocoTAC (six + and one ++ reaction) and six to SDS (three + and three ++). There were no positive reactions to the Alcohol C12-C15/E3.

The total number of positives over the 4 hours, from a panel of 32, for CocoTAC, Alcohol C12-C15/E3 and 20 per cent SDS was therefore 8, 0 and 24, respectively. If the results for the two test materials are then compared to those of the irritant positive control, 20 per cent SDS, then neither would be considered to be significantly irritant.

Results from testing 29 substances have recently been published (York *et al.*, 1996). Included in this work were materials with a wide range of skin irritation potential; all were safely evaluated in panels of human volunteers by controlling the exposure duration. On balance, human skin seemed more resistant to irritation than rabbit skin on which the pre-existing irritation classifications were based. However, the important point is that in an ethical and safe protocol, the skin irritation potential of undiluted substances could be assessed in the species of concern using the end-point of concern.

Skin Irritation – Risk Assessment

In the section above, the determination of intrinsic skin irritation hazard was considered. Such data is largely abstract information until it is put into the context of exposure. For example, the widely used preservative Kathon CG is corrosive to skin (Rohm and Haas, 1989) but is widely used in personal products such as shampoos where it has no significant irritant effect.

The explanation is fairly obvious; the high dilution in the product together with the limited skin contact time combine to reduce the skin exposure to the extent that neither corrosion nor irritation properties of Kathon CG can be expressed. So the purpose of this section is to describe the methodologies used to investigate in human volunteers the relationship between a known hazard and safe use conditions.

General strategies and test methodologies for the assessment of skin irritation risks have been described (e.g. Jenkins and Adams, 1989; Patrick and Maibach, 1991). It is important to recognise that the protocols employed will generally be customised to meet the specific needs of the individual safety evaluation process. Thus some substances or preparations may require assessment under single occluded patch-test conditions, whilst others may be best evaluated by repeated open application testing or assessment under conditions which approximate to intended use. Indeed, the results obtained in terms of relative irritation potential of various materials may vary according to the protocol, thus making it, in some circumstances, especially important to adopt the most relevant methodologies (e.g. Hannuksela and Hannuksela, 1995). To illustrate risk assessment practice, the approach taken for the examination of skin compatibility of a shampoo and a skin cream is described.

Prior to performing human skin irritation testing, the formulation concerned must be evaluated. A 'new' shampoo is likely to be a variation of an existing formulation with alterations to the levels of different components, or it may contain novel substances which require further evaluation prior to an irritation assessment.

When considering the irritation potential of the new shampoo, the main concern is to ensure that it is not likely to be more irritant than a similar existing marketed product with an extensive history of safe use. Therefore the irritancy of the new formulation is compared with a similar marketed product that has comparable skin contact in normal use.

Routinely this type of evaluation is performed using an occluded patch. The irritation potential of a dilute solution of the new shampoo is compared with a marketed control product and standard positive and negative control materials.

The use of the occluded patch provides conditions that are likely to elicit a positive, but not unacceptable response, i.e. localised visible erythema. The responses from the test and control materials need to be sufficient to allow recognition of different degrees of erythema by visual assessment.

Data for safety evaluation has reliably been produced using the following procedure. Four site patches are prepared using standard Al-test units and Leukosilk tape. A known volume of dilute solutions (2 per cent v/v in distilled water) of the new shampoo and the marketed control shampoo, plus distilled water (negative control) and the positive control, 0.3 per cent sodium dodecyl sulphate (SDS) are applied to individual sites on the patch, according to a randomised sequence. The patch is applied to the upper outer arm of the panellist and secured with further Leukosilk tape. After 23 hours the patch is removed, the sites are wiped clean, marked and then assessed one hour later, by a trained assessor. At this point, if distinct erythema is evident, the site will not be re-treated. The remaining sites have a further patch applied for 23 hours after which time the same procedure of wiping, marking and assessing is repeated. A further assessment is performed at 72 hours to check that any reactions are subsiding normally.

To allow for individual variation a panel of 33 people are usually selected for this type of protocol. The positive and negative controls are always included to ensure that the panellists are sufficiently sensitive to respond to a known irritant and that the majority have no reaction to the distilled water. Since individuals, and therefore panels of people will produce variable irritation reactions depending on the time of year and initial skin condition, the positive control also acts as a reference point.

The assessment scores of the new and current shampoo formulations are statistically compared with each other and also the positive control (two-tailed all-pairs modified Sign test). This enables a comparison of the irritancy of the new formulation with a known irritant and also with an acceptable marketed formulation. Providing that the new formulation is not significantly more irritant than the current marketed formulation then using this approach can provide some of the data required to support marketing of the new formulation.

A similar approach may be adopted for assessing products such as skin creams. An in-use evaluation of this type of formulation will provide potentially more relevant data on the likely irritation effects of repeated use of this type of product. Products such as skin creams are not expected to elicit visible or subjective reactions even when applied several times a day for several weeks. If this can be demonstrated using an exaggerated number of applications then it provides good support for unsupervised consumer testing, prior to marketing.

A number of sites are suitable for this type of repeated open application test – the elbow, the volar forearm and for some product types the dorsal forearm. Where a comparison of two or more skin creams is required, then the volar forearm would routinely be used as up to four treatment sites can easily be templated onto one forearm. A 'new' skin cream may not have a significantly different formulation from a currently marketed product. If this is the case then comparison of the two products under exaggerated simulated use conditions should be sufficient to indicate if either formulation is likely to produce irritation, and if so it should also highlight any differences in the degree of irritation produced.

In a volar forearm test a 5 × 5 cm matched site is templated on both forearms, one site for the new test product (new skin cream); the other for the control product (currently marketed skin cream); each individual is therefore their own control. Each panellist is supplied with both creams and is asked to apply each one (up to) six times a day to one of the templated sites on the volar forearm. Panellists are asked to use sufficient cream to cover the fingertip and to ensure that it is completely rubbed in.

Normally, a panel of 24 people is used, the panel is balanced for sex, hand dominance and initial skin condition prior to the start and all treatments are performed blind. Treatments are continued for 21 days unless adverse effects, such as significant erythema or dryness, are evident prior to this (the number of the treatment at which the panellist is stopped is an important factor when analysing the results). Visual assessments are taken eight times during the test and each panellist keeps a record of the number of treatments achieved each day. During these assessments the assessors score the templated site and monitor for adverse reactions to ensure any reactions produced do not exceed an acceptable level.

At the end of the test the amount of cream used by each panellist is calculated to ascertain whether there are any discrepancies in the amount applied within the panel. Any comments the panellists may have on subjective effects are recorded throughout the test to aid in the evaluation.

On completion of the test the number of erythema and dryness reactions of each grade associated with both the test skin cream and the control skin cream is compared for each assessment day, which provides an overall comparison across the whole group. The assessment scores for erythema and dryness elicited by the test product may be compared with those caused by the control product in the same person. Suitable statistical analysis may be performed (e.g. a two-tailed all-pairs modified Sign Test).

One advantage of this type of protocol is that it is flexible in the number of treatment sites and applications that can be used. It is feasible to compare up to eight formulations, as four sites can be templated onto each volar forearm. Also, for certain formulations where a more cautious approach is deemed appropriate, the number of treatments per day can be reduced for the initial stages and gradually increased over the following two weeks, assuming that the reactions observed are acceptable.

Other Methodologies

In brief format, a reasonable view of how skin irritation studies using human volunteers are carried out in practice is given. However, it is important to appreciate that there is a wide range of options available in terms of the test protocol. This is necessary not only in the context of the design of the most appropriate experimental method, but also to ensure that the test is safe and ethical. Examples of alternative types of assay include hand or arm immersion studies in which the test skin site is repeatedly immersed in a dilute solution of the test article. Commonly this will be a surfactant-based household product such as a dishwashing liquid, with the protocol effectively mimicking normal or slightly exaggerated domestic use. However, such protocols can also be used in other ways, e.g. to assess the impact of that type of domestic activity on allergic reactivity (Allenby and Basketter, 1993).

On the other hand, the type of protocol employed and indeed the way the end-points are assessed might depend very much on the nature of the product to be tested for skin irritation (e.g. Pierard *et al.*, 1994; Frosch and Kurte, 1994; Paye *et al.*, 1995). So for example, an underarm deodorant and/or antiperspirant product may well be evaluated by in-use, but closely monitored, application to the axilla. In fact, in-use tests in which normal or slightly exaggerated use is required, form a valuable part of the assessment of the risk of skin irritation (e.g. Bannan *et al.*, 1992; Hayakawa *et al.*, 1995).

Finally, mention should be made of subjective end-points which may come under the general heading of skin irritation (reviewed by Grove *et al.*, 1984). These include itching, stinging, burning, tightness of the skin (especially on the face) and several other relatively minor sensory responses. Many of these can be assessed in a properly monitored human volunteer study and can represent one of the major assets of such an approach over either *in vitro* or animal tests. Of these effects, only stinging has the benefit of a well-described protocol (Frosch and Kligman, 1977) and it is interesting to note that susceptibility to this effect does not seem to correlate with susceptibility to skin irritation (Basketter and Griffiths, 1993).

Summary and Conclusions

The brief review presented here demonstrates, in our view, that it is possible to undertake a variety of types of assay in human volunteers which measure intrinsic skin irritation potential and evaluate aspects of the risk presented by skin irritants in a manner which is both safe and ethical. In the final analysis, such an approach (when properly undertaken and evaluated) must be more reliable than extrapolation from non-human models since they use the end-point of concern in the species of concern.

Discussion

To the non-expert eye the four-hour patch test which is a hazard identification test seems very similar to the previously described patch test which is a risk assessment test. Why does one detect risk and one hazard?

The four-hour patch test was developed along the lines of the rabbit four-hour patch test and that is used for hazard classification purposes. Obviously using humans one has to take a cautious approach but similar sorts of materials that are used for the rabbit test may be considered. So for example, substances like benzalkonium chloride and similar materials which you would not normally apply to human skin, may now be considered. The risk assessment protocol uses *in-use* concentrations of shampoos or other product formulations.

Is it all actually based on previous toxicology tests on animals?

Most of the data is based on toxicology on animals, or in-use data that has been produced before. However, all subsequent experimentation for that particular product would not actually be on animals at all.

None of the tests described was blind. What is the reason for that?

All groups of panellists are balanced in that right- and left-handed people were used, for example, male, female. They know what material is on the patch but they do not know which one is on which site in the patch.

In an arm immersion study they know what is in the tank of water presumably – because one looked quite different to the other.

One tank has got bubbles on but the volunteer will not know which material is giving rise to the bubbles. Also, the person assessing the test site will not immerse the panellists' arms – this will be done by another individual so that the testing remains blind

Handedness is discussed. Obviously if someone is right-handed the hand might be more damaged, so is that taken into account?

All panellists are assessed prior to starting the study and all of the panels are balanced for initial skin condition.

All the volunteers in these trials are white people. Would the results also apply for coloured people in the same way?

Because of the location, and because site staff are used, there are only two or three coloured people that routinely take part in patch tests. A study has recently been set up with St John's Contact Dermatitis Clinic to look into the differences in different coloured skins.

For the hazard identification protocol what safety data would be provided before you would start your skin irritation testing?

All the information that the toxicologists would normally have on a substance is provided, but prior to using human volunteers a selection of screening processes is carried out. *In vitro* screening techniques are used to look at whether something could be positively corrosive before we apply it.

What about possible allergic reactions and sensitisation data?

A toxicologist would have evaluated all safety aspects prior to the testing being carried out.

References

ALLENBY, C. F. and BASKETTER, D. A., 1993, An arm immersion model of compromised skin. II. Influence on minimal eliciting patch test concentration of nickel, *Contact Dermatitis*, **28**, 129–33.

BANNAN, E. A., GRIFFITH, J. F., NUSAIR, T. L. and SAUERS, L. J., 1992, Skin testing of laundered fabrics in the dermal safety assessment of enzyme containing detergents, *Journal of Toxicology–Cutaneous and Ocular Toxicology*, **11**, 327–39.

BASKETTER, D. A., 1994, Strategic hierarchical approaches in acute toxicity testing, *Toxicology in Vitro*, **8**, 855–9.

BASKETTER, D. A. and GRIFFITHS, H. A., 1993, A study of the relationship between susceptibility to skin stinging and skin irritation, *Contact Dermatitis*, **29**, 185–8.

BASKETTER, D. A., WHITTLE, E., GRIFFITHS, H. A. and YORK, M., 1994, The identification and classification of skin irritation hazard by a human patch test, *Food and Chemical Toxicology*, **32**, 769–775.

DRAIZE, J. H., 1959, Dermal toxicity, in *Appraisal of the Safety of Chemicals in Foods, Drugs and Cosmetics*, Association of Foods and Drugs Officials of the United States, Littleton, CO, USA, pp. 46–59.

DRAIZE, J. H., WOODARD, G. and CALVERY, H. O., 1944, Methods for the study of imitation and toxicity of substances applied topically to the skin and mucous membranes, *Journal of Pharmacology and Experimental Therapeutics*, **82**, 377–90.

EC, 1988, Council Directive of 7 June 1988 on the approximation of the laws, regulations and administrative provisions of the Member States relating to the classification, packaging and labelling of dangerous preparations, *Official Journal of the European Communities*, **L18**, 14.

1991, Annex I to Commission Directive 91/325/EEC of 1st March 1991 adapting to technical progress for the twelfth time Council Directive 67/548/EEC on the approximation of the laws, regulations and administrative provisions relating to the classification, packaging and labelling of dangerous substances, *Official Journal of the European Communities*, **L180**, 34.

FROSCH, P. and KLIGMAN, A. M., 1977, A method for appraising the stinging capacity of topically applied substances, *Journal of the Society of Cosmetic Chemists*, **28**, 197–209.

FROSCH, P. and KURTE, A., 1994, Efficacy of skin barrier creams (IV). The repetitive irritation test (RIT) with a set of 4 standard irritants, *Contact Dermatitis*, **31**, 161–8.

GROVE, G. L., SOSCHIN, D. A. and KLIGMAN, A. M., 1984, Adverse subjective reactions to topical agents, in: Drill, V. A. and Lazar, P. (Eds), *Cutaneous Toxicity*, New York: Raven Press, pp. 203–12.

HANNUKSELA, A. and HANNUKSELA, M., 1995, Irritant effects of a detergent in wash and chamber tests, *Contact Dermatitis*, **32**, 163–6.

HAYAKAWA, R., SUZUKI, M., KATO, Y., UEDA, H., MATSUNAGA, K., IKEYA, Y., SANDA, T., USUDA, T. and SUZUKI, T., 1995, Study of the safety and usefulness of hypo-irritant skin care products (PHS-511: soap, shampoo, lotion) for children, *Environmental Dermatology*, **2**, 50–8.

JENKINS, H. L. and ADAMS, M. G., 1989, Progressive evaluation of skin irritancy of cosmetics using human volunteers, *International Journal of Cosmetic Science*, **11**, 141–9.

PATRICK, E. and MAIBACH, H. I., 1991, Predictive skin irritation tests in animals and humans, in: Marzulli, F. N. and Maibach, H. I. (Eds), *Dermatotoxicology*, 4th edition, New York: Hemisphere Publishing Corporation, pp. 210–22.

PAYE, M., MORRISON, B. M. and WILHELM, K.-P., 1995, Skin irritancy classification of body cleansing products, *Skin Research and Technology*, **1**, 30–5.

PIERARD, G. E., ARRESE, J. E., RODRIGUEZ, C. and DASKALEROS, P. A., 1994, Effects of softened and unsoftened fabrics on sensitive skin, *Contact Dermatitis*, **30**, 286–91.

ROHM and HAAS, 1989, Kathon CG Bulletin, p. 9.

World Medical Association, 1964, Declaration of Helsinki. *Recommendations Guiding Physicians in Biomedical Research Involving Human Subjects.* Adopted by the 18th World Medical Assembly, Helsinki, Finland, June 1964, amended by the 29th World Medical Assembly, Tokyo, Japan, October 1975, the 35th World Medical Asssembly, Venice, Italy, October, 1983 and the 41st World Medical Assembly, Hong Kong, September 1989. Proceedings of the XXVIth Conference, Geneva, 1993.

YORK, M., GRIFFITHS, H. A., WHITTLE, E. and BASKETTER, D. A., 1996, Evaluation of a human patch test for the identification and classification of skin irritation potential. *Contact Dermatitis*, in press.

13

Volunteer Studies using the Health and Safety Laboratory Exposure Chamber

KERR WILSON

The Health and Safety Laboratory (HSL) is an agency of the Health and Safety Executive (HSE). HSE's mission is to ensure that risks to people at work are properly controlled. Since 1983, the HSL has been involved in human volunteer studies using a specially designed exposure chamber for solvent vapours. The purpose of using an exposure chamber is to obtain experimental data from human subjects which is precise and not subject to the variabilities normally encountered in field trials. The aim of the work is to provide sound data to underpin biological monitoring and biological effect monitoring strategies.

In HSL there is a well-developed procedure for conducting volunteer studies. It is axiomatic that all studies must comply with health and safety laws and any relevant HSE guidance. In terms of the risk to the volunteers, all studies which are conducted by the HSL pose negligible risk. The level of exposure to a substance is never greater than the amount a worker is permitted to receive in the course of their daily work.

The first stage in setting up a study is to prepare a research proposal which is submitted to the HSE's ethics committee. The submission will include toxicology data, the scientific justification and protocol, and information to volunteers. After the ethics committee has given its approval for the study to proceed, volunteers are called for, usually from HSE staff or from an external institute with whom they collaborate. The volunteer selection is made by the medical officer appointed for the study. All volunteers must have a pre-exposure medical examination and if accepted for the study they are invited to sign the informed consent sheet. The medical officer must be present during the exposure period and ensure the volunteers are fit and well before they go home. Volunteers are asked not to drive home.

All data from the chamber studies are stored in a secure and retrievable fashion for at least 15 years.

This chapter will consider four typical examples of the work done at the HSL in the exposure chamber over the past 12 years. Over this period about 200 single exposures have been carried out without incident.

Structure and Operation of the Chamber

The HSL exposure chamber (2.5 × 2.5 × 2.5 m) is built around a metal frame and walled with perspex. Air and solvent vapour are introduced at the top of the chamber through 16 adjustable diffusers to ensure a uniform distribution of solvent vapour throughout the chamber. The extraction system consists of 16 similar exit ports, 12 cm below the perforated steel floor. The temperature and humidity were controlled. The concentration of solvent in the chamber is monitored independently and continuously by an infrared analyser (Miran) and a gas chromatograph. Television and video were provided for entertainment. A porthole allows breath or blood samples to be taken without the operator entering the chamber. The chamber is maintained under slight negative pressure so that the contents are contained (Wilson *et al.*, 1983).

1,1,2-Trichloro-1,2,2,-trifluoroethane

The first study to be considered in this chapter was a collaborative project between the HSL and ICI Central Toxicology Laboratory. The purpose of the exercise was to see whether a suitable biological monitor could be devised for the substance 1,1,2-trichloro-1,2,2,-trifluoroethane, FC113. It was known from previous studies and the literature that this is a lipophilic, non-metabolised solvent. The most suitable biomarker was considered to be the measurement of FC113 in blood or expired air. Six volunteers were exposed to FC113 at two air concentrations (1900 mg/m^3 and 3800 mg/m^3) for four hours. Blood and breath samples were collected during the exposure period and for several days post-exposure. The blood and breath concentrations of FC113 were dose related and showed individual variations. The low blood breath ratios observed were consistent with the low solubility of FC113 in blood. Blood concentrations of FC113 reached a plateau after 30 minutes' exposure and peak concentrations (0.69 and 1.2 μg/ml respectively) were dose related. Immediately on leaving the chamber the blood concentrations fell rapidly and had returned to baseline value after about seven or eight hours.

During the post-exposure elimination phase the breath concentrations from the two groups overlapped at some time points. If, however, the breath concentrations were normalised to the body fat content of the individual subject there was a clear separation between the dose groups at all time intervals. The breath elimination profile was described by a three-compartment model ($t\frac{1}{2}$ = 0.22 h, 2.3 h, 29 h). We interpreted these data to correspond to blood, tissue and fat depots respectively. FC113 could be detected in the breath seven days after a single exposure to 1900 mg/m^3. It was concluded that breath sampling was a suitable biological monitoring indicator for exposure to FC113 and that the predictive value of such a measurement could be improved if the results were normalised for body fat (Woollen *et al.*, 1990).

1,1,1-Trichloroethane

The second example is a volunteer study in which behavioural changes during exposure to 1,1,1-trichloroethane were examined and related to blood solvent concentrations. Twelve volunteers received three exposures in a design balanced for order effects and were tested in pairs. The exposure concentration was zero, 950 or 1900 mg/m^3 for 3.5 h. Peppermint oil was used to mask the smell of the solvent. The blood levels at 20, 60, 120, and 180 minutes after entry into the chamber were measured. Volunteers carried out a series of performance tests at set intervals. When test performance was adjusted for both pre-exposure baseline scores and corresponding zero exposure conditions, the profile of behavioural change that emerged closely followed the time course of blood solvent levels for many of the more sensitive tests. A pattern of performance deficits was found for some of the tests of psychomotor performance. The time course for these was rapid, occurring in some cases within 20 minutes of exposure. For those tasks shown to be sensitive to 1,1,1-trichloroethane exposure, the development of performance changes followed the time course of blood solvent levels. Different effects were found with the tests concerned with distractibility of attention and concentration (using a modified Stroop test (Hartley and Adams, 1974)) where enhanced performance was noted. However, the syntactic reasoning was found to be resistant to solvent effects (MacKay *et al.*, 1987). It was concluded that the observations of time-course effects in performance and their relationship to change in blood solvent levels have implications for psychological test selection and for examining field exposure.

Styrene and Alcohol

The third example is one in which the exposure chamber was used to solve a mystery. It is now established that monitoring workers exposed to styrene vapour is best accomplished by measuring mandelic acid in urine. In an earlier study (Wilson *et al.*, 1979) there was a detailed investigation of the daily excretion of mandelic acid in urine by two technicians building glass-reinforced plastic boats under controlled ventilation conditions. Both subjects showed maximum mandelic excretion some hours after the end of exposure. The report of this time lag in excretion caused some controversy. It was argued by others that maximum excretion occurs at or near the end of styrene exposure. Wilson *et al.* (1979) subsequently confirmed that under controlled exposure chamber conditions maximum excretion of mandelic acid does occur at the end of the exposure period. This apparent discrepancy required explanation. Among the factors considered was alcohol intake during the exposure period. The effect of alcohol on the kinetics of mandelic acid excretion in four volunteers exposed to styrene (220 mg/m^3) was investigated. It was found that alcohol delayed the excretion of mandelic acid so that the peak excretion was delayed for three hours. From this study it was noted that spuriously low concentrations of mandelic acid may be recorded if the worker has taken alcohol during the working day. The mandelic acid concentration in the 'end of shift' sample, after taking alcohol, was less than 30 per cent of the value obtained if no alcohol was taken. The current advice is that workers should be asked to refrain from alcohol on the day when sampling is taking place (Wilson *et al.*, 1983).

Xylene and Shift Patterns

Finally, some work currently in progress that has not yet been published will be mentioned. Recent work has involved volunteers being exposed to xylene for 12-hour and 8-hour shifts, both at steady state and fluctuating concentrations. Methyl hippuric acid in urine was used as an indicator of uptake. The data is currently being used from these exposure chamber studies to validate physiologically based pharmacokinetic models.

Summary

The Health and Safety Laboratory, an agency of the Health and Safety Executive of the UK, has conducted over 200 single exposures over the past 12 years using its exposure chamber. Substances are introduced at normal work exposures and breath and blood samples may be taken without the operator entering the chamber. Four examples are given of this type of work to illustrate: (1) whether a suitable biological monitor could be devised for FC113; (2) behavioural changes during exposure to 1,1,1-trichloroethane; (3) the effect of alcohol on the kinetics of mandelic acid excretion in volunteers exposed to styrene vapour and (4) validation of physiologically based pharmacokinetic models on volunteers exposed to xylene.

Discussion

Given that the work described is on substances which are already in use, could these studies in human volunteers have replaced animal studies which might otherwise have been done to try to elucidate those points?

The HSL does not have facilities for animal studies. Our work has been confined to working on existing chemicals for which there is sufficient toxicological information and occupational exposure limits.

One of the problems may be that this is normal work exposure, and therefore there is no reason not to use human beings. But had double the normal human exposure been required, what would the attitude of the HSL have been?

HSL would adhere strictly to Health and Safety Law. The HSE ethics committee would review the research proposal and if sufficient justification could be made, it might permit volunteers to be exposed to levels beyond that found in some industries. However, the levels would never exceed the occupational exposure limits either for an 8-hour time weighed average or short-term exposure limit.

Is the limit based on animal studies in the first place?

The occupational exposure limits are set by the Health and Safety Commission on the advice of the Advisory Committee on Toxic Substances. They will have at their disposal all the available human and animal data.

With regard to substances such as occupational sensitisers and isocyanates, would it be acceptable to expose volunteers to these kinds of substances that are known to induce, for example, occupational asthma in these chambers?

In principle the same rules apply, i.e., we comply with the HSE limits. HSL has no immediate proposals to do volunteer studies on sensitisers. Other research groups have published work on metabolic studies where volunteers were exposed to isocyanates.

Is it possible to conduct these types of studies with very low ascending doses of substances to which man has never been exposed before?

Volunteer studies are subject to clearance by the ethics committee. If the perceived benefit to mankind in exposing volunteers to increasing doses is considered justified the Committee may give approval for the study. In the case of potential carcinogens, however, the general view is that all exposures should be reduced to the lowest possible level.

Is there a psychologist on the HSL ethics committee?

Yes. The psychologist provides ueful input to the committee, particularly when behavioural studies are being considered.

Most of your volunteers are driven home; but they are exposed to things that people would normally be exposed to at work. This seems a little illogical.

It may appear to be unnecessary, but we take the view that in these exceptional circumstances and for the comfort and convenience of the volunteers it is the prudent thing to do.

This may be worrying for those people who are working with those substances every day, and still driving home.

References

HARTLEY, L. R. and ADAMS, R. G., 1974, Effects of noise on the Stroop test, *Journal of Experimental Psychology*, **102**, 62–6.

MACKAY, C. J., CAMPBELL, L., SAMUEL, A. M. and WILSON, H. K., 1987, Behavioral changes during exposure to 1,1,1-trichloroethane, *American Journal of Industrial Medicine*, **11**, 223–9.

WILSON, H. K., COCKER, J., PURNELL, C. J., BROWN, R. H. and GOMPERTZ, D., 1979, The time course of mandelic acid excretion in workers exposed to styrene under model conditions, *British Journal of Industrial Medicine*, **36**, 235–7.

WILSON, H. K., ROBERTSON, S. M., WALDRON, H. A. and GOMPERTZ, D., 1983, Effect of alcohol on the kinetics of mandelic acid excretion in volunteers exposed to styrene vapour, *British Journal of Industrial Medicine*, **40**, 75–80.

WOOLLEN, B. H., GUEST, E. A., HOWE, W., MARSH, J. R. and WILSON, H. K., 1990, Human inhalation pharmacokinetics of 1,1,2-trichloro-1,2,2,-trifluoroethane (FC113), *International Archives of Environmental Health*, **62**, 73–8.

14

The Limits of Human Studies

DOUGLAS SMITH

The Environmental Medicine Unit (EMU) at the Institute of Naval Medicine has been involved in human experimentation for some 20 years, undertaking trials and studies to assess the performance of subjects over a wide range of climatic and environmental conditions to which military personnel may be exposed. Climatic studies range from cold immersion through cold wet to hot and assessments range from maximum physical performance to sustained psychological performance. Environmental factors may include work in noisy environments and exposure to low levels of potentially toxic gases such as can be found in polluted or contaminated environments.

To conduct these studies on a sound ethical basis, an independent ethical committee structure has been established which reviews the work of the Institute. This committee has an agreed set of guidelines – the 'Schedule of Approved Procedures' – which defines the limits to which human volunteers may be taken.

In the bad old days scientists conducting, what they considered to be, extremely important work, were so bound up with their research that ethical considerations tended to assume a low profile. There are examples, where the effects of this lack of control resulted in the most abominable, so-called, scientific work. In recent years, before ethics committees became the norm but the concept of ethical procedures was accepted, scientists tended to resort to experimenting on themselves in the absence of willing volunteers and if they thought the dangers of a procedure were rather high. Fortunately, this situation has become more formalised in approach, and for the Royal Navy such studies are extremely tightly controlled, without imposing unnecessary constraints. It is not believed that the formulation of these procedures has in any way interfered with research work. In fact, quite the converse situation has occurred as the procedure of assessing in detail scientific and ethical considerations generates improved experimental protocols, and has actually improved the quality of the science. In this chapter some of the limits to which volunteers are taken will be considered.

The process used to approve and conduct a study follows the pattern described below. First, the need to conduct a piece of work is agreed. The example taken will be for a new item of protective clothing. The Navy wishes to know to what degree this will affect performance of a sailor working on the upper deck of a ship in the heat. To assess this, a series of climatic chamber studies using volunteer sailors as subjects will be carried out.

A project officer is appointed to conduct the study. He or she will be a scientist experienced in the field and will usually be supported by a group of junior scientists. Their first job is to produce a scientific protocol – a detailed description of what they intend to do, and how they intend to do it. This protocol will also include details of the potential risks to subjects, what safety limits will be used and what supporting safety back-ups will be required. It will also include a subject information sheet and a consent form.

An independent medical officer is appointed. This individual is unconnected with the study and has sole responsibility for ensuring the safety of the subjects. The individual will therefore have to be satisfied that the protocol is safe and is responsible for providing medical cover for the trial itself. During the trial they will ensure that no procedures are added nor safeguards ignored. If asked by any volunteer subject, they will be their adviser and spokesperson.

The next step is to scrutinise this protocol fully from both a scientific and ethical point of view, according to strict rules set by the Ministry of Defence (MOD) (Navy) Personnel Research Ethics Committee. This is a totally independent organisation, chaired by an eminent Professor of Physiology, who is supported by specialist scientists from a wide range of fields. Also included on the committee are representatives of the legal and religious community. They meet twice a year (or more often if necessary) to review research programmes both of the Institute and the work of the Defence Research Agency's (DRA) establishment which conducts diving and hyperbaric research.

Over the years a large number of protocols have been approved by this committee. Instead of submitting protocols in which the methodology and risks are practically identical to those approved earlier, a *Schedule of Approved Procedures* has been agreed to minimise the workload. This document lists, in detail, those procedures which may be approved locally, by an in-house committee. The headings of the Schedule are shown in Figure 14.1.

The chairman of the committee, a senior statistician with much experience of research, determines whether all procedures within a protocol, submitted for approval, are clearly listed in the schedule of approved procedures (Figure 14.1). If not, then the protocol is sent to the chairman of the MOD(N) ethics committee. If it is felt that the procedures, whilst not listed in this schedule,

SCHEDULE OF APPROVED PROCEDURES

- Administration of drugs
- Collection of samples
- Exercise testing
- Psychological experimentation
- Modifications to sleep and rest patterns
- Nutrition
- Exposure to noise and vibration
- Exposure to motion challenge
- Thermal stress
  immersion
  exposure to cold air
  exposure to hot air
  field trials
- Exposure to gases
- Diving and compression chamber experiments
- Submarine escape and rescue
- Equipment trials

Figure 14.1 Headings of Schedule for approved procedures

are straightforward, chairman's action can be taken to approve the protocol, or the protocol can be sent to one or more experts on the committee for comment. Alternatively, the work can be discussed in more detail at a full committee meeting, in which case the project officer will attend to present the proposals (Figure 14.2).

If all the procedures *are* within the schedule, then the protocol undergoes an in-house review. The review culminates in a meeting which includes scientists not involved in the trial, an ethical review by non-scientists and final approval by the Medical Officer-in-Charge. Part of this process involves an assessment of the scientific content. In the Navy it is believed that for studies using human volunteers, *if the work is not scientifically valid, it is not ethically acceptable*. Once approved internally, a copy of the protocol is sent to the chairman of the MOD(N) ethics committee. Once these procedures have been completed, volunteers are recruited and the study commenced.

The use of volunteers is strictly in accordance with guidance provided by the Declaration of Helsinki (Figure 14.3). Subjects must be true and fully informed volunteers. The concept of a senior officer 'volunteering' subjects for a trial is unacceptable and does not occur. They must fully understand the nature of the study, and the procedures to which they will be exposed. They must also have explained to them any possible risks associated with the procedures. Of particular importance, particularly in a military organisation, is that they must be able to refuse to take part in or withdraw from the study at any time without penalty and without having to give a reason. They can be paid a test allowance, but this pay should be seen as a reward for discomfort, and not as an inducement to volunteer; it should never be viewed as danger or inconvenience money. For this reason, rest pay is set at a low level.

PROCEDURE FOR ETHICAL APPROVAL

- Are all of the procedures within the schedule of approved procedures?

- If 'no' protocol referred to chairman of MOD (Navy) personnel research ethics committee.
  - His options
    - Chairman's action
    - Members review
    - Full meeting
- If 'yes' can be reviewed in-house:
  - Scientific review by peers from unconnected groups
  - Review meeting to consider protocol in detail
  - Ethical scrutiny by unconnected in-house personnel

Figure 14.2 Procedure for ethical approval

The practical implications of the above strategy are: first, that the procedures will be explained to the subject in clear English, and the subject will be given the opportunity to discuss the trial with both the project officer and the independent medical officer; second, each subject will be given time to consider a decision to volunteer; third, for assistance, the volunteer will be provided with a written information sheet. If content, the volunteer will then be invited to sign a consent form. The wording of both the consent form and information sheet will have been agreed by the ethical committee. It will be explained that, at any time during the trial, the subject, the project officer, or the independent medical officer has the right and obligation to terminate the study if it is felt that the subject may suffer unacceptable distress.

It is worth pointing out that most of the studies are physiological trials. A subject who is overstressed is no longer a physiological subject, but is showing pathological changes, and this is not the aim of the study.

Figure 14.1 lists the schedule of approved procedures. Volunteers can be given drugs, the limitation being that only proprietary drugs approved by the Committee for the Safety of Medicines – to the limit of dose levels recommended – can be used. Clinical drug testing is not carried out. For blood sampling the limit is 500 ml per three-month period, the same as a blood donor. In a study involving the measurement of sodium balance, urine and faeces may be collected. Subjects can be exercised to exhaustion, on bicycles or on treadmills, or can be bored conducting psychological performance tests while staring at a screen for lengthy periods. Their performance during shift work, as would be found in naval watchkeeping schedules, can be observed. They can be deprived of sleep or woken up in the middle of the night to assess their performance. They can be fed special diets, for example, in trials to look at the effects of different intakes of salt during acclimatisation to the heat, or to study the performance of subjects who have been living on a packet of barley sugars and a pint of water a day for a week. They can be subjected to loud noises or bounced around in small boats, to

DECLARATION OF HELSINKI

'DRAFT CODE OF ETHICS ON HUMAN EXPERIMENTATION' presented to the World Medical Association at Helsinki in 1961 and as amended thereafter. To comply with this code the following rules will apply:

Subjects

- Must be true volunteers
- They must understand the nature of the study
- They must understand the risks involved
- They must be able to refuse to take part with no penalty
- They may be paid but this pay should not be an inducement to volunteer

Figure 14.3 Declaration of Helsinki – rules applying to the subject

look at the effectiveness of ear defenders or to assess the problems of small boats travelling at 50 knots. The effects of motion can be studied by spinning them around in rotating chairs, or they can be put into survival suits, or life rafts, and allowed to bob on the sea.

In the range of thermal stress trials, volunteers can be immersed in cold water to follow their performance over several hours or their initial responses to immersion observed. They can be exposed to cold air in studies to look at the effectiveness of Arctic clothing, or the aetiology of cold injury. They can be heated in a hot chamber, which can reach temperatures of 50°C, for example, to look at the use of firefighting clothing where subjects need to be protected from the heat of a fire, but still perform physical work – a difficult compromise to make. There is access to firefighting training rigs which can be fired up to much higher temperatures. In this case observations started with a dummy to convince the ethics committee of feasibility and safety, and slowly worked up to environmental temperatures of 180°C. For the ultimate study of the effects of fire, a dummy is used. Finally in this area, field studies can be conducted to get subjects to exercise in the actual environment in which they are expected to work. A number of studies have been carried out at the southern end of the Red Sea, where even at night the temperature never falls below 34°C, with a relative humidity of 100 per cent. Subjects tend not to do very well when wearing protective clothing. Ethical considerations for this type of study are clearly important.

Volunteers can be subjected to various gases, be it to assess the toxicity of CO_2 to set safe levels in ambient air in submerged submarines or to look at low levels of atmospheric pollutants. There is a separate ethical subcommittee which deals solely with hyperbaric experiments, as safety in this field is clearly critical. When the considerations are not only compression and decompression, also the problems of thermal equilibrium associated with the environment temperature, the clothing worn and the breathing-gas composition, both ethical committees may be involved jointly.

One area very specific to the Navy is that of submarine escape and rescue. This covers the unlikely scenario of a submarine being stranded on the bottom of the sea with the problems of getting personnel out of it. There are two options: rescue by another submersible which locks on to the sunken submarine and transfers survivors to another vessel, or escape of the submariners to the surface. The latter procedure is to rapidly compress submariners in a tower to the ambient water pressure, opening the top hatch and allowing them to shoot to the surface, at which point they inflate their suits, and have then to survive on the surface, possibly for several hours. Clearly the physiological problems of these manoeuvres are quite considerable.

One area which is often raised in discussions of ethics is whether military personnel should be *expected* to take part in trials if, 'the stresses are similar to those to which they may be exposed to during their normal duty'. It is felt at the EMU that this is totally unacceptable. Armed forces personnel, by definition, put their lives at risk when they join the forces. Exposure to *unnecessary* risk for scientific reasons is a completely different matter.

This prompts discussion of the limits which a scientist should reasonably expect an experimental subject to tolerate. The example is the limits set for a heat stress trial where personnel are working in a thermally severe environment, wearing restrictive clothing and undertaking physical work. What are the aspects of physiology with which we are concerned? The first is, clearly, how hot the subject gets, so there is a requirement to monitor body temperature. This can be done using a number of methods, most commonly rectal temperature and temperature recorded in the ear canal – the aural temperature (not to be confused with oral) – other methods such as swallowed radio pills are also a possibility. There are pros and cons of these methods, but the Navy approach in the heat is to use aural temperature. This has the advantage that it has a rapid response whereas rectal temperatures respond more slowly – and after all it is the brain temperature which causes subjects to collapse. The limits that have been set are shown in Figure 14.4. Historical studies carried out over many years, culminating in a large series of studies in the early 1970s, have indicated that a situation defined as 'imminent collapse' is reached at a core temperature of around 39.5°C. This is the level above which performance starts to drop off, and the risks of collapse or heat illness are markedly increased. Thus, the top limit is set at 39.5°C in all situations. For personnel exercising, particularly if they are wearing restrictive clothing, the limit at which *exercise* is stopped is set 0.5°C lower. This is to take into account any overshoot, but if post-exercise body temperature continues to rise, subjects are again withdrawn at the 39.5°C point.

Another aspect, generally only encountered in extremely hot environments, is the temperature of the breathing-air. The limits set for inspired air are as follows: exposure to air temperatures above 80°C dry bulb or 50°C wet bulb will only be permitted if breathing apparatus is worn. This considers

EXPOSURE TO THE HEAT

- Maximum allowable aural temperature 39.5 °C. At this level subjects will be removed from the heat, undressed and cooled down.
- Exercising subjects whose aural temperature reaches 39 °C may remain in the heat but must stop exercise.
- Exposure to air temperatures above 80 °C dry bulb or 50 °C wet bulb will only be permitted if subjects are breathing dry air (normally via breathing apparatus).
- At air temperatures above 80 °C dry bulb inspired air temperatures will be recorded and subjects removed from the heat if inspired temperature reaches this level.
- Subjects will be removed from the heat if skin temperature at any site reaches 42 °C.
- Subjects will be withdrawn from the heat if heart rate is in excess of 210 − age.
- Subjects will be withdrawn from the heat if cardiac arrhythmias or ectopic beats appear at a frequency of more than five per minute or ectopic beats show coupling.
- A subject may withdraw if he feels he cannot continue (or for any other reason).

Figure 14.4 Exposure to heat

the relative heat transfers to the respiratory passages and the lungs by convection and the heat losses by evaporation. It is surprising, but true, that the heat loss by evaporation is greater than the heat gain by convection at temperatures up to about 80°C, providing the air is dry. Above this limit, when breathing apparatus is worn, the air temperature will be measured and the experiment will be terminated if the temperature of the breathing-air reaches 80°C. The third thermal limit is skin temperature. Mild skin burns and pain start occurring above 43–45°C, and therefore a level is set at 42°C below which skin burns are very unlikely.

The next consideration is stress on the circulatory system. It is inappropriate for subjects to work at their maximum heart rate for extended periods as the physical stress and the potential dangers are likely to be too high. The problem with setting a single number for a maximum heart rate is that maximum heart rate decreases with age, so a limit of say 180 beats per minute for a 17-year-old may be only 85 per cent of his maximum, but this limit may be above the maximum heart rate for a 40-year-old. For this reason, a limit of 210 less the subject's age is used. This corresponds to around 90 per cent of the predicted maximum. As this is a fairly severe limit it is constrained by a number of factors: (a) heart rate must be monitored continuously; (b) the appearance of irregular beats at a frequency of more than five per minute (ectopics show coupling); and (c) the ECG becomes unreadable (generally a function of technical difficulties); and these are grounds for termination of the study.

The final limits to which a volunteer may be subjected are based on signs, symptoms and subjective feelings: thus the trial will be stopped if the subject collapses, complains of pain, breathlessness, nausea, dizziness or becomes confused or wishes to pull out. Of course, the volunteer can decide to withdraw at any time, and encouragement to continue should be balanced against enthusiasm. It is well known that highly motivated, fit subjects are those most likely to push themselves to the limit. However, the physiological constraints applied should be such that this limit is not reached and the experiment can be completed in safety. Experience shows that the above approach works. The Independent Medical Officer has an important role to play in safeguarding the enthusiastic or very determined volunteer.

Ensuring that all these variables are recorded effectively means the subject is extensively wired to recording equipment. Subjects have thermistors in their ears, a set of four skin temperature probes and a set of ECG electrodes. These are fed to monitoring equipment so that physiological state can be monitored continuously. Additionally, to make data analysis easier, subjects are generally wired into a data logger which records up to 16 channels of information for off-loading into a computer on completion of the trial. This is also important for trials on ships, where the state of the subjects can be easily monitored.

The Institute of Naval Medicine is very satisfied with this system – it has proven to be safe and has a major practical advantage in that it ensures reproducibility between trials. It is now policy that all work within the MOD should be covered by such a system, and it is hoped this will be adopted nationally.

Discussion

It seems that there are many controls like those used in animal experiments: the independent medical officer, the humane end-points, built in. Is there a computerised data logger because it helps to establish a diagnosis very quickly because somebody could collapse?

This system also provides a permanent record.

How many things can be put on the data logger?

There are 16 channels and it records events or voltage, so temperature, heart rate as a number of beats can be recorded, but not ECG. Medilog-type recorders for EEG have been used but the decoding is very difficult. Transcutaneous recorders are also being examined.

Is there any comparable data on suffering some sort of adverse reaction or needing hospitalisation, and are there interaction studies with alcohol?

There is no problem with any long-term lock-up experiments as studies are controlled for a few days anyway. Breathalysers have been used occasionally when one volunteer is suspected of drinking alcohol the night before contrary to instructions; the subjects have then been removed from the experiment. There was a case on survival trials where barley sugar and water were fed and an individual started to produce ketone bodies, but then it was discovered that the barley sugar was not being eaten.

How do the heat tolerance experiments compare with saunas which are widely used?

The experiments are a combination of exercise, clothing and heat. Quite a lot of environmental heat can be tolerated if the subject is not doing anything, but as soon as volunteers start generating internal heat there can be a problem. The wet sauna is the most stressful.

15

Magnetometry – The Ultimate Non-invasive Neurophysiological Technique?

GRAHAM HARDING

Functional imaging of the human brain has been the goal of many neuroscientists for the last 20 years. Neuromagnetometry may well represent the ultimate non-invasive technique for studying the brain, since it does not even require placement of electrodes on the surface of the scalp, unlike electroencephalography. This chapter is a description of the history and some of the current applications of magnetometry as a non-invasive method for studying brain function. Some of the advantages of this technique over other imaging systems are also discussed.

Available imaging techniques can be divided into two basic categories. First, slow techniques include such procedures as Positron Emission Tomography (PET), Single Positron Emission Computerised Tomography (SPECT), or functional Magnetic Resonance Imagery (fMRI). The first two approaches involve invasive procedures with radioisotopes to measure various activities in the brain, such as oxygen consumption, glucose metabolism or blood flow. For this reason the frequency of testing is severely limited. The fMRI method is based on blood flow alone, and does not involve invasive procedures. Unfortunately, all these techniques require seconds of time, and contrast with the faster imaging techniques of Electroencephalography (EEG) and Magnetoencephalography (Harding, 1993).

The EEG has been utilised since Berger's original recordings of the human brain (Berger, 1929). However, although electroencephalography has contributed to significantly more areas of clinical work, such as epilepsy and a few areas of psychology, the complexity of the resulting EEG signals prevented accurate localisation, until the advent of computerised brain maps. Even with these techniques, the resolution of the EEG was always poor due to the smearing of electrical signals by intervening tissues such as skull and scalp. These intervening tissues, however, are transparent to the equivalent magnetic currents and, therefore, magnetoencephalography offers an attractive alternative with similar spatial resolution to PET, SPECT and fMRI, and the millisecond by millisecond temporal resolution of EEG. Measurement of these tiny magnetic currents is intrinsically difficult, however.

In 1908, the Dutch physicist Onnes liquified helium, and found that its boiling point was 4 ° Kelvin (K). After reducing its temperature to 1.4 ° K, he investigated the conductivity of a variety of metals between this temperature and the boiling point of helium (Onnes, 1911). He discovered that a wide variety of metals lose all resistance at these extremely low temperatures and described the condition as 'superconductivity'. In 1957, Bardeen *et al.* (1957) explained this peculiar behaviour of materials, by showing that electrons become paired at these low temperatures, and each pair can be described in quantum theory by a common wave function. If this wave is applied to a closed ring below the critical resistance temperature, the quantum flux can be trapped. The closed ring has a narrow portion, or Josephson Junction, which at these extremely low temperatures will allow one flux quantum to pass if the total current exceeds this amount. The behaviour of this ring is then monitored, and the output used as the signal from the Superconducting Quantum Interference Device (SQUID). Use of this device allows the measurement of minute magnetic signals emanating from the brain. The signal is sensed by a simple flux transformer in the form of a detection coil maintained with the SQUID at superconducting temperature, a combination known as a Magnetometer. Modifying the configuration of this coil so that the single coil is replaced by a form of winding giving two coils in opposite directions makes the device become a gradiometer, which is sensitive to currents affecting only one coil, but is insensitive to distant currents which affect both coils equally. This is essential in cancelling the distant massive magnetic signals such as the Earth's magnetic field (10^{10} femtoTesla), whilst at the same time being sensitive to near, but minute, signals such as those from the brain (10^1–10^3 femtoTesla).

Cohen (1968) succeeded in recording magnetic signals from the human brain using an ordinary induction coil. He confirmed these results with improved detection equipment using SQUID technology (Cohen, 1972). His studies pioneered the development of magnetoencephalography (MEG) as a complementary, or competing, technique to electroencephalography. As both techniques have the ability to respond to functional changes in the brain, which take place on a millisecond-to-millisecond basis, they permit the study of the *sequence* of cortical events, an ability not shared by other imaging techniques.

MEG differs from EEG in a number of ways. The magnetic fields are orthogonal (at right-angles) to the electrical potentials. Theoretically, electrical potentials detected by the EEG are those which represent the volume currents outside the nerve cells, whilst MEG detects the magnetic field produced by post-synaptic dendritic potentials of pyramidal cells within the cortex (Williamson and Kaufman, 1990). In addition, MEG does not require a reference for its current, whereas EEG does for its potentials and although many techniques have been used to overcome this difficulty (Harding, 1988), no completely satisfactory solution has been found. To record the EEG, it is essential that electrodes are placed in contact with the scalp; whilst this is a relatively innocuous procedure using the 20 electrodes of a standard clinical EEG, it becomes a serious restriction as the number of channels, and therefore the number of electrodes, increases (Gevins *et al.*, 1994). From this point of view, MEG currently represents the ultimate non-invasive technique. The sensing coils contained in their super-cooled dewar only have to be moved close to the scalp in order to sense the currents.

There is evidence that EEG records both radial and tangential components of a signal, with emphasis on the radial component. Theoretically, MEG will only record tangential sources, but this restriction does not appear as severe as first thought. The majority of the cortex is contained in fissures, and therefore all these areas are amenable to MEG recording. In addition, the gyri of the human brain are rarely exactly tangential to the scalp and therefore their sources are picked up as well.

Modern multi-channel MEG systems usually have between 10 and 100 detectors contained in a liquid helium dewar. This allows the magnetic field to be recorded around the head at a single moment in time. Most devices are still currently contained in a recording dewar, which is placed over the particular area of the head which is being studied, but helmet-type systems, containing between 60 and 100 channels to give whole-head recordings, have been developed already. To cancel outside magnetic noise, it is usual to carry out the recordings in a magnetically shielded room.

Having measured the magnetic field, or mapped the electrical potentials coming from the scalp, it is necessary to produce what is called the inverse solution. Thus, the generating source of these signals within the brain must be deduced from the magnetic field or electrical potential map. Unfortunately, there is rarely a unique solution, as many different current distributions within the head could explain the recorded activities. Previously available information, such as limiting the spatial extent of the sources, allows reduction of the problem to something which is soluble, however. Usually the technique involves restricting the solution to a single equivalent dipole. A further technique allows application of a distributed source solution (Ioannides *et al.*, 1989). Other techniques fall between these two solutions, and are considered as constrained sources (Bedford and Harding, 1992).

In studying both the location and timing of function within the human brain, EEG and MEG make use of the technique of averaging (Dawson, 1951). This author surmised that any response in the brain to a particular stimulus must be time-locked. Even though the response may be tiny compared with the spontaneous electrical or magnetic activity, if the stimulus is repeated a large number of times, and the resultant electrical potentials or magnetic fields superimposed, each of the small events occurring at the

SPATIAL AND TEMPORAL RESOLUTION OF EXPERIMENTAL TECHNIQUES

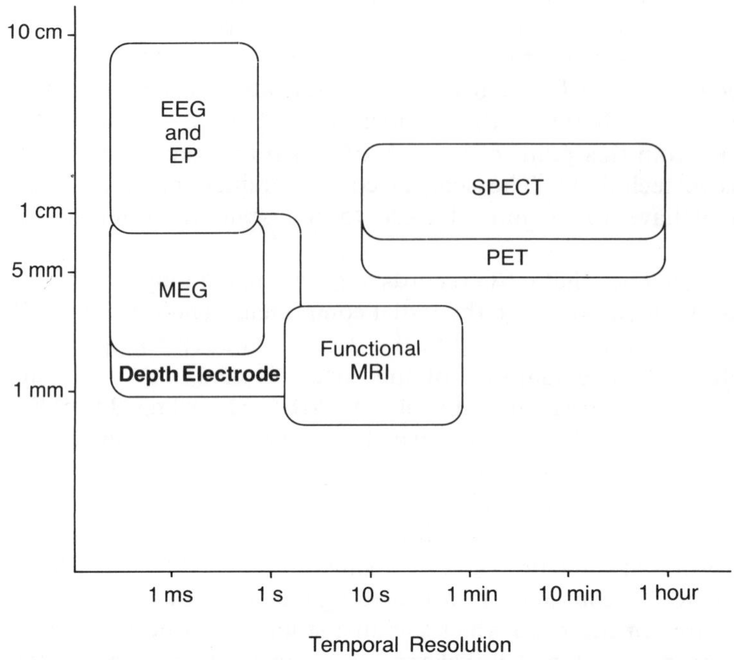

Figure 15.1 This figure shows the spatial and temporal resolution of various experimental imaging techniques which can be used to study the human brain. It can be seen that the slow (second plus) techniques of SPECT, PET and functional MRI are clustered to the right of the illustration, whereas the fast techniques, such as EEG and evoked potentials and MEG, as well as the invasive technique of depth recording, can provide information on a millisecond-by-millisecond basis. It should be noted that MEG has similar resolution to slow techniques being better than PET or SPECT but not as good as functional MRI.

same time interval from the stimulus add, together, whereas the spontaneous activity, or other noise sources, being random with respect to the stimulus, cancel (Harding, 1988). This technique gives EEG and MEG their marked advantage over other functional imaging techniques (Figure 15.1). It is possible by this procedure to study the sequential responses to a stimulus, millisecond by millisecond. By combining this technique with the spatial resolution of electrical brain mapping, or magnetic fields, it is feasible to localise which area of the brain is responding to a particular stimulus, the timing of the response, and how the responses from the different areas of the brain interrelate.

The development of highly detailed anatomical images of the brain, utilising magnetic resonance imagery, has provided the perfect platform on which to place functional information. The difficulty is, however, in co-registering the MRI data with those provided by MEG. Many of the earlier studies used co-registration with marks or positions on the head, determined from bony landmarks, such as the nasion and the two cochas or pre-auricular depressions. These positions can be recorded in relation to the dewar during MEG measurement and can be located on the MRI by marking with oil capsules. Unfortunately, this does not solve the problem of head movement during the MEG investigation, and various other techniques, such as small coils attached to the scalp (Ahonen *et al.*, 1991), have been used to generate a magnetic field which can then be sensed by the magnetometer. These devices have to be positioned with regard to the bony landmarks. The bite bar is a more sensible solution, which is utilised by our group. A dental impression of the individual subject is made on a bite bar, which has an open-ended triangular frame fitting around the head. This frame contains small holes full of oil markers and these points can be digitised using a Polhemus Navigational Sciences system, in relation to the dewar. The patient uses the same bite bar during the MRI, and the oil markers show up as white spots. During magnetometry, the bite bar is clamped so that the subject has the head fixed in a particular orientation in relation to the dewar during the whole period of the investigation. This is, in fact, a very comfortable procedure, since subjects can release themselves in between each investigation and always can return the head to exactly the same position.

The MEG system at the University of Aston (Figure 15.2) consists of 19 channels of magnetometers. The magnetometers, in a liquid helium dewar, are distributed in a planar hexagonal array with a diameter of 17.5 cm. The dewar can be moved into any position around the head, and can be raised, lowered and tilted. In addition to the 19 channels, a vector magnetometer records fluctuations for adaptive noise cancellation. The system resides in a magnetically shielded room. Signals are sampled at a rate greater than 1 kHz, and are amplified, band-pass filtered and then averaged. Somatosensory stimulation is provided electrically, and visual stimulation is generated using a specialised graphics system with the display monitor outside the shielded room, and viewed via a system of front-silvered mirrors.

Similar techniques have been used for MEG studies of somatosensory, auditory and visual cortex. Wood *et al.* (1985) succeeded not only in resolving conflicting theories of the generators of the somatosensory evoked potential recorded by EEG, or electro-corticography (ECoG), but also demonstrated mapping of the cortical representation of the human hand. The inability of EEG, or ECoG, to distinguish between radial dipoles and tangential dipoles prevented accurate localisation. Thus, in the somatosensory evoked potential, the earlier N20–P30 components of the evoked potential could be explained, either as two cortical sources on the gyri of the central sulcus with radial dipoles, or as one tangential dipole in the central sulcus itself. Since an N20–P30 magnetic field was easily recorded, the latter explanation had to

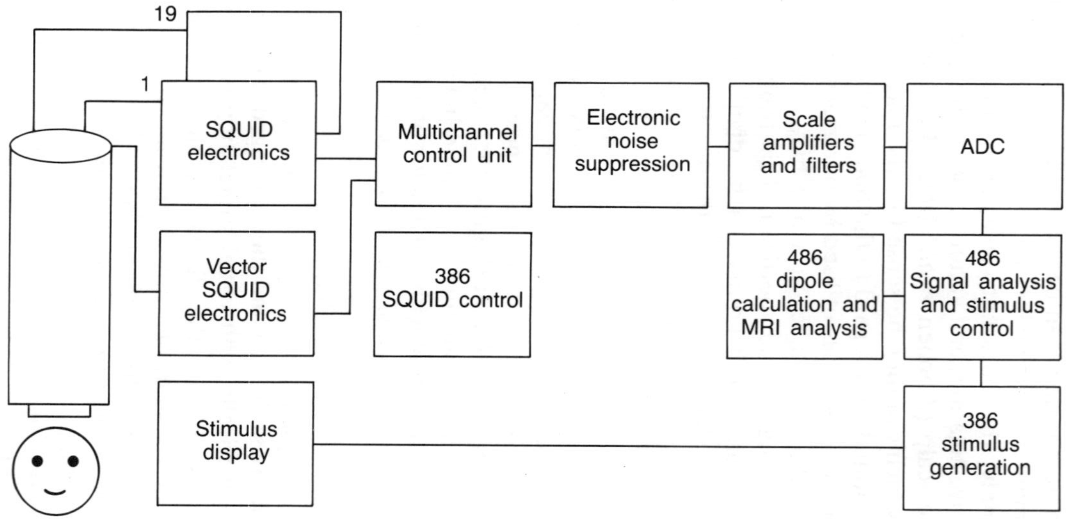

Figure 15.2 The Aston 19 channel neuromagnetometer system is shown in this block diagram. The 19 SQUID channels are shown in a dewar on the left, coupled by their SQUID electronics to a multi-channel control unit. In addition, this control unit has an input from a single channel which measures the ambient noise in three vectors, allowing noise to be deducted from the signals from the 19 recording channels. A 386 computer controls the squids at their optimum recording parameters. An electronic noise suppression system follows this to remove very low-frequency noise, not excluded by the magnetically shielded room in which the dewar and the subject are sited. Amplification and filtering is then performed and a standard analogue-to-digital converter then precedes signal analysis averaging and control of the stimulus. This is backed by a 22 transputer array allowing on-line source analysis. The visual stimuli are produced by a Cambridge Systems 386 generating system, and displayed through surface-silvered mirrors into the magnetically shielded room.

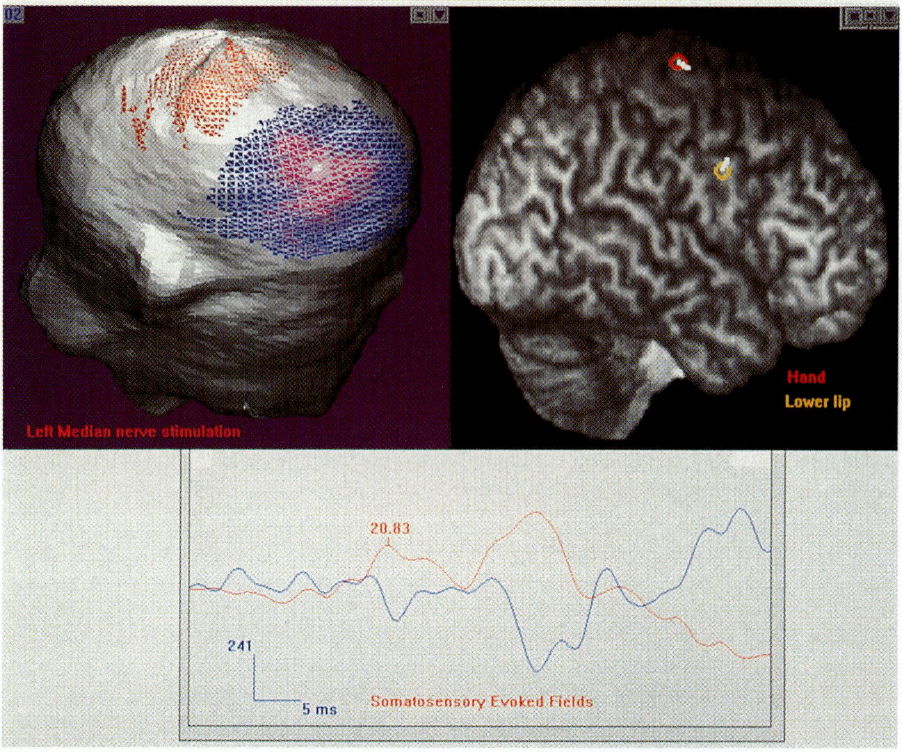

Figure 15.3 Shows the somatosensory-evoked fields from left median nerve stimulation. The lower traces show the response to left median stimulation with red indicated as the maximum outgoing field, as shown on the top view of the head (left upper) and blue-purple is the maximum ingoing field. The localisation at 22 ms is then indicated on the surface reconstruction of the subject's MRI on the upper right illustration as a red area for the location of the single equivalent dipole, with the arrow indicating the orientation of the dipole. The localisation seen in yellow is for stimulation of the lower lip.

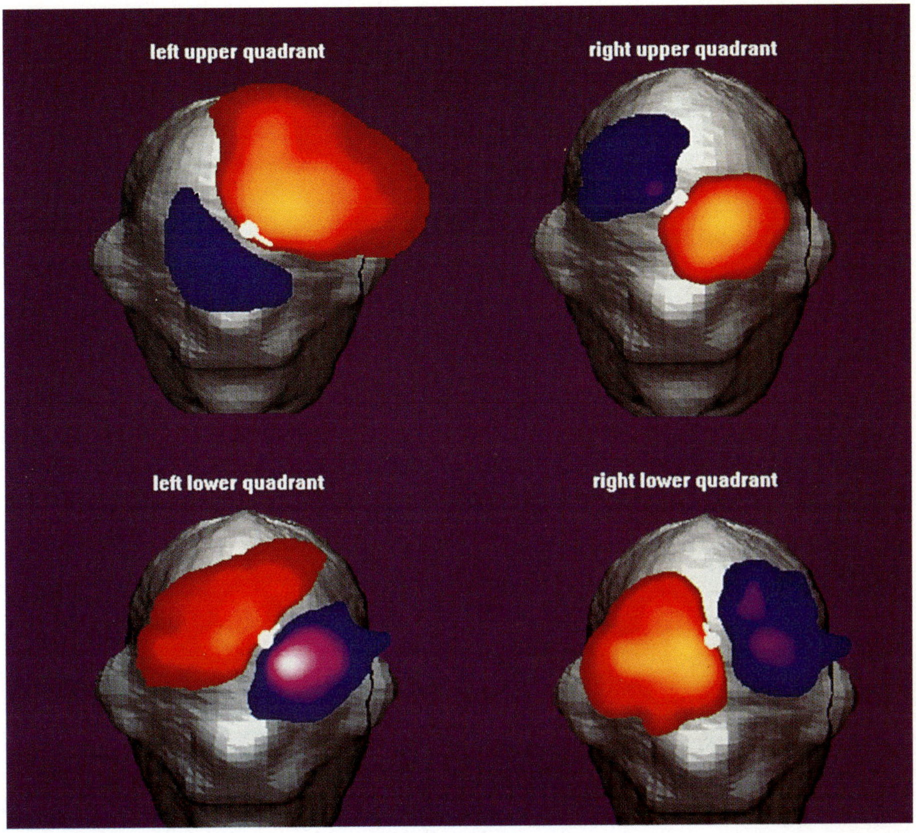

Figure 15.6 This figure shows the outgoing magnetic fields (in red yellow) and ingoing magnetic fields (in blue), as well as the single equivalent dipole position, and its orientation on the rear surface of the head. The response is seen to left upper, left lower, right upper and right lower quadrants of the visual fields. It can be seen that on each occasion the dipole is orientated in the direction that one would expect when either the floor of the calcarine fissure and the lingual surface are stimulated by the upper quadrants of the visual fields, or the ceiling of the calcarine fissure and the cuneal surface are stimulated by the lower quadrant. In addition, the orientation changes according to whether right calcarine fissure or left calcarine fissure is stimulated. These responses were to isoluminant chromatic stimuli.

be correct, and the inverse solution showed a tangential dipole situated in the posterior bank of the central sulcus. In addition, however, simultaneous EEG recording showed a radial generator for an N25–P25 component of the SEP, which was not seen in the MEG, and which was located in the anterior crown of the post-central gyrus. Although the MEG showed better spatial accuracy than the scalp EEG, this finding illustrates the essential, complementary nature of the two techniques. More recently, both ourselves (Furlong *et al.*, 1995), and others, have shown (Figure 15.3, see colour plate section) that it is possible to record the somatosensory evoked potential to both foot, hand and lip stimulation. The spatial organisation found on the cortex is the same as the somatosensory humunculus, described by Penfield and Rasmussen (1950), and Penfield and Jasper (1954). Baumgartner *et al.* (1991) demonstrated the somatotopy of the human hand, utilising both magnetic and electrical recordings. Yang *et al.* (1993) localised 14 facial, 44 hand and 8 arm sites bilaterally, using MEG and by mapping their results onto magnetic resonance images (MRI). The utilisation of the readiness potential by Kornhuber and Deecke (1965) allows comparable studies of the motor cortex. These authors demonstrated that a negative motor potential could be observed prior to voluntary movement. Using MEG, Deecke *et al.* (1982) demonstrated the humuncular organisation of the human motor cortex, and this was confirmed by Cheyne *et al.* (1991).

This non-invasive method for studying the human humunculus is not only of academic interest, but is a great advantage in pre-surgical work-up. Whenever neurosurgery is undertaken close to an eloquent functional area, the surgeon is always concerned about possible post-operative losses, due to damage to the functional cortex. Under present circumstances, the only way to identify the functional significance of the tissues surrounding a tumour is for the surgeon to localise both the somatosensory and motor areas at operation, by recording responses from exposed cortex or by electrically stimulating presumed motor areas. The patient needs to be conscious for such studies and therefore has to be awake during this part of the procedure. This restricts the operation to those who are able to face the stress and it obviously cannot be used in children. Magnetoencephalography allows localisation to be performed entirely non-invasively prior to the surgery itself, and permits the functional localisation to be presented to the surgeon as a Monte Carlo analysis on a surface-rendered image deduced from the MRI, with a resolution of 1.3 mm (Figure 15.4). Both ourselves (Furlong *et al.*, 1995) and Gallen *et al.* (1994) have found this to be a highly effective technique.

Studies of auditory-evoked responses have resulted in the identification of a 19 msec peak occurring after a click stimulus deep inside the Silvian fissure in the primary auditory cortex (Scherg *et al.*, 1989). The auditory-evoked magnetic field shows a series of deflections in the next few hundred milliseconds, with a marked N100 magnetic response, equivalent to the N100 recorded at the vertex in electrophysiological investigation (Jones *et al.*, 1980), but with a clear equivalent dipole orientated perpendicularly in the

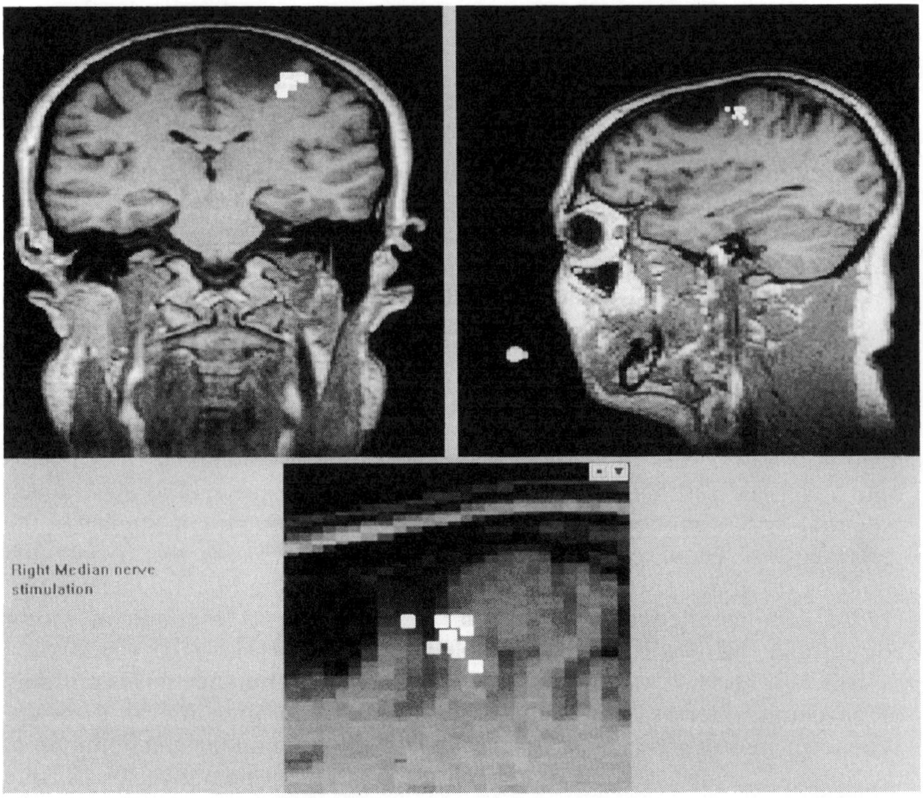

Figure 15.4 Shows the MEG localisation of right median nerve stimulation over laid on the MRI images of a patient with an astrocytoma. The tumour can be seen as the dark area in the sagittal view just in front of the median nerve localisation. The lower illustration shows this area enlarged with the tumour indicated by the arrow. The axial view shows the localisation just to the right of the tumour. The small white dot in front of the mouth in the sagittal view is part of the localisation from the bite bar.

Silvian fissure, pointing towards the neck and the vertex (Yamamoto *et al.*, 1988; Pantev *et al.*, 1990). The equivalent electrical potential is recorded at the vertex, since electrical potentials are recorded best from a radial disposition of the dipole. With EEG, it is exceptionally difficult to differentiate activity from the two auditory cortices, but this is straightforward using MEG. Papanicolaou *et al.* (1990) demonstrated that the equivalent dipole for the N100 was located more posteriorly and medially when stimuli were contra-lateral. Pantev *et al.* (1988, 1990) demonstrated a tonotopic arrangement of these responses, with the depth of the equivalent dipole generating the N100 increasing with the logarithm of the stimulus frequency.

Past functional studies of the visual cortex have been divided between those that are performed on animals using micro-electrode techniques, and psychophysical studies of human vision, or a combination of this technique with a study of deficiencies produced by specific accidental damage in humans. It is known that in primates the retinal image is processed by separate pathways arriving at different layers of the striate visual cortex (areas V1 and V2). Following this, spatial form and colour are processed in area V4 and motion, with probably motion flow and depth vision, in area V5 (Zeki, 1993; Zeki and Shipp, 1988; De Yoe and van Essen, 1988). On the other hand, Campbell and Robson (1968), for example, used pioneering psychological techniques to delineate the discrimination characteristics of the different pathways of the human visual system, on the basis of human individual responses to specific visual stimuli, with defined temporal and spatial frequencies. Until recently, no attempt had been made to combine these two techniques, but Watson *et al.* (1993) reported the functional separation of colour and motion centres in human visual cortex, using PET techniques. Their experimental design, however, was necessarily crude to allow for the long temporal sequence of PET sampling.

Magnetoencephalography (MEG) overcomes these problems completely, and allows both the study of the functional organisation of different areas of the visual cortex and their temporal relationship. Teyler *et al.* (1975) were the first to visualize evoked magnetic responses to brief light flashes. Later studies, such as those of Kouijzer *et al.* (1985) and Aine *et al.* (1989), used stimuli in which there were no overall changes in luminance, but simply local areas of luminance change of either checker boards, or bars, which appeared or disappeared, or reversed. Using these types of stimuli, they were able to demonstrate retinotopic organisation, as well as at least double dipoles. It is known that the striate visual cortex shows retinotopic representation down the Calcarine Fissure, and Maclin *et al.* (1983) showed that, as the stimulus was moved away from the central visual field, the single equivalent dipole reached greater depth as would be expected by the visual field distribution down the Calcarine Fissure. In our own laboratory, we have demonstrated that, using pattern onset stimuli in which the stimulus appears from a neutral background and then disappears into it again, there appears to be differences between responses to chromatic patterns and to achromatic patterns. Evoked magnetic responses were recorded to isoluminant red-green stimuli, as well as achromatic stationary gratings of 1 cycle per degree occupying a visual field of 4 by 6 degrees which was positioned in each quadrant (Fylan *et al.*, 1995a and b). Using the chromatic stimuli, both C2 responses around 92 to 110 ms and C3 responses around 180 to 260 ms were obtained. With the single equivalent dipole inverse solution, there was clear evidence that the C2 component originated in striate cortex (Figure 15.5), whereas the C3 component was undoubtedly extra-striate and appeared to originate from an area equivalent to that of V4 in primates. The C2 component showed clear retinotopic organisation consistent with the anatomy of the Calcarine Fissure

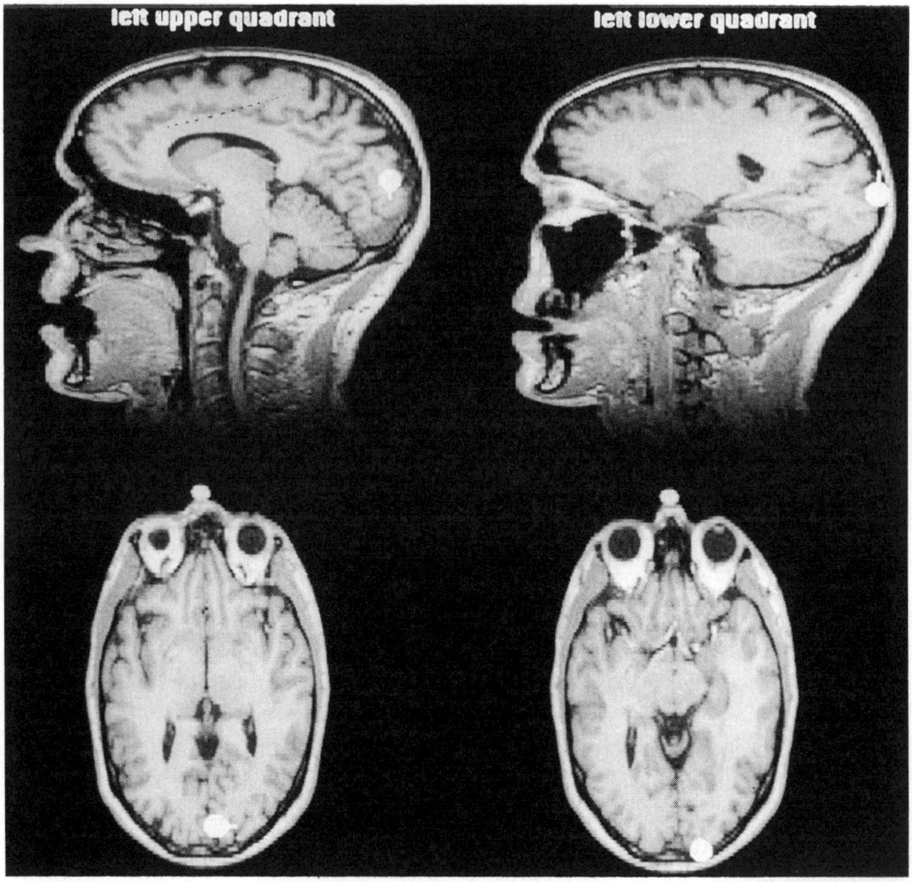

Figure 15.5 Shows MRI sections giving the localisation of the single equivalent dipoles to left upper quadrant, and left lower quadrant visual field stimulation. It can be seen that the localisation is as expected, with that from the left upper quadrant being placed on the lower surface of the Calcarine Fissure in a more ventral position, and with the opposite orientation to the response from the left lower quadrant, which is clearly dorsal on the upper surface of the occipital lobe.

(Figure 15.6, see colour plate section). Surprisingly, however, the achromatic responses were much more variable, and failed to show retinotopic representation. Since both chromatic and achromatic stimuli are processed in areas V1 and V2 it may well be that the representation in area V2 of achromatic stimuli is more diffuse due to its dual projection (Zeki, 1969). Current research involves investigating the temporal relationship and sequencing between these two areas and studies of the behaviour of the motion area V5.

Summary and Conclusions

In conclusion, it is clear that the above studies illustrate the great advantage of the MEG system over previously developed imaging methods. Its spatial resolution is good, in the case of the Aston 19-channel system (the largest in the UK), the resolution and the accuracy of the system are around 1.5 mm. This compares favourably with PET, is almost equivalent to fRMI, and is far better than SPECT. The great advantage of MEG, however, is in the ability to decode the temporal sequence of processing within the brain, and this will prove critical in studies of visual, somatosensory and auditory cortex. Although there is little doubt that neuromagnetometry will make significant contributions to neurosurgery, it is in studies of normal brain function that this technique is likely to make the most significant contribution.

Discussion

Can one use magnetometry to look at brain function below the level of the cortex?

This is not possible because the distance problem with magnetometry means that one is probably limited to about 5 cm. It might be possible to detect a space-occupying lesion in the cortex if it gives a signal. Magnetometry is used, for instance, to locate epileptogenic foci which produce spikes because these can be recorded, and then back-averaged to locate where the signals are coming from. In some cases it is not necessary to do this because magnetic resonance imaging is so good that it is possible to locate the source of the abnormality. Thus, a good clear signal is necessary for location of lesions by magnetometry, but spatial resolution drops rapidly when these become deeper.

Magnetometry is a spatial technique in the sense that the localisation is very good, as long as enough cortical neurons become involved to enable the signal to be localised.

Also, it is possible to look at the effects of drugs on brain function using the technique, and the treatment of epilepsy is an example, instead of using EEG. In modern drugs, it is possible to study what is happening to a localised epileptogenic lesion during partial seizures. The method has not as yet been used to study migraine, although this is a possibility, particularly as it can be applied to detecting evoked potentials in patients who get clear abnormalities, perceptions in the visual field, and localised abnormalities occur. This can be monitored electrically, and it is only useful using a magnetic approach if a very small resolution is needed. It is complicated by the fact that the patient must keep very still, and MRI and PET have the problem of movement artefacts.

The question arises as to whether magnetometry offers the potential presently, or in the near future, to replace some animal experiments and, if so, which experiments.

It seems completely stupid to do the cross-species jump that has had to take place in the past where these techniques make it possible to do otherwise. Apart from fortuitous accidents on humans, which are either where humans have a localised lesion which produces some particular functional abnormality, or where they have to have an operation, and you actually decide while you are there where one or two other bits are represented. Obviously that is an ethical question. These techniques, PET, fMRI and magnetometry, have the advantage that one can do human studies either completely non-invasively or relatively non-invasively, as with PET. Given that, all the work that has been done on the visual cortex with the macaque monkey, and there have been vast numbers used simply because their visual system seems closest to the human brain, becomes unnecessary. What one actually wants to know is not what macaque monkeys see, but how the human visual system works. Whereas those animals were used in the past in the classical studies for locating all the various visual areas, V1 to V5, that is no longer necessary. In fact, more and more studies are changing over. Equally, for some work on photosensitive epilepsy there has always been an animal analogue. This is a photosensitive Singhalese baboon, *Papio papio*. There is absolutely no reason to use this animal, because it is possible to locate where the occipital spikes occur with MEG. The only reason that it has been done in the animal in the past is that this is a good way of doing drug trials. But, since the mechanism is different in *Papio papio*, the incorrect answer could be obtained.

Acknowledgements

These studies would not have been possible without the support of the Dr Hadwen Trust for Humane Research, and Project A20/20 of the EC AIM Initiative. I am most grateful to the Aston MEG team, Steve Anderson, Paul Furlong, Fiona Fylan, Ian Holliday and Krish Singh. I am also grateful to the Dr Hadwen Trust for meeting the cost of the colour reproductions.

References

AHONEN, A. I., HÄMÄLÄINEN, M. S., KAJOLA, M. J., KNUUTILA, J. E. T., LOUNASMAA, O. V., SIMOLA, J. T., TESCHE, C. D. and VILKMAN, V. A., 1991, Multichannel SQUID systems for brain research, *IEEE Transactions Magazine*, **27**, 2786–92.

AINE, C. J., GEORGE, J., MEDVICK, P., SUPEK, S., FLYN, E. and BODIS-WOLLNER, I., 1989, Identification of multiple sources in transient visual evoked neuro-magnetic responses, in Williamson, S. J., Hoke, M., Stroink, G. and Kotani, M. (Eds) *Advances in Biomagnetism*, pp. 193–6. New York: Pergamon Press.

BARDEEN, J., COOPER, L. N. and SCHRIEFFER, J. R., 1957, Theory of superconductivity, *Physics Reviews*, **108**, 1175–204.

BAUMGARTNER, C., DOPPELBAUER, A., SUTHERLING, W. W., ZEITLHOFER, J., LINDINGER, G., LINDL, C. and DEECKE, L., 1991, Human somatosensory cortical finger representation as studied by combined neuromagnetic and neuroelectric measurements, *Neuroscience Letters*, **134**, 103–8.

BEDFORD, J. L. and HARDING, G. F. A., 1992, Dual analysis of visually evoked magnetic and electrical responses, in Dittmar, A. and Froment, J. C. (Eds) *Proceedings of Satellite Symposium on Neuroscience and Technology*, pp. 37–41. Annual International Conference, Lyon, France: IEEE Engineering Medical Biological Society.

BERGER, H., 1929, Über das elektrenkephalogrann des menschen, *Archiv für Psychiatrie und Nervenkrankheiten*, **87**, 527–70.

CAMPBELL, F. W. and ROBSON, J. G., 1968, Application of Fourier analysis to the visibility of gratings, *Journal of Physiology*, **197**, 551–66.

CHEYNE, D., KRISTEVA, R. and DEECKE, L., 1991, Humuncular organisation of human motor cortex as indicated by neuromagnetic recordings, *Neuroscience Letters*, **122**, 17–20.

COHEN, D., 1968, Magnetoencephalography: Evidence of magnetic fields produced by alpha rhythm currents, *Science*, **161**, 784–6.

1972, Magnetoencephalography: Detection of the brain's electrical activity with a superconducting magnetometer, *Science*, **175**, 664–6.

DAWSON, G. D., 1951, A summation technique for the detection of small signals in a large irregular background, *Journal of Physiology (London)*, **115**, 2–3P.

DE YOE, E. A. and VAN ESSEN, D., 1988, Concurrent processing streams in monkey visual cortex, *Trends in Neuroscience*, **11**, 219–26.

DEECKE, L., WEINBERG, H. and BRICKETT, P., 1982, Magnetic fields of the human brain accompanying voluntary movements: Bereitschafts-magnetfeld, *Experimental Brain Research*, **48**, 144–8.

FURLONG, P. L., WEALE, P., SINGH, K. D., HARDING, G. F. A. and CHAVDA, S., 1995, Magnetoencephalography and functional magnetic resonance imaging for presurgical evaluation, *Human Brain Mapping, Supplement 1*, New York: Wiley, p. 345.

FYLAN, F., HOLLIDAY, I. E., SINGH, K. D., ANDERSON, S. J. and HARDING, G. F. A., 1995a, Evoked magnetic responses to chromatic and luminance patterns differ in area V1 in humans, *Investigative Ophthalmology and Visual Science Supplement 1*, **36**, 1053.

1995b, Cortical origins of visual evoked magnetic responses differ in humans for chromatic and luminance stimuli, *Human Brain Mapping, Supplement 1*, New York: Wiley, 51.

GALLEN, C. C., SCHWARTZ, B., REIKE, K., PANTEV, C., SOBEL, D., HIRSCHKOFF, E., BLOOM, F. E., 1994, Intra-subject reliability and validity of somatosensory source localisation using a larger ray biomagnetometer. *Electroencephalography Clinical Neurophysiology*, **90**, 145–56.

GEVINS, A., LEE, J., MARTIN, N. K., BRICKETT, P., DESMOND, J. and RYTER, B., 1994, High resolution EEG: 124 channel recording, spatial deblurring and MRI integration methods, *Electroencephalography Clinical Neurophysiology*, **90**, 337–58.

HARDING, G. F. A., 1988, Neurophysiology of vision and its clinical application, in Edwards, K. and Llewellyn, R. (Eds) *Optometry 1988*, pp. 44–60, London: Butterworth.

1993, How surgeons could navigate the brain, *New Scientist*, **140** (1903), 28–31.

IOANNIDES, A. A., BOLTON, J. P. R., HASSEN, R. and CLARK, C. J. S., 1989, Localised and distributed source solutions for the biomagnetic inverse problem II, in Williamson, S. J., Hoke, M., Stroink, G. and Kotani, M. (Eds) *Advances in Biomagnetism*, pp. 591–4, New York: Pergamon Press.

JONES, L. A., HARDING, G. F. A. and SMITH, P. A., 1980, A comparison of auditory cortical evoked potentials, BSEPs and PAMPs in normals and patients with known auditory defects, in Barber, C. (Ed.) *Evoked Potentials*, pp. 337–444, Lancaster, UK: MTP Press.

KORNHUBER, H. H. and DEECKE, L., 1965, Hirnpotential änderungen bei willkürbewegungen und passiven bewegungen des menschen; bereitschaftspotential und reafferentepotentiale, *Pflügersarchive*, **284**, 1–17.

KOUIJZER, W. J. J., STOCK, C. J., REITS, D., DONAISKI, Z., LOPES DA SILVA, F. H. and PETERS, M. J., 1985, Neuromagnetic fields evoked by pattern on-offset stimulus, *IEEE Transactions on Biomedical Engineering*, **BME-32**, 455–8.

MACLIN, E., OKADA, Y. C., KAUFMAN, L. and WILLIAMSON, S. J., 1983, Retinotopic map on the visual cortex for acentrically placed patterns: first non-invasive measurement, *Nuovo Cimento*, **D2**, 410–19.

ONNES, H. K., 1911, *Leiden Comms.*, 124C.

PANTEV, C., HOKE, M., LEHNERTZ, K., LÜTKENHÖNER, B., ANOGIANNAKIS, G. and WITTKOWSKI, W., 1988, Tonotopic organisation of the human auditory cortex revealed by transient auditory evoked magnetic fields, *Electroencephalography Clinical Neurophysiology*, **69**, 160–70.

PANTEV, C., HOKE, M., LEHNERTZ, K., LÜTKENHÖNER, B., FAHRENDORF, G. and STÖBER, U., 1990, Identification of sources of brain neuronal activity with high spatio-temporal resolution through combination of neuro-magnetic source localisation (NMSL) and magnetic resonance imaging (MRI), *Electroencephalography Clinical Neurophysiology*, **75**, 173–84.

PAPANICOLAOU, A. C., BAUMANN, S., ROGERS, R. C., SAYDARI, C., AMPARO, E. G. and EISENBERG, H. M., 1990, Localisation of auditory response sources using magnetoencephalography and magnetic resonance imaging, *Clinical Neurophysiology*, **47**, 33–7.

PENFIELD, W. and JASPER, J., 1954, *Epilepsy and the Functional Anatomy of the Human Brain*, Boston, USA: Little Brown and Co.

PENFIELD, W. and RASMUSSEN, T., 1950, *The Cerebal Cortex of Man*, New York: Macmillan.

SCHERG, M., HARI, R. and HÄMÄLÄINEN, M., 1989, Frequency-specific sources of the auditory N19-P30-P50 response detected by multiple source analysis of evoked magnetic fields and potentials, in Williamson, S. J., Hoke, M., Stroink, G. and Kotani, M. (Eds) *Advances in Biomagnetism*, pp. 97–100, New York: Pergamon Press.

TEYLER, T. J., CUFFIN, B. N. and COHEN, D., 1975, The visual evoked magnetoencephalogram, *Life Science*, **17**, 683–92.

WATSON, J. D. G., FRACKOWIAK, R. S. J. and ZEKI, S. M., 1993, Functional separation of colour and motion centres in human visual cortex, in Gulyas, B., Ottoson, D. and Roland, P. E. (Eds) *Functional Organisation of the Human Visual Cortex*, pp. 317–28, Oxford, UK: Pergamon Press.

Williamson, S. J. and Kaufman, L., 1990, Evolution of neuromagnetic topographic mapping, *Brain Topography*, **3**, 113–27.

Wood, C. C., Cohen, D., Cuffin, B. N., Yarita, M. and Allison, T., 1985, Electrical sources in human somatosensory cortex: identified by combined magnetic and potential recordings, *Science*, **227**, 1051–3.

Yamamoto, T., Williamson, S. J., Kaufman, L., Nicholson, C. and Llinás, R., 1988, Magnetic localisation of neuronal activity in the human brain, *Proceedings of the National Academy of Sciences (USA)*, **85**, 8732–6.

Yang, T. T., Gallen, C. C., Schwartz, B. J. and Bloom, F. E., 1993, Non-invasive somatosensory humunculus mapping in humans by a large-array biomagnetometer, *Proceedings of the National Academy of Sciences (USA)*, **90**, 3098–102.

Zeki, S., 1969, Representation of central visual fields in pre-striate cortex of monkey, *Brain Research*, **14**, 271–91.

Zeki, S. M., 1993, *A Vision of the Brain*, Oxford, UK: Blackwell Scientific Publications.

Zeki, S. M. and Shipp, S., 1988, The functional logic of cortical connections, *Nature*, **335**, 311–17.

16

Pharmacokinetic and Pharmacodynamic Assessment in Early Drug Development – Current Approaches and Future Developments

STEPHEN TOON

Pharmacokinetic and pharmacodynamic assessment forms a fundamental component of the early clinical evaluation of new medicines. This chapter focuses on the use of healthy volunteers and patients to obtain such measurements and discusses how this information should be used, in conjunction with pre-clinical animal data, in making decisions on drug efficacy and safety.

Phase I volunteers (i.e. normal healthy volunteers) play an important role in the drug development process, sitting as they do between pre-clinical evaluation in animals and the assessment of new medicines in the targeted patient population. There is much ethical concern and debate about the use of animals in pre-clinical evaluation. There are also concerns however about the patient, as it is of paramount importance that the chance of new medicines reaching the market with unanticipated side effects or other problems is minimal.

In clinical development it is essential that responsible scientists and physicians maximise the amount of relevant information that is obtained from the Phase I programme. Certainly pharmacokinetics and pharmacodynamics have very important roles to play at this stage in the development of a new medicine. Pharmacokinetic information can be used to relate the administered dose to the systemic concentration at any point in time post-dosing. These concentrations can in turn be related to observed efficacy and to any observed toxicity. Pharmacokinetic information is important for turning drugs into medicines by impacting upon formulation design and, through rigorous and detailed evaluation in Phase I, for enabling us to anticipate any clinical problems that may arise later on in the development programme.

Having established the pharmacological activity of a drug, the primary objective in the drug development programme is to identify and quantify potential sources of variability, as it is at the extremes of any such variability that lack of effect and toxicity can arise. In many respects, the development programme is comprised of specific studies aimed at quantifying and identifying these sources of variability. Such an approach seems an eminently suitable and sensible way in which to go about developing a medicine, but occasionally medicines do get onto the marketplace and to the patient, only to exhibit unpredicted toxicities, or other problems. So what are the flaws in such a developmental strategy? Undoubtedly, part of the problem is the extrapolation of pre-clinical observations in animals through to man – in other words, problems with interspecies differences. Additionally, there are problems in extrapolating observations that are made in non-patient volunteers through to patients *per se*.

So how can the above problems be overcome? More often than not, the first study in humans is of a dose-escalation design. Typically, the study would aim to assess the tolerability to a new drug at six dose levels, with each dose being evaluated in a group of six healthy young male volunteers, four of whom would receive active drug, and two the placebo. The first dose is selected from pre-clinical toxicological observations and can equate to one tenth of the no-effect dose in the most toxicologically sensitive animal. Following each dose administration, rigorous analysis of tolerability, clinical chemistry and ideally pharmacokinetic data is undertaken before proceeding to the next dose. Such a study can go to completion (i.e. administration of all six dose levels) or it could be curtailed due to adverse events or to a realisation that clinical effectiveness is likely to occur at a lower dose than initially anticipated. This design also allows one to gain an initial evaluation of inter-subject variability in response and pharmacokinetics. A more robust design is one where each individual receives more than one dose of the drug. A typical format for such a study again would involve six dose levels, but demands two groups of nine volunteers. Within each group of nine, six would receive alternating doses within the escalation (i.e. group 1 would receive dose levels 1, 3 and 5, and group 2 would be administered dose levels 2, 4 and 6). Within each group of nine, placebo would be randomly allocated to three volunteers such that on study completion each volunteer would have received two active doses plus placebo. This design is far more robust than that initially described as it enables multiple observations in any one given individual to be made, and thereby allows an assessment of intra-subject variability. Moreover, if one has been sufficiently foresighted and has gathered both pharmacokinetic and pharmacodynamic data from the study, then an initial feeling for the shape of the concentration-pharmacological response surface can be gained.

While historically the first studies in humans were designed to simply assess the tolerability of a new drug in the healthy volunteer, such objectives are indeed very limited. With the availability of sophisticated methods for non-invasive measurement of the pharmacological response, results from early quantitative pharmacological assessment, related to *in vivo* drug concentrations, enable one to make considerable advances in understanding how drugs behave in humans. Early pharmacokinetic evaluation can also provide other important information. In the first human studies it is likely that the range of dose levels investigated will not be studied again within the entire development programme. This is an ideal opportunity to estimate the extent of non-linearity in the pharmacokinetics (i.e. an indication of any disproportionality between dose and systemic concentration). Early pharmacokinetic evaluation in humans enables the identification of similarities between humans and the animal species that have been used in pre-clinical evaluation. This in turn allows one to determine the more relevant species for use in longer-term toxicology studies. Pre-clinical toxicological evaluation has historically been based on dose–response relationships. If, however, observed toxicity is related to dose some quite drastic assumptions have to be made. Given that dose–toxicity assessments are conventionally undertaken following extravascular administration (normally oral), then without a knowledge of systemic concentration, one has to assume complete availability (i.e. that the entire dose being administered is entering the systemic circulation). Similarly, if toxicity is being assessed over a wide dose range, then without quantifying systemic concentration, a proportionality between dose and toxicity has to be assumed. The major problem is that, when a lack of effect or no toxicity is observed, it is unclear if this is really due to a true inactivity of the molecule, to poor absorption or to a very high first-pass metabolic loss.

In relation to the typical medicine consumer, the issues of intraspecies comparisons and extrapolation from the young healthy volunteer to the patient are important considerations. The typical medicine consumer is often ill, and therefore he or she could have some abnormal underlying physiology. Often such individuals are receiving multiple drug therapy. So the typical medicine consumer is the antithesis of the typical Phase I volunteer, who is more often than not male (although this is changing quite radically now), Caucasian, young (between the ages of 18 and 35 years), within strict boundaries of weight for height, with normal haematology and biochemistry, not receiving medication, mostly a non-smoker with no unusual dietary habits. This, therefore, raises the question as to what relevance data gathered in the Phase I programme can have to the patient population. As stated earlier, one of the primary objectives in medicines development is the identification and quantification of sources of variability in drug response. If this is really what is required, then measurements have to be made against relatively invariant basal observations. For instance, if an answer to the question, 'Does gender have an effect on the pharmacokinetics for a particular drug?', is required then it is necessary to initiate a study in which a group of males and a group of females take a dose of the drug and subsequently undergo pharmacokinetic evaluation. Statistical comparison between the pharmacokinetic parameters associated with the two groups would then be made. If subsequently it was found that within each group there were individuals of wide weight range, of different ethnic backgrounds receiving multiple therapy as well as smokers and non-smokers, then this would confound attempts to address the specific point above, as to whether gender has, as opposed to the other variables, affected the pharmacokinetics of the drug. The Phase I volunteer can, therefore, be considered to provide the human pharmacological baseline, against which therapeutic and pharmaceutical variability can be quantified.

In the context of the practical development of a new medicine, how does one progress from the normal volunteer through to the patient? It is well known that there are many factors which potentially affect drug response and pharmacokinetics. These factors include, in particular, diet, gender, concomitant medication and age. Specific studies could therefore be undertaken to identify and quantify those potential sources of variability which might have a real effect. Any clinical development plan, however, has to be based on sound scientific and clinical reasoning. Unfortunately, there are occasions when modulations and adjustments are made because of political or public pressure. While such changes are often well intentioned their implementation is often founded on emotion, rather than on scientific reasoning. As a consequence, they can impede, rather than aid, clinical development. Partly in response to unanticipated adverse events in elderly patients receiving the new NSAID benoxaprofen, it was deemed appropriate that a detailed Phase I pharmacokinetic study should be performed in elderly volunteers, if a drug is specifically targeted for the elderly population. There are some concerns with this approach. For instance, in terms of pharmacokinetics and drug response, it is not easy to decide if someone is old, and what the characteristics are of such individuals. A typical set of inclusion criteria for an elderly volunteer study would indicate that such individuals are over the age of 65, that they have no history of any clinically relevant disease, are generally healthy, in good physical condition and are without any significant medical problem. These individuals are able to understand the nature of the study and any hazard relating to their participation (i.e. they are able to give informed consent), and are not in need of any other medication. It is likely, however, that most people would feel these criteria do not typify the average geriatric patient or the average elderly person for the reasons given above.

With regard to the use of elderly patients, in a study that was undertaken by Medeval a few years ago (Toon *et al.*, 1987), the pharmacokinetics of a new antibiotic were being investigated in elderly male volunteers. As the drug was primarily eliminated by the kidneys, the influence of renal function on drug clearance was evaluated. A linear correlation between renal clearance and glomerular filtration rate (GFR) was found. Even though all six volunteers participating in the study were over 65 years of age, three of the individuals had renal function of people half their age. Thus, chronological ageing and physiological ageing are not necessarily the same. From the pharmacokinetic and therapeutic point of view, it is physiological ageing that is likely to cause clinical problems, and of concern is the fact that the conventional approach to recruiting healthy elderly volunteers for Phase I programmes is likely to bias these studies to those individuals who are chronologically, but not necessarily physiologically, old. It is important to see beyond this potential problem, otherwise the results of studies will be undertaken in the targeted geriatric patient probably with more confidence than is merited from the available data.

Clearly then, extrapolation of observations from the normal volunteer to the patient has to be undertaken with care. It could be argued that, if there is a problem with extrapolating observations from the normal volunteer to the patient, why should not all studies be undertaken directly in the targeted patient group? Indeed, for some medicines this has to be done. Thus, for some cytotoxic agents and certain immunosuppressants, it is necessary to study the pharmacokinetics and to obtain a primary evaluation of the pharmacology of the drug in the targeted patient group. Interpretation of pharmacokinetics and basal pharmacology of new chemical entities in such patients is no mean task, and certainly could be compromised by the presence of underlying disease and/or multiple drug therapy.

With progression from Phase I through to Phase III of the clinical development programme, participating volunteers more closely resemble the targeted patient group. Perhaps, therefore, ways of undertaking pharmacokinetic evaluation in the Phase III programme should be investigated. Pharmacokinetics are assessed conventionally in a relatively small number of homogenous individuals, by making a relatively large number of drug concentration measurements. Following pharmacokinetic analysis, pharmacokinetic parameters are summarised using descriptive statistics. If a comparison between different groups is required, for example a group of males and a group of females, a statistical comparison between the two groups is undertaken to ask if there was a significant gender effect on the pharmacokinetics of the compound. This conventional approach is known as the standard two-stage method, and it represents a data-rich situation, consisting of many observations in relatively few homogenous individuals, with variability quantified by use of conventional statistical methods.

Normally, many hundreds of patients are used in the Phase III programme, and therefore it would obviously not be practical to do a full pharmacokinetic evaluation with every patient. It may be possible, however, to take a few (1–5) post-dosing blood samples from such individuals as they attend outpatient clinics. A database can therefore be constructed that is made up from relatively few observations taken from a large number of the targeted patient group. Such data are known as sparse observational data. By applying sophisticated statistical procedures to these data, a pharmacokinetic model for the drug in the targeted patient population can be developed. Part of the problem in generating such a model based on sparse data, is that one cannot assess the variability in the pharmacokinetic data within the population in a conventional manner. Population pharmacokinetics, as the method is known, simultaneously provide both estimates of the pharmacokinetic parameters and also estimates of the variability of these parameters within the population *per se*. Undertaking population pharmacokinetics, therefore, affords the possibility of obtaining general pharmacokinetic and response information from sparse observational data within the targeted patient group. Moreover, it provides confidence limits which can be placed around the predicted plasma drug concentration-time profile within a given population group, which in turn enable an identification of concentrations that fall outside the predicted boundaries of variability. The question can then be asked, what is it in these individuals that is giving rise to these abnormal concentrations that could in turn be ineffective (lower than predicted) or toxic (higher than predicted)? Application of population analysis allows this to be extended, and a covariate analysis to be undertaken to look at the underlying characteristics of the patients that are yielding these unanticipated observations. Also, this might enable an identification of subgroups within the population that could be at risk from higher, or lower than anticipated, drug concentrations arising from a standard dosing regimen.

Population pharmacokinetics has been seen by some as replacing the need to undertake conventional pharmacokinetic analysis in the Phase I environment. This is not so. Successful population analysis depends heavily upon our ability to provide reliable initial estimates for the model parameters, and such estimates are most readily obtained from rigorous pharmacokinetic evaluation in the normal healthy volunteer. Additionally, even though population analysis can identify potential clinical conditions that unexpectedly impact upon pharmacokinetics, only a conventional and detailed pharmacokinetic evaluation of the drug in such individuals will provide data of sufficient detail as to afford an understanding of the underlying basis of the observation.

Summary and Conclusions

In conclusion, as responsible scientists and clinicians, it is our duty to maximise the amount of relevant information gathered from volunteer studies. We should recognise that such individuals are receiving no therapeutic benefit from participating in these investigations, but that they indeed have a pivotal role to play. We have, therefore, to design good studies, and to analyse these studies rigorously to yield the maximum amount of relevant information to facilitate logical clinical development of the new medicine. While medicines development is necessarily undertaken in a piecemeal fashion, the overall objective should always be kept in mind when designing specific studies. It is imperative that studies are designed to answer a specific question, and not to try to answer every question in a single go. At the same time, however, it is most important to keep in mind the overall development objective, and why it is that such studies are being performed in the first place. Early assessment of pharmacokinetics enables a drug to be turned into a medicine and it might allow the anticipation of problems, both pharmaceutical and clinical, that could occur later on in the development programme. Every attempt should be made to assess the concentration response surface at an early stage. With the availability of sophisticated non-invasive methodology to facilitate the quantification of certain types of pharmacological response even in volunteers, it is important not to compromise such techniques by trying to simply relate pharmacological observations to dose alone. Population analysis will obviously have an important role to play in medicines development. It is a formidable tool to add to the existing statistical armamentarium, but it will only realise its full potential when applied prospectively to appropriately designed studies. Successful population pharmacokinetic analysis necessitates a good understanding of the basic pharmacokinetics of the compound in question. Finally, in population analysis, sparse data do not mean *ad hoc* data. They are observational data (i.e. blood samples) taken from individuals as they come into the clinics, but it is essential we know the relationship between those samples and the time the drug was ingested. In other words, observational data are gathered according to a strict protocol; the quality of such data is of paramount importance.

The welfare of the non-patient volunteer, participating in the drug development programme, is of overriding importance. Of no lesser importance, however, is our duty to ensure that the studies in which they participate are appropriately designed, analysed and interpreted. The dilemma facing the drug developer is, therefore, extrapolating observations made in animal models through to human volunteers, and in turn through to human patients. The solution has to lie with well-planned and executed studies.

Discussion

It could be argued that undertaking pharmacokinetics is not always a good way of establishing efficacy and toxicity of a drug.

For example, if one looks at the efficacy of a drug like Warfarin, subjects with the same INR might have approximately a thirtyfold variation in the blood levels. Thus, there can be much more to efficacy than just the blood level of a drug. Thus the pharmacodynamics of drug receptor interaction is important. Nevertheless, understanding the pharmacokinetics of a drug is important in relating dose to systemic concentration, and in relating that concentration through to effect and for observing variability in response. This should also be coupled with good pharmacodynamic measures, where they exist, such as the INR, which can help to interpret pharmacodynamic data. Obviously, drug efficacy cannot be studied by investigating pharmacokinetics alone. It is merely a tool to relate dose to response and is only part of the picture. Pharmacokinetic information is not just concerned with determining plasma levels, it also provides information about systemic and target organ concentrations.

The issue of subject variability is very important and much neglected and involves the effects of genetic polymorphisms on drug response. In prospective studies, however, variability might not be important if the therapeutic window is very wide.

This is a problem which is encountered clinically, and if the therapeutic window is very wide, the problem can be ignored, but not so if it is narrow. It should be possible to routinely use information from studies on molecular pharmacology and metabolising enzymes at an early stage in the drug development plan. Also, at the Phase I stage it is becoming possible to genotype individuals for their metabolism of certain drugs, using only a small amount of blood.

Reference

Toon, S., Hopkins, K. J., Garstang, F. M., Aarons, L. and Rowland, M., 1987, Pharmacokinetics of imipenem and cilastatin after their simultaneous administration to the elderly, *British Journal of Clinical Pharmacology*, **23**, 143–9.

17

The European Dimension

INGRID KLINGMANN

This chapter provides an overview of the recommendations for the use of volunteers for research and testing in several European countries including France, Germany, the UK, Belgium and Spain. The situation in the new Member States, Sweden and Austria, is also described.

In the European general situation, the need to explain the different roles and constitutions of ethics committees in Europe stems from the fact that the CPMP Note for Guidance, Good Clinical Practice for Trials on Medicinal Products in the European Community (CPMP, 1990), requests the use of ethics committees but is not legally binding. It merely describes the state of the art. However, EU Directive 91/507/EEC (Commission of the European Communities, 1991) of July 19, 1991, requires that every clinical trial of whatever phase is performed according to Good Clinical Practice Standards, that is, according to the Note for Guidance. Such directives are legally binding and must be incorporated into national law. Hence, there are considerable variations in the approaches to ethics committees taken by EU member states, many of them arising from the way in which the Note for Guidance is worded.

The use of ethics committees is defined in Chapter 1 of the Note for Guidance. 'The Sponsor and/or Investigator must request the opinion of relevant Ethics Committee(s) regarding suitability of clinical trial protocols (including annexes) and of the methods and material to be used in obtaining and documenting Informed Consent of the subjects.' Here, Member States have differed on whether both sponsor and investigator should request an opinion or whether it falls to one or the other. There are also differences in interpretation of the exact meaning of 'opinion' and in determining which is the 'relevant' committee. The Note continues: 'Subjects must not be entered into the trial until the relevant Ethics Committee(s) has issued a favourable opinion on the procedures and documentation. Sponsor/Investigator should consider recommendations made by the Ethics Committee(s).' In this paragraph there is also considerable scope for variation.

Even the definition of an ethics committee is open to debate as the Commission acknowledges in the glossary to the Note that an ethics committee is 'an independent body, constituted by medical professionals and non-medical members'. It also includes the statement: 'The legal status, constitution and regulatory requirements pertaining to Ethics Committees, Review Boards or similar institutions may differ among countries'.

Each European country, except Italy, has adopted the EU directive. In Denmark, France, Ireland, Germany, Greece, The Netherlands and Spain it has been translated into national law. In Belgium and the UK it exists in the form of guidelines. In Italy ethics committees are in practice always consulted, although as yet they are not mandatory.

National approaches to the establishment of ethics committees vary from being centralised to being decentralised. Germany, for instance, has one ethics committee established in each local medical council, and in each medical faculty. One or two medical councils exist in each Bundesland, and thus there are only 58 committees in the entire country. France has one ethics committee for each of the 83 regions, with 40 of them in Paris. Belgium, with a population of only 9 000 000, has 112 ethics committees associated with hospitals or local physicians groups. There are, however, concerns that countries with large numbers of ethics committees will have difficulty in ensuring that each has the same level of knowledge and experience.

Ethics committees in France are governed by legislation passed in 1980, which was amended in 1991. The health ministry authorises committees and designates the number per region. Members are named by the government representative in each region, drawn at random from individuals nominated by authorised organisations such as large hospitals, consumer organisations, the National College of Physicians, churches and legal authorities.

Some important practical issues are clearly defined by the French government. For instance, the health ministry sets the rate of duty paid by the sponsor, which helps to finance the costs for operating the system. The duty is set at a lower level for individuals and for non-commercial organisations that wish to sponsor trials. It is however the investigator, not the sponsor, who formally applies for an opinion. Twenty-four members are required to sit on an ethics committee in France, of which half are permanent members and the other half are alternate members. Six members are required at a meeting before a vote can take place. Of the total membership, one third must be experienced researchers, one third other health professions (e.g. GPs, pharmacists and nurses) and the remaining third should be qualified in ethics, social work, psychology or law.

An advantage for conducting multi-centre clinical trials in France is that principal investigators can consult any committee sitting in their region, and that only one favourable vote, issued as an opinion and not a decision, is required. That opinion is then given officially to other investigators involved in the trial, with the relevant committees merely informed rather than being consulted. In the case of an unfavourable opinion, the committee informs the health ministry, which has two months to prohibit the study from being conducted. If the ministry does not respond within two months, the trial study can go ahead. This contrasts with the situation in Belgium, Ireland, The Netherlands, Spain and Germany (the latter since August 1995), in which *positive* opinions must also be submitted to the respective health ministries. In Denmark, the drug agency itself scrutinises the ethics of a trial.

In Germany, rules governing ethics committees are in a state of transition, and the situation is consequently complex. Until 17 August 1995, committees have not been required by national law. However, the German physicians' code of conduct requires that any physician who wishes to take part in a clinical trial must be advised by an ethics committee. Under new legislation, known as the Fifth Amendment which was passed in August 1994, the situation is different. The new law, which came into force in August 1995, makes ethical assessment of clinical trials mandatory. Each investigator agreeing to participate in a clinical trial must receive a favourable opinion from the respective local ethics committee. It was not the intention of legislators to cover GCP issues when drafting the Fifth Amendment, but they were forced to include the 1991 Directive following pressure from Brussels and at home.

As a consequence, the hastily adopted Fifth Amendment has left several areas unclear in Germany. For example, it calls for ethics committees to be constituted according to the law of their relevant Bundesland, few of which currently have these laws in place to govern committees established by the local medical council or university. It is unclear whether other ethics committees, accredited by the Bundesland, will be acceptable.

Ethics committees in Germany are appointed by the board of the local Medical Council, or Faculty of Medicine. They must have a minimum of five members, of whom four must be physicians. Two of these should be experienced clinicians, one an expert in theoretical medicine, and the other must have knowledge of legal medicine. It can happen that there are no women on German ethics committees, and consumer organisations do not have the right of representation. If required, experts can be invited to give information, but they do not have the right to vote. Individual ethics committees decide on the fees to be paid by the sponsor. Details of a trial including the names of investigators, protocol and the votes of committees must be submitted to the health authority before the trial can commence. If there is a positive opinion, the study can be started after confirmation of the health authorities that the documentation has been received and is complete. If there is a negative opinion, or one negative opinion amongst positive opinions, health authorities can reject the study within 60 days.

In contrast to the Drug Law Amendment, the recently changed German law for Medicinal Products requires that a favourable opinion for the principal investigator alone is sufficient in multi-centre trials. Those ethics committees of other participating investigators only need to get this single vote for information.

Ethics committees in Belgium are covered by legislation passed in 1992. Committees have eight members, the majority physicians, with at least one lay member. Committees must have both male and female members. Belgium is the only Member State which has the added requirement that at least one physician per committee must be independent from the committee it works with. Belgium also is more explicit than many countries in laying down the way in which a vote must work. A two-thirds majority is required for a favourable opinion.

Spain incorporated the CPMP Note for Guidance into its national law in 1993. Ethics committees are accredited by health authorities in each autonomous community, which must then inform the General Directorate of Pharmacy and Health Products, with the Ministry of Health and Consumer Affairs, of the sphere of action of the committee and its method of selection.

Clinical trials in Spain require the authority of the Directorate as well as the corresponding ethics committee. However, in trials involving drugs which are already registered in Spain for other indications all that is necessary is for one application to be made to the committee. If there is a favourable opinion, the committee must send the documentation and vote to the Directorate. The application must come from the sponsor but the principal investigator must sign this and then report regularly to the committee. In the case of an unfavourable opinion, the health authority has 60 days to raise objections and to obtain comments from the sponsor, with a further 30 days to reject it.

Spanish ethics committees have a minimum of seven members, five of whom must be present for a vote. Two must be laymen and there must be some physicians, one a clinical pharmacologist as well as a hospital pharmacist and a nurse. Unlike many other countries, there is no charge to the sponsor. Neither the ethics committee nor any of its members are allowed to receive any remuneration directly or indirectly from the sponsor.

A comparison of the requirements for ethics committee review procedures in laws and guidelines in France, Belgium, UK, Germany, Spain, Ireland, Japan, Australia and the USA, shows that the guidelines from the World Health Organisation (WHO), the Council for International Organisations of Medical Science (CIOMS) and the GCP Note for Guidance all suggest that ethics committees should comment on risk–benefit, the adequacy and size of the investigation, insurance and indemnity and any adverse events. Patient information and consent are also important in all the above cases. Payments to patients, volunteers, investigators, institutions or government agencies are mentioned in all the requirements except those for Japan. All guidelines, except those for Spain and Japan, refer to the patient's right to privacy and confidentiality. Only in guidelines for the UK, Nordic countries, Australia and the WHO and CIOMS recommendations, is any reference made to the science of the protocol. UK and CIOMS guidelines recommend that committees should look at publication agreements.

Only in Spain does the law give detailed instructions of the constitution, organisation and performance of ethics committees. In the UK, various organisations have put forward proposals for Standard Operating Procedures (SOPs (Royal College of Physicans, 1990)), but there has been little progress on this issue made elsewhere in the EU. In the absence of any initiative from the European Commission or Member States, impetus for harmonisation is likely to come from individual scientists upwards. The draft SOP proposal for ethics committees of the European Forum for Good Clinical Practice (EFGCP), which calls for minimum standards and requirements, aims for the harmonisation at least of the organisation and performance of ethics committees so that multi-centre clinical trials can be handled in a more efficient way, and also in order that patients across Europe receive similar security and ethical considerations. Adoption of this draft proposal will accelerate drug development, thus providing new treatments to patients at an earlier stage.

Summary and Conclusions

Thus, the composition of ethics committees varies from country to country, and members are appointed by different bodies or institutions, although the tasks of the committees are more or less clearly defined. The application process requires much administrative effort, and approval procedure is handled individually by every ethics committee; very often it is not defined in the SOP. Follow-up requirements for long-term studies and for serious adverse effects are of varying importance to the different ethics committees within the EU. Directive 91/507/EEC is having an increasing influence on the manner in which ethics committees operate throughout the European Union.

Discussion

If a non-patient or patient volunteer comes to permanent harm as a result of taking a drug then the possibility of compensation arises. He or she is likely to sue the investigator, hospital and anyone else connected in any way with the study. The question is whether members of ethical committees are open to such action and, if so, how they are indemnified.

If an ethics committee gives a positive opinion and subsequently something goes wrong this is a very critical point, and is the reason why all ethics committees would normally insist on giving an opinion and not an approval, in order to reduce any risk of liability. This might be handled differently according to country, but it is unlikely that individual assurance exists. However, there is no record of any member of an ethics committee having been sued in connection with a study.

Under the terms of UK guidelines, district health authorities are encouraged to offer indemnity to all members of local research ethics committees in respect of the work that they do as members of LRECs. Anyone on an LREC who is already employed by the organisation is covered by the arrangements for clinical negligence indemnity in respect of any negligent harm that occurs to anyone as a result of participating in any trial that the committee has passed. Negligence is the only thing that is covered. There is no legal liability for non-negligent harm. If there was any question of someone being sued for negligence, there are far more likely individuals, such as the person who actually perpetrated the negligent act, who will be sued long before anyone goes to an ethics committee.

In the rest of Europe, however, there is a considerable uncertainty for ethics committee members as to their situation. This problem arose during discussions at the European Forum, when the question was raised as to whether the members of ethics committees should be publicly known. There are some countries which require publication of the membership lists. There are many good reasons why it would be very helpful to have easy access to these names. There is a very strong resistance in several countries for leaving this situation anonymous, because committee members are afraid of liability.

Payment for participation in ethics committees may complicate the issue of liability, as it could lead to claims of corruption, particularly if the money comes from the company involved, rather than from an independent third party.

It is likely that most ethics committees have a system in which sponsor money goes into one account, and is then distributed to the different members of the ethics committees according to the amount of work or time they spent for the meetings, or the preparations for the meetings. It is unclear whether in some countries there is any direct payment from the sponsor to the ethics committee members, which might influence a decision. This problem is likely to be the good reason why the Spanish government decided that no financial payments at all should be made.

References

Commission of the European Communities, 1991, *EEC Directive 91/507/EEC, relating to the Marketing Authorization for Medicinal Products for Human Use*, O.J. No. L270 of 26.6.91, Brussels: Commission of the European Communities.

CPMP, 1990, *CPMP Note for Guidance: Good Clinical Practice for Trials on Medicinal Products in the European Community*, Brussels: Commission of the European Communities, p 57.

Royal College of Physicians, 1990, *Guidelines on the Practice of Ethics Committees in Medical Research Involving Human Subjects*, London: Royal College of Physicians.

18

The Future of Ethics Committees

JOE COLLIER

This chapter presents the views of someone who is neither an ethicist, nor currently a member of an ethical committee, but who is nevertheless someone who can act as an interested lay person and raise some important questions which require answers. Such questions have been prompted by my experience as a clinician, from editing a bulletin (*Drugs and Therapeutics Bulletin*) and from my previous experience of sitting on the ethics committee of St George's Hospital, London. Ethics committees are now known as Research Ethics Committees. It is unclear whether this change in name was due to a political decision, but it was clearly an important change since in practice they act as research review committees with almost no expertise on ethics and consequently cannot function correctly in the way that the hospital community and patients would wish for.

Nevertheless, ethics committees have altered considerably. In the 1970s the ethics committee at St George's hospital used to sanction requests almost solely on the basis of the personalities involved. It took several years in the early 1980s to rectify this situation and required the committee to produce guidelines and terms of reference. The result was that almost immediately a 95 per cent initial acceptance rate was reduced to 5 per cent, although the situation has improved gradually, due to increased understanding of the issues involved.

Any hospital needs access to both research review and ethics committees, perhaps combined as a research ethics committee. Use of the phrase 'ethics committee', however, raises real problems, as within them real ethical issues are rarely addressed by trained ethicists. In more developed countries like France, the USA and Australia, bioethics committees exist with a clear background in ethical issues. While in the UK research review committees can deal with many of the issues raised by applicants wishing to do research, there is no easy way of tackling the time issue of ethics. Nevertheless, the two functions should be kept separate.

The committee at St George's Hospital has 12 members, with one of the two lay members in the chair. Other members include a nurse, pharmacist, surgeon, physician, general practitioner, clinical pharmacologist, obstetrician, member of the church, psychiatrist, and a member of the public health service, to comply with the requirements of the Department of Health (DoH). There is, however, no one who is strictly a trained ethicist and who truly understands all of the principles involved, despite all members being caring and educated individuals. Of all the developed countries, only France seems to require expertise on ethics. Thus, guidelines in France require that one third of the people available to sit on ethics committees should be trained in ethics, social work or a related subject. On the contrary, in the UK there is no requirement to have members with such backgrounds, although outsiders may be co-opted. Thus, the DoH booklet on ethics committees states that the committee should have hospital medical staff, nursing staff, general practitioners, two or more lay persons and 'co-opted members to cover ethical or other issues beyond the core of members' expertise'.

The ethics committee at St George's is accountable to and appointed by the district health authority. It is autonomous, meets monthly and takes decisions which are unlikely to be overturned by the health authority. Every health authority has a similar committee, which means that several hundred such committees exist, with a concomitant duplication of work, and time wasting for members and applicants alike.

Somehow, such duplication needs tackling. There needs to be more integration in the organisation and operation of ethics committees. This will require the use of common guidelines and application forms, as well as reciprocal arrangements for recognising approval from other committees, especially those for multicentre trials. If 10 applications are being assessed at St George's for a multicentre trial, then it follows that applications for these same trials are being filed all over the country. This causes an unnecessary burden on the community. It is important to reduce the time spent vetting and writing duplicate applications. More centralised and reciprocal arrangements are needed. This will be made easier in part by having a standardised application form.

In my view, ethics committees should become closely integrated into the whole medical system. The committee at St George's is closely integrated with the Drug and Therapeutics Committee (DTC). No drug can be stocked or dispensed, therefore, without the prior approval of one of these two committees. Moreover, the two share some common membership with the clinical pharmacologist on both. I believe such close integration is essential. In the absence of such an arrangement, drug use is no longer controlled and so neither the requirements of the ethics committee or the DTC can be met. If nothing else, such integration allows for more efficient policing of pharmacies.

There is also a need for openness in the working of the ethics committees. Every year or so the LREC produces a booklet about 15 or 16 pages long, in which the names of all the members are published. This valuable information indicates what is expected of applicants in the various areas of the submission form, together with the terms of reference. The booklet is freely available and is recommended reading. It is designed for the members of staff at St George's, and aims to 'facilitate medical research in the interest of humankind, protect subjects of research of possible harm and preserve their rights, protect research workers from unjustified attack'. It also states that approval of the committee is a legal requirement prior to embarking on a trial. In fact it is only a quasi-legal requirement in terms of the DoH itself, and certainly severe consequences could arise, probably also with the DoH, if a study proceeded without the correct authorisation.

Surely the statement, 'facilitate medical research in the interest of humankind', is a potent reminder of the ethical considerations that need to be taken by the committee, and yet members have little formal knowledge or training in ethical issues. The phrase, 'in the interest of humankind' has little or no meaning to a physician. These are complex ethical issues, yet there are no ethicists on the committee to consider them. It is expected that the committee 'protects subjects of research of possible harm and preserve their rights'. Now the word 'rights', as used here, does not refer to medicine, but to ethics. Again, the phrase, 'unjustified attack', is an ethical issue, as an attack may be justifiable under certain circumstances. Thus, hospitals are establishing ethics committees, which are making judgements around ethical issues but for which members do not have the necessary expertise. What they are very competent to do is to look at the research issue, the actual trial, the data, questions relating to the competence of the researcher, also to question the scientific aims and objectives, and whether the results will be useful and publishable. What these LRECs cannot do at present, is to consider important ethical issues properly, despite the very real need for hospitals to have decisions relating to such issues taken. As a consequence, both hospitals and patients are being failed.

When the definitions for ethics committees, set by the DoH, are considered, it becomes even more obvious that ethics is a crucial component of the issues that these committees should be discussing. Ethics is the study of morals, and morality can be defined as the rules of conduct and bad conduct. Morality therefore governs the way people treat each other. If an individual hits someone else, it could be seen as either ethical or unethical, but this analysis is complicated by the fact that an act is morally good if it has the good of humanity as its objective. Thus, if a needle is inserted into someone's forearm in the course of undertaking a study, but actually the desired end-point is obvious discomfort and pain to the subject, that could be considered to be unethical. If, however, this reason is not declared the act may well be deemed to be ethical. If the patient is informed that the study is being conducted to develop a particular research field and receive money from a sponsor, most patients would consider the work unethical. If this situation was not revealed, and yet sponsorship was forthcoming, then it would probably be seen as legitimate. These are real dilemmas, which cannot be tackled without the input of an ethicist. Using people as an end in itself is unethical, but this position is not necessarily realistic as in reality some people inevitably have to suffer for the good of the greater majority. Some would maintain that is ethical. Solutions to these problems are complex, but they have to be resolved, but difficulties arise because of the general absence of trained ethicists on committees.

It has to be recognised that ethics is a specialised subject with an academic base. I suspect that the English do not really understand this. In France an understanding of ethical issues is widespread, with ethics being taught at intermediate and higher levels in secondary schools. On the other hand, in England ethics and philosophy are subjects considered to be obscure and best avoided. In England, by co-opting extra members ethical issues in ethics committees are tackled. As a consequence, it would not be surprising to find very few committees with ethicists involved.

Ethical issues cannot be resolved by nice people thinking together. This is a dilemma, however, as ethicists assert that they do not resolve problems, but just raise questions. So a trained ethicist would be present at discussions, to allow other responsible committee members to resolve issues. The trouble is they are not there at all and these important issues will not be resolved satisfactorily, despite the extensive efforts of others.

It is important to remember that ethics and law are not synonymous, although they share some features. Thus, whilst laws can change overnight, ethics are more general and intransigent. Thus, the presence of a lawyer on a committee will cover legal problems, but not ethical ones, especially if the lawyer is a forensic physician.

According to the DoH booklet, a committee has to think about whether the scientific merit of the proposal has been properly assessed. It is, however, very difficult to undertand precisely the meaning of the phrase, scientific merit. This is a really difficult issue, since it is unclear whether society demands that the clinical trial must show some effect before it is considered or that it cannot proceed if a literature analysis has not been undertaken to establish whether the same subject has not been previously studied. This is a really crucial issue, since no one can afford to have patients put at risk in a repeat trial or in one that will not proceed properly. This is an important, potential ethical problem about which an LREC might have to come to a decision. One way to resolve questions about money, independence, risk and potential benefit, is by ensuring that the proper procedures are being used for obtaining consent because if all the issues are spelled out to the potential volunteer, he or she can make an informed decision and that allows them to share the burden of decision making. Moreover, members of the committee are well placed to judge the consent form.

There are two features of ethics committees which require improvement.

First, there must be trained ethicists on the committee that deals with research and secondly, there should be a (bio)ethics committee dealing with other matters. Clearly ethicists will be needed on the bioethics committee to help tackle institutional and individual dilemmas such as confidentiality, policies on organ transplantation, screening and resuscitation, as well as conflicts of interest. In my view the days of the LREC, as it is now, are numbered. Essentially it is necessary to acknowledge directly that the predominant work of this particular committee involves reviewing research. In such a research review committee there must also be ethicists, but to call it a research ethics committee is incorrect. Doctors and their managers need access to a second, bioethical committee (a bioethics committee), the establishment of which is needed urgently. It is unnecessary to have one of these in every hospital, instead one, perhaps in every region, would suffice. Nevertheless, research and ethics policies should be integrated into those of the whole institute. Danger can arise if there is an ethics committee that sits in a corner, deliberating ineffectively, and a research committee that is very powerful, and listened to, deliberating in the boardroom.

Summary and Conclusions

What is required is that ethics committees recognise their dual role and either ensure that their membership reflects this, or split to give two separate committees, one dealing with ethics and the other with the science of medicine. Medical ethics is now much too important an issue to be left solely to those without an ethical training. The most logical way forward is to have trained ethicists on all relevant committees to facilitate complex and important decision making.

Discussion

One possibility would be to have two levels of committees, one which checks the real ethical aspects and the other the scientific aspects.

This possibility has been discussed previously because there is much information from large clinical trials where, for example, 75 ethics committees were involved from all over Europe, and none of these committees asked the question whether the protocol as such was scientifically meaningful. All the ethics concerns dealt with informed consent problems and local insurance issues for example. The vast majority of these ethics committees can only deal with the local needs of patients. That is very helpful and important to cover, but a large number of ethics committees simply do not have the experience and expertise to ask these very important detailed ethical questions.

In Hungary, there is one committee that reviews the scientific and ethical aspects of the programme and then the local ethics committee just considers the local needs of the patients. That system worked well at the beginning but now this central committee has become a bottleneck apparently. There are very long waiting lists and the problem has not been solved. Having two kinds of committees is a good idea, but only if this arrangement does not delay drug development.

The two committees should work in harmony. There is a hospital in Sydney, Australia, which has a bioethicist and a committee called the bioethics committee, which discusses certain issues, and bioethicists can be called upon by the management. They have a representative on the research committee, and the interaction between the two is very interesting and effective. It is a very satisfactory arrangement, but it is necessary to find an ethicist, and this is an impossible task for most general hospitals. There is a feeling, however, that there are far too many ethics committees in the UK, and it may just be that a regional ethics committee might be the answer.

The idea that members of ethics committees are not expected to have any competence in ethics is debatable.

The first paragraph on ethics committee membership in the UK Department of Health *Red Book* states, 'An LREC should have 8–12 members. This should allow for a sufficiently broad range of experience and expertise so that the scientific and medical aspects of the research proposal can be reconciled with the welfare of research subjects and broader ethical implications.' That paragraph makes it quite clear that people on research ethics committees are expected to think about ethics. The point about co-option which does appear in the *Red Book* is that there can be issues which raise specific ethical questions which may well be beyond the competence of the average ethics committee. An example would be discussions on gene therapy, a topic which raises a whole range of issues which may not have arisen before gene therapy was invented. The DoH viewpoint is that it is only sensible that for an LREC to do its job competently it should seek outside advice where it is conscious itself that it needs a little more expertise. It could be argued, however, that the above wording is vague. It says, for instance, that members should be familiar with ethical issues, but that might not mean much to the everyday person. In France, for example, the wording would be sufficient, because there is much more general awareness of ethical matters. If information about difficult ethical issues is required then it is necessary to use a trained ethicist, and these individuals are certainly not very common in the UK, and are not routinely members of ethics committees.

It could be argued that it is unethical for a committee to allow a project to commence with only a two-thirds majority, as was mentioned in the French model.

Perhaps this should be a unanimous decision if it is meant to be a quasi-legal committee. The word 'legally' is a little awkward, however, and in principle it is necessary to have majority ethical approval, due to the fact that there will always be someone who will object. Again, the presence of an ethicist on the committee would be helpful for resolving disputes. In most cases committees tend to create a unanimous feeling with no objections, and that certainly should be the intention. If there are problems, such as insufficient patients being used, then these need to be resolved in committee discussion.

It is possible that being well instructed in moral philosophy is not a good criterion for knowing what is right and wrong and for being a member of an ethics committee.

It certainly is important to have questioning people on committees, who will not automatically rubber-stamp things. With regard to ethics committees charging for their services: in the north-west region of the UK probably one in seven of the ethics committees charge. The normal fee seems to be between £200 and £400, and in one case a Merseyside ethics committee charged a drug company £3000 to consider their application because of the amount of time taken. The biggest problem that the majority of ethics committees face is getting people to serve on them. If ethics committees are to be amalgamated, and there are very many good arguments for that course of action, then it is likely that members will have to be paid a fee commensurate with the large amount of time and effort necessary to consider applications. One way of raising the necessary finances would be to charge applicants.

However, in general it is desirable to remain as independent as possible of the company that is sponsoring a study. If payment is to be forthcoming, perhaps it should go to the institution undertaking the assessment. A good, busy committee involved in assessing important applications should attract members easily.

The need for trained ethicists on committees to offer views on morals might not be necessary because surely lay members and clerical members can perform this function.

Certainly many of the ethical issues that laypeople often have to struggle with can be resolved. Nevertheless, trained ethicists could play a very important role, as lawyers do for legal issues. The UK is in its infancy on this issue. Ethicists can help steer discussions by asking pertinent questions to facilitate solutions. This kind of input cannot be provided by laypeople. Nevertheless it is important that ethicists do not take over committees and make the decisions. It is necessary that people understand why decisions are made, and therefore ethicists should not go beyond their roles as facilitators.

Declaration of Helsinki

Recommendations guiding physicians in biomedical research involving human subjects. Adopted by the 18th World Medical Assembly, Helsinki, Finland, June 1964, and amended by the 29th World Medical Assembly, Tokyo, Japan, October 1975, the 35th World Medical Assembly, Venice, Italy, October 1983 and the 41st World Medical Assembly, Hong Kong, September 1989.

Introduction

It is the mission of the physician to safeguard the health of the people. His or her knowledge and conscience are dedicated to the fulfilment of this mission.

The Declaration of Geneva of the World Medical Association binds the physician with the words, 'The health of my patient will be my first consideration', and the International Code of Medical Ethics declares that 'A physician shall act only in the patient's interest when providing medical care which might have the effect of weakening the physical and mental condition of the patient'.

The purpose of biomedical research involving human subjects must be to improve diagnostic, therapeutic and prophylactic procedures and the understanding of the aetiology and pathogenesis of disease.

In current medical practice most diagnostic, therapeutic or prophylactic procedures involve hazards. This applies especially to biomedical research.

Medical progress is based on research which ultimately must rest in part on experimentation involving human subjects.

In the field of biomedical research a fundamental distinction must be recognised between medical research in which the aim is essentially diagnostic or therapeutic for a patient and medical research the essential object of which is purely scientific and without direct diagnostic or therapeutic value to the person subjected to the research.

Special caution must be exercised in the conduct of research which may affect the environment and the welfare of animals used for research must be respected.

Because it is essential that the results of laboratory experiments be applied to human beings to further scientific knowledge and to help suffering humanity, the World Medical Association has prepared the following recommendations as a guide to every physician in biomedical research involving human subjects. They should be kept under review in the future. It must be stressed that the standards as drafted are only a guide to physicians all over the world. Physicians are not relieved from criminal, civil and ethical responsibilities under the laws of their own countries.

I. Basic Principles

1 Biomedical research involving human subjects must conform to generally accepted scientific principles and should be based on adequately performed laboratory and animal experimentation and on a thorough knowledge of the scientific literature.

2 The design and performance of each experimental procedure involving human subjects should be clearly formulated in an experimental protocol which should be transmitted for consideration, comment and guidance to a specially appointed committee independent of the investigator and the sponsor provided that this independent committee is in conformity with the laws and regulations of the country in which the experiment is performed.

3 Biomedical research involving human subjects should be conducted only by scientifically qualified persons and under the supervision of a clinically competent medical person. The responsibility for the human subject must always rest with a medically qualified person and never rest on the subject of the research, even though the subject has given his or her consent.

4 Biomedical research involving human subjects cannot legitimately be carried out unless the importance of the objective is in proportion to the inherent risk to the subject.

5 Every biomedical research project involving human subjects should be preceded by careful assessment of predictable risks in comparison with foreseeable benefits to the subject or to others. Concern for the interests

of the subject must always prevail over the interest of science and society.

6 The right of the research subject to safeguard his or her integrity must always be respected. Every precaution should be taken to respect the privacy of the subject and to minimise the impact of the study on the subject's physical and mental integrity and on the personality of the subject.

7 Physicians should abstain from engaging in research projects involving human subjects unless they are satisfied that the hazards involved are believed to be predictable. Physicians should cease any investigations if the hazards are found to outweigh the potential benefits.

8 In publications of the results of his or her research, the physician is obliged to preserve the accuracy of the results. Reports of experimentation not in accordance with the principles laid down in this Declaration should not be accepted for publication.

9 In any research on human beings, each potential subject must be adequately informed of the aims, methods, anticipated benefits and potential hazards of the study, and the discomfort it may entail. He or she should be informed that he or she is at liberty to abstain from participating in the study and that he or she is free to withdraw his or her consent to participation at any time. The physician should then obtain the subject's freely given consent, preferably in writing.

10 When obtaining informed consent for the research project the physician should be particularly cautious if the subject is in a dependent relationship to him or her or may consent under duress. In that case the informed consent should be obtained by a physician who is not engaged in the investigation and who is completely independent of this official relationship.

11 In case of legal incompetence, informed consent should be obtained from the legal guardian in accordance with national legislation. Where physical or mental incapacity makes it impossible to obtain informed consent, or when the subject is a minor, permission from the responsible relative replaces that of the subject in accordance with national legislation.

Whenever the minor child is in fact able to give a consent, the minor's consent must be obtained in addition to the consent of the minor's legal guardian.

12 The research protocol should always contain a statement of the ethical considerations involved and should indicate that the principles enunciated in the present Declaration are complied with.

II Medical Research combined with Professional Care (Clinical Research)

1 In the treatment of the sick person, the physician must be free to use a new diagnostic and therapeutic measure, if in his or her judgement it offers hope of saving life, re-establishing health or alleviating suffering.

2 The potential benefits, hazards and discomfort of a new method should be weighed against the advantages of the best current diagnostic and therapeutic methods.

3 In any medical study, every patient – including those of a control group, if any – should be assured of the best proven diagnostic and therapeutic method.

4 The refusal of the patient to participate in a study must never interfere with the physician–patient relationship.

5 If the physician considers it essential not to obtain informed consent, the specific reasons for this proposal should be stated in the experimental protocol for transmission to the independent committee (I.2).

6 The physician can combine medical research with professional care, the objective being the acquisition of new medical knowledge, only to the extent that medical research is justified by its potential diagnostic or therapeutic value for the patient.

III Non-therapeutic Biomedical Research involving Human Subjects (Non-clinical Biomedical Research)

1 In the purely scientific application of medical research carried out on a human being, it is the duty of the physician to remain the protector of the life and health of that person on whom biomedical research is being carried out.

2 The subjects should be volunteers – either healthy persons or patients for whom the experimental design is not related to the patient's illness.

3 The investigator or the investigating team should discontinue the research if in his/her or their judgement it may, if continued, be harmful to the individual.

4 In research on man, the interest of science and society should never take precedence over considerations related to the well-being of the subject.

Guidance Relating to Clinical Research: National

Examples

Belgium

- Bioethical questions (Belgian Association of Physicians 1992)
- Ethical Rules (Belgian Association of Physicians 1990)

Nordic Countries

- Clinical Trials of Drugs (NLN No. 11 – Nordic Council on Medicines 1983)
- Good Clinical Trial Practice (NLN No. 28 – Nordic Council on Medicines 1989)
- Quality assurance in clinical drug research (Nordic Council on Medicines 1993)

Portugal

- The Code of Medical Deontology Act 59–66

The Netherlands

- The Health Organisation Rules of Conduct
- The Institute for Medicinal Scientific Research Guidelines

Germany

- Principles relating to the proper execution of clinical trials in medicinal products 9.12.87 (B Anz S16617)
- Releases of various state ministries
- Guidelines relating to trials in military and public hospitals
- Release regarding Protection of Healthy Persons subjected to clinical trials of medicinal products marked with radioactive substances 20.6.76(GMB1 S366)
- Procedural principles for medical ethics committees adopted by working group of medical ethics commissions in the Federal Republic 1986 onwards and others dealing with insurance, trials of new products by GPs, data protection and information

Spain

- Ethical and Deological Code (Art 32) (Spanish Medical Association)

Main Ethical Guidelines relevant to the Evaluation of Clinical Research conducted in the UK

General

- The Declaration of Helsinki; The World Medical Association Inc., 1964 (amended 1975, 1983, 1989)
- Proposed Guidelines on Biomedical Research; Council for International Organisations of Medical Sciences (CIOMS), 1982 as amended October 1993
- Note for Guidance, Good Clinical Practice for Trials on Medicinal Products in the European Community 111/3976/88-EN; The Committee for Proprietary Medicinal Products, July 1990 ('CPMP Guidelines')
- Guidelines on the Practice of Ethics Committees; RCP, January 1990
- Health Service Guidelines HSG (91)5: Local Research Ethics Committees
- The Relationship between Physicians and the Pharmaceutical Industry; RCP, October 1986
- Relationships between the Medical Profession and the Pharmaceutical Industry; ABPI
- Guidelines for payments to GPs Participating in Clinical Research; Royal College of General Practitioners (RCGP)
- Ethics related to research in nursing; Royal College of Nursing (RCN), 1977
- Guidelines for preclinical and clinical testing of new medicinal products; ABPI, 1987
- Guidelines for ethical approval of human pharmacology studies carried out by pharmaceutical companies; ABPI, 1990

- Clinical Trial Compensation guidelines; ABPI, 1991
- Responsibility in investigations on human participants and material, and on personal information; Medical Research Council (MRC) 1992
- Guidelines on Good Clinical (Research) Practice; ABPI, 1988 as amended 1992

Patient/Therapeutic – Research

- Guidelines on Post Marketing surveillance; (ABPI/British Medical Association (BMA)/Committee on Safety of Medicines (CSM)/RCCP), 1988
- Research involving Patients; RCP, January 1990
- Clinical Trial Compensation Guidelines; ABPI 1991
- A Guide to consent for examination or treatment; Department of Health (DoH) Circular HC(90)22; revised by Health Service Guideline HSG(92) 32
- Code of Practice for the clinical assessment of licensed medicinal products in General Practice; ABPI, 1992

Healthy Volunteer/Non-therapeutic Research

- Research on Healthy Volunteers; RCP, October 1986
- The Medicines Commission Advice to Health Ministers on Healthy Volunteer Studies (1987)
- Guidelines for Medical Experiments in non-patient human volunteers; ABPI, March 1988
- Facilities for Non-patient Volunteer Studies; ABPI

Special Subject Categories

- *Medical Research with children; ethics, law and practice*; Nicholson, R. H. (Ed.), Institute of Medical Ethics, Oxford University Press, 1986
- A checklist of questions to ask when evaluating proposed research during pregnancy and following birth; British Paediatric Association and Royal College of Obstetricians and Gynaecologists 1991
- Guidelines for the Ethical Conduct of Medical Research involving children; British Paediatric Association (BPA), 1992. (Updates Guidelines to aid ethical committees considering research involving children; BPA, 1980)

- Guidelines for Research Ethics Committees on psychiatric research involving human subjects; the RCP, *Psychiatric Bulletin* (1990), **14**, 48–61
- The Ethical Conduct of Research on Children; MRC December 1991
- The Ethical Conduct of Research on the Mentally Incapacitated; MRC December 1991
- Guidelines for Psychological Research; B Psych
- Introduction to the revised ethical principles for conducting research with human participants; British Psychological Society, 1990
- Statement of Ethical Practice; British Sociological Association
- National Union of Students (NUS) Guidelines for students participating in medical experiments; NUS
- International Guidelines for Ethical Review of Epidemiological Studies; CIOMS 1991
- Report on the Ethics of Gene Therapy; Clothier Committee 1992
- The Ethical Conduct of AIDS Vaccine Trials; MRC, 1991

Index